# Geoff Lawson's

## Diary of the

# ASHES

# GEOFF LAWSON'S
# DIARY OF THE
# ASHES

## AS TOLD TO MARK RAY

ANGUS
& ROBERTSON
PUBLISHERS

## ACKNOWLEDGMENT

The publishers would like to thank Allsport/Adrian Murrell, Philip Brown, Geoff Lawson, Graham Morris, News Ltd and Mark Ray for the use of their photographs, and Richard Willson/*The Times,* London for reproduction rights to the caricatures of the Australian Ashes series cricket team.

*AN ANGUS & ROBERTSON BOOK*

*First published in Australia in 1990 by*
*Collins/Angus & Robertson Publishers Australia*

*Collins/Angus & Robertson Publishers Australia*
*Unit 4, Eden Park, 31 Waterloo Road, North Ryde*
*NSW 2113, Australia*

*Collins/Angus & Robertson Publishers New Zealand*
*31 View Road, Glenfield, Auckland 10, New Zealand*

*Angus & Robertson (UK)*
*16 Golden Square, London W1R 4BN, United Kingdom*

*Copyright © Geoff Lawson and Mark Ray, 1990*

*National Library of Australia*
*Cataloguing-in-Publication data*

*Lawson, Geoff, 1957-          .*
  *Geoff Lawson's diary of the Ashes.*

  *ISBN 0 207 16664 1.*

  *1. Lawson, Geoff, 1957-          . — Diaries. 2. Cricket players*
  *— Australia — Diaries. 3. Ashes (Cricket*
  *test series). I. Ray, Mark. II. Title.*
  *III. Title: Diary of the Ashes.*

*796.358092*

*Designed by Leonie Bremer-Kamp*
*Typeset in 11pt Times Roman by Post Typesetters, Brisbane*
*Printed in Australia by Globe Press*

*5   4   3   2   1*
*95  94  93  92  91  90*

I am delighted to be able to pay tribute to one of the most successful Australian cricket teams ever to tour England.

I had the great pleasure of seeing the team play at Lord's on the second day of the second Test. The team went on to win the series four-nil, and, but for the weather, would almost certainly have won six-nil. In doing so, they achieved a feat last performed by Bill Woodfull's team in 1934.

Their individual performances will stand comparison with anyone's — well, nearly anyone's. Don Bradman put England to the sword in 1930 to the tune of 974 runs at an average of 139. It would of course be sacrilege for any subsequent Australian player to aspire to surpass this record but, for a while, Mark Taylor gave the aggregate a shake and Steve Waugh fell just short of the Don's average.

The top six — Mark Taylor, Geoff Marsh, David Boon, Allan Border, Dean Jones and Steve Waugh — performed with superb consistency and, equally importantly, provided bright and aggressive batting throughout the series.

The bowlers were also superb. It was very good to see Geoff Lawson back in top form, bowling with fire and cunning. Terry Alderman's second haul of 40 wickets in an Ashes series was a truly wonderful effort, and Merv Hughes took important wickets when they were needed.

Ian Healy played his part by hanging on to every chance which came his way and, most importantly, the fielding and catching of Border's team were in the best tradition of Australian cricket.

It was obviously important that the other touring players — Greg Campbell, Tim May, Tom Moody, Carl Rackemann, Mike Veletta and Tim Zoehrer — performed well throughout and, however frustrating it must have been to watch the Tests from the rooms, still contributed by their support and competitiveness to the outstanding success of the tour.

Allan Border's leadership on this tour was outstanding, whether in the aggressive innings he played on the first day at Headingley, which set the tone for the series, the assured and purposeful manner in which he handled his bowlers and set his fields, or in the delighted but modest way he accepted victory.

I also want to pay tribute to Bob Simpson and Lawrie Sawle for their work in preparing the team for performance on the field and keeping them such a happy and united bunch off it.

A measure of the 1989 team's success can be gauged by the fact that the commentators continually reached for their history books to determine which record had just been broken and what the next one would be. Their magnificent performances in England brought an inner warmth to the hearts of their fellow Australians during the 1989 winter and made us all very proud of them.

*Extract from the Prime Minister's speech of 27 September 1989 delivered at the Ashes dinner, Melbourne, reproduced with the kind permission of the Prime Minister.*

# CONTENTS

# INTRODUCTION

AT 5.41 PM ON TUESDAY, 1 AUGUST 1989, the players' balcony at the Old Trafford cricket ground in Manchester erupted into shouts of triumph. David Boon had swept English spinner Nick Cook past the outstretched arms of Neil Foster to the square leg boundary for the winning runs in the fourth Test of the 58th Ashes series. Australia had reclaimed the Ashes for the first time in England since Bill Woodfull's 1934 side.

When the ball crossed that rope, Australia regained the Ashes it had lost in 1985 and had failed to regain in the 1986–87 home series. It was a truly sweet moment for the Australian cricket team, the team supporters and for myself — it's a memory I'll cherish for the rest of my life. This was my third tour of England and my last chance to be part of a successful team. The 1981 and 1985 series had been frustrating and bitterly disappointing. The weather had often been damp and cold, many of us suffered injuries that healed slowly in the cold and our cricket was not up to scratch when it counted. But on 1 August the bad memories, nightmares even (certainly of Headingley in 1981), of past tours were erased in the time it took a cricket ball to travel to the square leg boundary. That's what it seemed like at Old Trafford on that day.

This victory was not the result of any one team member's work. Unlike some of the Australian teams of the mid–1980s, which were carried in many ways by skipper Allan Border, this was a team effort. Every member of the party did his bit and, like all successful teams, the whole was well and truly greater than the sum of the parts. A cliché perhaps, but one that certainly applied to the 1989 Australians.

Still, three months before that day in Manchester things

1

were not so certain. The make-up of the touring party was a matter of conjecture right up to the time it was announced, on Friday, 17 March.

Towards the end of the 1988–89 Australian season doubts surrounded three of the players who would later excel in England. Steve Waugh, Terry Alderman and Dean Jones were respected cricketers but their futures at Test level were far from assured.

Waugh was a fine limited-overs performer but after 41 Test innings had yet to make a century — his Test average an unflattering 30.52. Jones had ended what had been a horrid domestic season, salvaged only by his 216 against the West Indies in the last Test at Adelaide. Mind you, a double century is a good way to break a drought, especially against the big lads from the Caribbean. Alderman, having just regained his baggy green cap after his sojourn in South Africa, had played two home Tests when injury forced him out of the final Test of the Australian season.

Of the others, Merv Hughes after a superb effort of thirteen West Indian wickets in the Perth Test could manage only one more in the next three Tests. Carl Rackemann had struggled through another injury-plagued season. And could Geoff Lawson come back from another serious injury at the ripe old age of thirty-one? With Alderman already thirty-three, Hughes and Rackemann still unproven and the fifth paceman, Greg Campbell an unknown from Tasmania, there were some serious doubts about the quality of the fast bowling. Could we bowl out a strong England batting line-up often enough to win the series? Many people thought Mike Whitney, my new-ball partner for New South Wales, would be on that Qantas jet after his fifty-eighth first class wicket which included nine in his only Test. But that was not to be and, hindsight being 20–20, his left-arm variation could not have been more successful than the efforts of those chosen ahead of him.

There were questions being asked about the rest of the side as well. Off-spinner Tim May had finished the Sheffield Shield season with the player of the year award but with a badly lacerated spinning finger. His South Australian captain, David Hookes, had even publicly advocated not bowling him until the first Test on 8 June. That would probably have done his finger a lot of good, but I'm not sure it would have been as helpful to his form.

The other spinner, Trevor Hohns, had played his first two Tests that summer without setting the scene alight, as had opening batsman, Mark Taylor. At least the wicket-keepers, Ian Healy and Tim Zoehrer, were healthy and in good form. Tom Moody was in great touch after two 150s in the Shield final, but he had yet to play a Test. Mike Veletta had begun the season well but had faded a little towards the end.

Allan Border was always going to lead the tourists but there was a lot of talk in cricket circles about the search for a new captain — someone younger and less burdened by the weight of past failures. After several years of carrying the side with his batting and of constant media attention he was frequently short-tempered — 'Captain Grumpy' as we often called him. The pressure on AB in England would be as great as ever. If we failed he would be the first Australian captain to lose three consecutive series to England. That would have been a severe blemish to AB's great record and he was desperate to avoid it.

So there we were, seventeen players of widely varying ages, shapes, abilities, fitness and form. What chance Australia?

The seventeen were, of course, dismissed by the English media as unable, unsuitable and unworthy. We were written off as 'the worst Australian tourists since 1788'. Still, this label is dragged out every four years and was not taken too seriously. In fact I think we would have been a little disappointed had the British press, with its less than salubrious reputation, not branded us as the worst team in Test history.

What did come as a surprise was that the newly appointed England captain David Gower and Ted Dexter, the chairman of selectors, agreed with the judgment of their cricket press. This was about the only time they would agree on anything all summer. Even before our squad was chosen we

3

heard from England that whoever bothered to come to the Old Dart stood absolutely no chance of grabbing the little urn. It was not so much the words themselves as the arrogance with which they were delivered that got us a little hot under the jockstraps. Our resolve to win, however great before those statements, increased enormously. Cricketers, like all sportspeople, don't take too kindly to arrogance from their opponents. These criticisms pushed us to practise hard from day one right through to the end of an arduous 122-day campaign. We didn't slacken off until that last day at the Oval in late August and as well as steeling our resolve, I'm sure these statements put a lot of unnecessary pressure on the England players.

AB was certainly not impressed by what he read or heard from the England camp. Many people have said that he was a much tougher captain on this tour and he was certainly less friendly with the opposition on and off the field. I'm sure this was a direct reaction to the early comments from England. There were no more smiles and chit-chat, this time around it was 'you talk a good game, let's see how you play'. Though the friendship, with David Gower in particular, remained throughout the series, it was always business on the field.

**GEOFF LAWSON 'HENRY'**
Age 32, New South Wales

**BOB SIMPSON 'SIMMO'**
Age 53, Coach

**ALLAN BORDER 'AB'**
Age 34, Queensland

**DAVID BOON 'BOONIE'**
Age 29, Tasmania

**STEVE WAUGH 'TUGGA'**
Age 24, New South Wales

**GEOFF MARSH 'SWAMPY'**
Age 31, Western Australia

**TIM ZOEHRER 'ZIGGY'**
Age 28, Western Australia

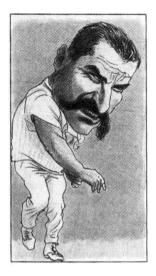

**MERVYN HUGHES 'SWERV'**
Age 28, Victoria

**DEAN JONES 'DEANO'**
Age 28, Victoria

**CARL RACKEMANN 'MOCCA'**
Age 29, Queensland

**TERRY ALDERMAN 'CLEM'**
Age 33, Western Australia

**MARK TAYLOR 'TUB'**
Age 25, New South Wales

**TREVOR HOHNS 'CRACKA'**
Age 36, Queensland

**IAN HEALY 'HEALS'**
Age 25, Queensland

**TIM MAY 'MAYSIE'**
Age 28, South Australia

GREG CAMPBELL 'CAMBO'
Age 25, Tasmania

MIKE VELETTA 'WAG'
Age 26, Western Australia

TOM MOODY 'BIG TOM'
Age 24, Western Australia

9

# ITINERARY

## MAY

5: Cricket League Conference XI
7: Duchess of Norfolk's XI
9: Sussex
11: MCC
13–15: Worcestershire
17–19: Somerset
20–22: Middlesex
23: Yorkshire
25: England
27: England
29: England
31–June 2: Warwickshire

## JUNE

3–5: Derbyshire
8–13: First Test, England
14–16: Lancashire
17–19: Northamptonshire
22–27: Second Test, England
28: Combined Universities

## JULY

1–3: Glamorgan
6–11: Third Test, England
15: Scotland
17: Minor Counties
19–21: Hampshire
22–24: Gloucestershire
27–Aug 1: Fourth Test, England

## AUGUST

2–4: Nottinghamshire
5–7: Leicestershire
10–15: Fifth Test, England
16–18: Kent
19–21: Essex
24–29: Sixth Test, England

# THE TOUR
# BEGINS

THE SERIOUS BUSINESS OF THE TOUR began for me on 17 March when the team was announced. You never know about selections no matter how good a season you've had. There's always some uncertainty until your name is read out. Having battled back into the Test team after a two-year absence, I was out again after having used my face instead of my bat against a short one from Curtly Ambrose in Perth. But the broken jaw had healed quickly enough for me to finish the season in good form and among the wickets.

Just to help me cope with that tad of uncertainty that always remains, I headed off that morning to St Michael's golf course in Sydney for a round with Greg Livingstone, an old friend and University of New South Wales Cricket Club teammate of mine. It must have been that nagging doubt that led me to my first ever golfing loss to 'Livo', but as we came off the 18th green a man came over from the clubhouse to congratulate me on my selection — and to tell me of Mike Whitney's bad luck.

This was mixed news. I was rather depressed that 'Whit' had missed out. He works so hard at his game and is so proud of playing for Australia that I knew how disappointed he'd be. Also, he is great company and I was very much looking forward to touring England with him.

The news did mean that training would have to continue and fitness would have to be maintained. Fortunately I'd finished the season without any injuries so I didn't need a spell of rest and recuperation. It was back to tackling those familiar hills around Coogee, a Sydney beach suburb.

11

The weeks before we left were very busy: trips into the country to Wagga Wagga and Narrabri to visit my family and my wife, Julie's, parents; a few speaking engagements and generally organising my life for a 24-week absence. Pay the bills; make sure the cat is looked after; do my part of the preparations for the University of New South Wales Cricket Club annual dinner which is always a highlight of the end of each Sydney season. The six weeks between the announcement of the team and the flight out seemed a long time, but it went quickly enough.

## FRIDAY, 28 APRIL

My wife, Julie, dropped me at the Ansett terminal for my 9 am flight to Melbourne to link up with rest of the team. She went on to the international terminal to catch her flight to London. Although the Australian Cricket Board (ACB) has decreed that wives will not be allowed to travel with the team until the last month of the tour, Julie will be in England for the duration. She reckons she's not covered by an ACB contract and, anyway, I couldn't stop her. She'll be staying with her sister in Suffolk and shouldn't get me into strife with the authorities.

The team met in Melbourne and after facing the cricket media headed off for fitness tests at a college in Footscray — they hit you hard early on.

The new boy Greg Campbell (Cambo) missed his first bus trip with the Australian team. He was set up by his mischievous Tasmanian teammate, David Boon. After the press conference Cambo, like most of us, went to his hotel room to get ready for the trip to Footscray. Apparently Max Walker wanted an interview with Cambo and when he couldn't find him asked Boonie to relay the message. Spotting a chance to initiate a new boy, Boonie didn't bother to pass the word until a few minutes before the bus was due to leave. Cambo, no doubt eager to please, obliged Walker and was duly left behind. He eventually caught a cab and after a calculatedly cool reception,

12

smiles replaced the stern expressions and he realised he'd been had.

The fitness tests can be a pain — Merv Hughes almost drowned in the vat that was used to test our body fat levels — but it was over soon enough.

Back at the hotel we collected loads of official team gear from the tour sponsors, Castlemaine XXXX. The ACB hosted a dinner with the Board members present at which Ian Redpath gave a suitably inspiring speech. Allan Crompton, one of the New South Wales delegates, spent two hours trying to convince Steve Waugh, Mark Taylor and myself that Graeme Hick should play for the Blues (New South Wales Cricket Team) next season. He lost 3-1.

## SATURDAY, 29 APRIL

Cambo made the bus — to a standing ovation. The flight was delayed but the Qantas captains' club lounge was comfortable enough. Merv, Clem (Terry Alderman), Ziggy (Tim Zoehrer) and Mocca (Carl Rackemann) began the first game of 500 of the tour.

The crowds at Tullamarine wished us well. I hope they're in a similar mood when we return. We travelled business class for the first time. Usually we fly economy which is not too good if you're like me (1.9 metres tall) or Tom Moody (2 metres tall). At least we'd arrive with backs and knees in good shape.

A 24-hour delay in Sydney was not appreciated. A stopover at Bangkok airport in the middle of the night allowed a quick walk around the duty free shopping areas. Most of the sales assistants were curled up asleep on makeshift mattresses behind the counters. It already felt like a long trip.

# PREPARATION
# IN ENGLAND

SUNDAY, 30 APRIL

Before we landed at Heathrow, the Qantas captain wished us luck and warned of some 'minor turbulence and flak over Fleet Street — nothing you can't handle' and expressed the hope that we bring back the Ashes and break a few records.

We arrived about five hours late, in mid-morning. It was a lovely day in London, 11°C and the sun shining. I hope we're not seeing the best of the summer too soon.

After checking into our hotel, the Westbury in Mayfair, we went straight to a large press conference in one of the reception rooms. AB handled it well, deflecting some ridiculous questions down the leg side for easy singles. 'Do you think you can win?' 'Many people say this is the worst ever Australian team to come here. Do you agree?' 'Will the team be drinking a lot of XXXX on tour?' What sort of answers do they expect? 'No, I don't think we can win. We've just come here for a holiday.'

Merv was the only one apart from AB to be asked a question and his were even less related to cricket. Swerv handled it well, playing up to the dumb yobbo image they have of him: 'Back home they throw rocks at me if I don't take wickets.' They loved that one. Still, it's obvious we'll have to be on the lookout with this lot.

Cricketers spend a lot of time in hotels and they usually

14

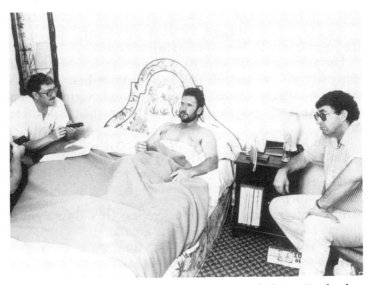

*The most relaxed press conference since John and Yoko? AB interviewed at the Westbury by Terry Brindle (l) of the* Australian *and Jim Woodward of the Sydney* Daily Telegraph.

assess the pros and cons of a new pub pretty quickly. We've never stayed at the Westbury before, but it looks alright so far, the rooms are quite good and the staff efficient and friendly.

A few of us spent the afternoon at Wembley for the Simod Cup final. As expected, I was very weary by the evening and passed out pretty quickly once I got to bed.

## MONDAY, 1 MAY

A public holiday in London today and more sunshine, 16° C. Two fine warm days in a row is a bit much to take in England in May. What's going on here?

Although still jet-lagged, we headed off to Lord's for practice at 9.30 am. Before the session began, Simmo (Bob Simpson) chatted to Clem and myself about working with Cambo and Merv. Clem will bowl in the same net as Cambo and help him develop his swing bowling as well as advise him on English conditions. I'll work with Swerv, mainly on the right length to bowl on English wickets.

The practice tracks were okay, especially for this time of the year. We trained all day in two three-hour sessions stopping to eat lunch on the team coach, a luxurious set-up which we'll all get to know well over the next three months.

A reporter from the *Daily Mail* interviewed me while I was bowling in a net with Merv.

**DM:**   How's your back?
**GL:**   Much better now.
**MH:**   (interrupting between deliveries) He's always got a bad back when the wickets are flat.
**DM:**   You were ill during the 1985 tour?
**GL:**   Yes I had bronchial problems all tour.
**MH:**   He's got no ticker you know.
**DM:**   What's going to be your biggest hurdle on this tour?
**GL:**   That's quite obvious. Merv Hughes!

A 36-hour flight followed by six hours in the nets and we were knackered. Still, I managed to drag myself out to one of my favourite Covent Garden restaurants from the previous tours — Maxwell's — before collapsing at about 9 pm. I'm glad I ran all those kilometres back home.

### TUESDAY, 2 MAY

Practice in the morning — the usual 9 am start. After practice we attended the traditional British Sportsmen's Club luncheon in the splendid Savoy Hotel. It's a very proper English function where you get plenty of 'What ho!' 'Jolly good show' and 'the very best of luck to you' and all that pucker English palaver. There were about 1,000 people present, all wearing grey pinstripe suits. My clearest memory is that of the smell of cigar smoke in the air. Don't you hate it when the MC says 'Gentlemen, you may now smoke'.

16

After the luncheon I called Reebok and ordered some boots, an important item on a four-month tour, especially for a fast bowler.

The team was photographed in the afternoon for the XXXX beer advertisements. We all had to wear caps — something I never do so I'll look pretty strange in the pictures — and stare at Merv who suffered sticky cream, as an imitation of the foam of XXXX beer, over his moustache. The price of fame I suppose.

## WEDNESDAY, 3 MAY

Another very full day. Before practice we dressed in creams and blazers for an official photo session with Patrick Eagar in the garden behind the pavilion at Lord's. The first picture was a straight team shot and the last a classic with all of us, including Simmo and the Colonel (manager Lawrie Sawle), wearing bright yellow XXXX caps with built-in radios with their antennae fully extended. Photo sessions like this are necessary for sponsors, but when they produced the 'radio hats', this session began to deteriorate. Lawrie was dumbfounded but said he would go along with it as long as the pictures weren't published anywhere. We must have looked pretty silly, especially in the hallowed grounds of Lord's.

We practised both morning and afternoon again and although we weren't at our sharpest after five sessions in three days, we have to make the most of the good weather. In 1985 we arrived at the nets to practise with new balls, and with the wickets looking pretty green and sporting, the bowlers were told to bat first. We hardly laid bat on ball and everyone got out several times but luckily no one was hurt. Things are a little different this time around.

Back at the Westbury in the evening, the XXXX people briefed us on what is expected of us on tour. We're to make pub appearances in groups of four or five, pose for a few pictures behind the bar and chat to the locals. All up each of

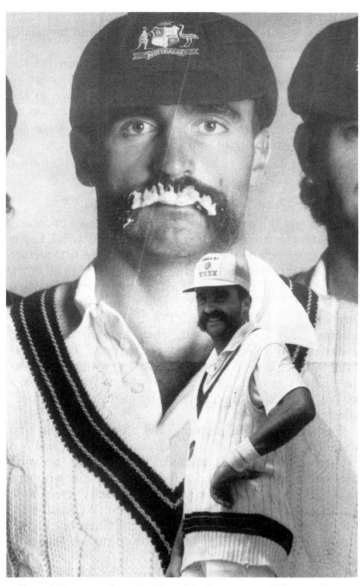

*The real Merv meets the media Merv: this advertisement will be seen all over England this summer.*

us has to do seven appearances. They also showed us a video of the advertisements they'll be doing — they're obviously putting in a big effort and it looks like our faces are going to be seen all over the country.

Tonight the team attended the traditional Taverners' dinner at Lord's. Lord Deedes gave a very inspiring speech on the spirit of cricket. AB replied and though he doesn't like public speaking, he is better at it than he thinks. However, at this dinner he told his sailing joke for the fifth year in a row. We're all sick of it now. Even if it's the only joke he knows, he could at least change the names or something to ease our pain.

## THURSDAY, 4 MAY

Jackhammers started about 8 am down in Conduit Street so a sleep-in was impossible. It was just as well though as Tub (Mark Taylor) and I took two hours to pack our gear for the bus trip north to Birmingham tonight.

We practised at Lord's in the early afternoon, our last session of a warm, sunny and productive week. It's been a hard week physically, but we've been lucky to have good weather and excellent facilities. With our first game coming up tomorrow, most of the guys feel confident and in reasonable nick. I think it's a mistake to talk too much about cricket, so I haven't overdone the coaching bit with Merv who anyway is a good listener and is very keen to learn and to put things into practice. He's obviously psyched-up to do well.

We left for Birmingham from Lord's and arrived at about 9 pm. We're staying, yet again, at the Albany. Birmingham is not the most beautiful city in England. It looks okay in the sunshine, but I hate to think what it's like in the depths of winter. I dined at Gino's Italian around the corner from the hotel, a place well frequented over the years by touring Australian cricketers.

# WARMING-UP IN THE COUNTIES

## FRIDAY, 5 MAY

Our first game was against a Cricket League Conference side which included Simon O'Donnell, the Indian spinner Maninder Singh, as well as two guys I played with at Haslingden last year, Brian Knowles and Mike Ingham, so there were plenty of familiar faces in the dressingrooms. I wasn't playing, so after a run I wandered around the small ground which is across the road from the home of the West Bromwich Albion soccer club, running into several of the Vics (Victorian Cricket Team) — Michael Dimattina, Jamie Siddons and Paul Reiffel — as well as Graham Smith from New South Wales.

The wicket was quite good and our guys got in some handy practice, Deano (Dean Jones) making a hundred and smashing a couple of big sixes out of the ground and across the road. We made 326 and they managed 5-161 thanks mainly to some good hitting from Simon. A good start for us and for the spectators.

We drove back to London after the match and went straight to bed when we got there. A tiring day.

**AUSTRALIA 3-326, CRICKET LEAGUE CONFERENCE XI 5-161**

## SATURDAY, 6 MAY

We were back at Lord's for another net session, though because we played yesterday, it wasn't too intense. While some of the guys went off to play golf at Moore Park in the afternoon, I stayed at the Westbury to finish writing an

20

article on last season's FAI Cup for the *Channel 9 Yearbook*. Later about fifteen of us ate at an Indian restaurant near the Westbury. Most of the side, after having spent a lot of time on the sub-continent in the past few years, are very keen on Indian food (though I'm not). I must admit the food was very good though a little expensive — which means very expensive by Australian standards. We are in Mayfair after all.

## SUNDAY, 7 MAY

We left at 7.30 am this morning for the drive south to Arundel Castle in Sussex and the match against the Duchess of Norfolk's XI. Being a warm, sunny Sunday the roads out of London were packed but the trip was pleasant enough. The ground next to the castle, which is set on a hill in the middle of the village, was full. There must have been 10,000 people there — according to local officials the best crowd they've had for a tour opener for many years. It looks like we're going to be popular this tour. I ran into a few friends from the University of New South Wales Cricket Club and there were plenty of other Australians about. Let's hope they keep coming to support us.

We made plenty of runs and won easily enough. AB caused a few worries when a six he smashed over mid-wicket hit a woman on the side of the head. He was out a few balls later and walked straight across to see if she was alright — a gesture that was warmly applauded. I think the woman was taken off for a few stitches but came back to the ground later on.

I bowled alright for my first outing, making sure the run-up was right and not stretching the body too much at this stage.

Arundel Castle is a beautiful spot at the worst of times, today it was superb. After the game we drove the short hop along the south coast to Brighton for Tuesday's one-dayer against Sussex.

AUSTRALIA 6-314, DUCHESS OF NORFOLK'S XI 5-194

## MONDAY, 8 MAY

Glorious sunshine again. We practised in the morning at the county ground at Hove on some sporting wickets. I seem to have strained a thigh muscle yesterday but was still able to practise okay. Some of the guys played golf in the afternoon while I rested the leg and finished that article. Afterwards Clem and I went for a walk along the promenade — plenty of bare, white English torsos catching the sun. We played a few video games at the Pier, had a toffee apple like all good tourists and then headed back to the pub to pack our gear for the drive to London after tomorrow's game.

## TUESDAY, 9 MAY

Another lovely sunny day, about 24°C. It was a 50-over a side game against Sussex but I sat this one out. Those of us not playing had a long net session before play started. A fairly typical exercise at this stage of a tour.

The wicket was a little uneven and Deano hit too early at a bouncer from Tony Pigott and copped a nasty blow to the cheekbone. Clem, Mocca and I were walking around the ground at the time and heard a distinct dull thud as the ball made contact. It didn't sound too good. Deano was in shock when he first came off but settled down pretty quickly and eventually volunteered to go back out as Tugga (Steve Waugh) neared his hundred. It didn't seem necessary in a 50-overs game against Sussex but at that stage his face didn't look too bad. It got a lot worse later that night.

We only made 154 which was not enough, but Tugga did play some great shots in his 86. The locals had seen him play for Somerset last season and so warmly applauded his better shots.

Towards the end of the game we suffered our second setback when Mocca twisted his knee trying to take a catch at mid-on. It looked funny at the time, the big fella

*Bruised but happy: Dean Jones manages to hide his battered eye and fractured cheekbone from a press camera, but he can't hide that smile.*

stumbling backwards up the hill with one eye on the ball and the other keeping a watch for possible dips in the surface (common on English grounds). He came off and we are all worried because of his history of injuries. It isn't clear just how serious the problem is but he's not moving too well.

We're not too happy about losing even though it was a fairly insignificant game. We can play a lot better.

We arrived back in London about 10.30 pm. Straight to bed for me.

AUSTRALIA 154, SUSSEX 6-158

## WEDNESDAY, 10 MAY

No practice today. It has been pretty intense recently so Simmo decided to give us the day off. The word is not good about Mocca's knee. It has stiffened up overnight and looks like it will need a fair amount of treatment. One out of action means more work for the rest of us.

It was actually hot today. Swa (Ian Healy) was my partner at golf against Simmo and Swampy (Geoff Marsh) who both tend to take it a touch seriously. We lost.

Europcars, who are providing cars for this tour, delivered a couple of Sierras and a Rover to the course. After the first month of the tour, those of us not playing in a match will be allowed to take the cars and head off somewhere for a break. The only drawback is that the cars carry stickers saying: 'Australian cricket touring team'. That can occasionally sway a friendly policeman but it can also attract unwanted attention. It would be better to have privacy when resting from the touring grind, but at least we are mobile.

The staff of the Westbury hosted a cocktail party for the team this evening after which I drove to Chelsea for a meal. When I got back the Reebok gear had arrived — five pairs of bowling boots, some batting boots and some clothes. The boots look very good, especially the bowling ones — the lightest I've seen. AB's gear arrived with mine and I had to sort it all out which was, I suppose, appropriate, as I had ordered it for him in the first place.

*Opposite: A rare day off: Simmo recovered from this setback to partner Marsh in a win against Healy and myself.*

24

We played a 55-overs game against the MCC at Lord's today. The wicket was good and Boonie and Swampy put on 277 for the first wicket. Carnage! Boon 166, Marsh 102. We bowled pretty well and won by 100 runs. Gatt (Mike Gatting) made a fine 86 and looked in good touch. He was lucky early but one six off me over mid-wicket was memorable. I beat him all ends up next ball which was typical of one-day cricket. I always have an interesting duel with Gatt, but I wasn't exactly pushing myself today. It's going to be a long summer and my aim was to show some skill while working on my rhythm. I'll see Gatt again no doubt.

Pat Cash, who is a cricket enthusiast, dropped into our rooms during the day. He is still on crutches after his achilles injury and, like most sportspeople who are injured, was not overly happy.

This was a typical busy day on tour. We packed all our gear on to the bus, left the hotel at 8.30 am, arrived at the ground about 9 am and were in the nets ready for the warm-up at 9.15 am. The game started at 10.45 am and finished sometime around 6.45 pm. After that, we showered, packed our cricket gear into our 'coffins' (the cricket bags), had a few hurried drinks (this time with Dave Gilbert who's playing in the Kent league) and were on the bus for the drive to the next venue, Worcester. No wonder we were all tired when we pulled in at the Giffard at about 11.15 pm.

**AUSTRALIA 4-309, MCC 208**

# THE FIRST CLASS
# MATCHES BEGIN

It was cold and cloudy this morning. I had breakfast with some of the Combined University players who were staying at the Giffard after beating Worcestershire in a Benson and Hedges game yesterday. They should be through to the quarter-finals and were in great spirits. Practice was not until the afternoon, so a group of us did the rounds of the shops, helping Swa and Maysie (Tim May) look for presents for their wives. There were a few amusing scenes as Australian cricketers were spotted checking out the lingerie sections of various boutiques.

I pulled the longjohns out for practice today. That might have been a slight over-reaction but it was decidedly chilly. The weather, combined with some ordinary practice wickets, made this the least satisfactory net session so far.

Tomorrow we play our first first class game, against the reigning county champions. Boon, Zoehrer, Campbell, May, Rackemann and Jones will not be playing.

Rang Julie and copped a bollocking for not ringing earlier.

We won the toss, batted and were all out by lunch. Mind you, Worcestershire were all out by 5.30 pm and we were 4–51 in our second innings by stumps. You could say the wicket was ordinary, I've never known twenty-four wickets to fall in one day of a first class match. It was certainly a bit of a joke, though I think we could have batted better. It looks like the guys are still in one-day mode, playing shots when they need a bit more discipline. Not a great start to the first class program and there's already talk of a one-day game on Monday to cover for the early finish.

A few of us went to a XXXX appearance tonight at the Little Sauce Factory, a great little pub with bottles of Worcestershire sauce set into a picture rail around the walls. I was eventually driven out by the cigarette smoke in the crowded bar. Yes, it is something of a sore spot as any teammate who's ever roomed with me will testify. Before I went to bed I poked my head in the bar at the Giffard where a sixty-strong Welsh male choir was in full swing. Apparently they'd been singing across the road in Worcester cathedral in the afternoon. In the middle of the group sat the Colonel, Mike Walsh, our scorer, and Austin (Aussie), our bus driver — looking nicely at home among the predominately elderly men.

**AUSTRALIA 103 AND 4-51, WORCESTERSHIRE 146**

## SUNDAY, 14 MAY

AB and Tugga, batted well this morning. Tugga made a great 60 on a very difficult track. I played and missed dozens of times for a superb 17 — a pretty good score in the circumstances. We left them 163 to win which they managed on the last over of the second day with three wickets remaining. It was disappointing to lose but seeing that thirty-seven wickets fell in two days we weren't overly upset. I bowled well enough, beating the bat but not having a lot of luck.

This game gave us our first look at two celebrated cricketers, Ian Botham and Graeme Hick. Beefy (Botham) bowled a very gentle medium-pace and batted in his typical aggressive style. He certainly looks fit, but it's too early to say how effective he will be for England this summer. Hick failed in the first dig, but, after being dropped early, made a good 40 in the second and hit a few memorable off-drives off me. I tried a slower ball on him and he leaned forward in what looked like a defensive shot but the ball sped away to the mid-off fence. He's certainly a good timer of the ball though I'm not convinced he hits it any better than Tugga. In the end, Hick's 40 was probably the difference between a win and a loss. I tried to search him out for a chat about the New South Wales business but I got the impression he was avoiding me.

That the game ended in two days is typical of county matches at the moment. There is a lot of speculation, not to say controversy, about the effect of the Reader balls with their high seams. Phil Newport certainly swung and seamed it around a lot in this game taking eleven wickets for the game and winning the man of the match award. We might be seeing more of him in the first Test next month.

The day ended with Duncan Fearnley, the Worcester chairman, arguing in our rooms for a one-day game tomorrow. AB was totally unimpressed, saying there was no point playing anything on that wicket. So, a free day tomorrow.

**AUSTRALIA 103 AND 205, WORCESTERSHIRE 146 AND 7-163**

## MONDAY, 15 MAY

We left Worcester for Taunton in Somerset at 10 am. We're at the County, an old world hotel with winding staircases and not too many mod cons. A hotel with character.

We practised at 2.30 pm and with Simmo accompanying Dean to the doctor in London there was a good chance we wouldn't get flogged but as the wickets were good, we worked fairly hard anyway. X (Mark Ray), my old University of New South Wales teammate who is covering the tour for the Melbourne *Herald*, dismissed Boonie

29

with an unplayable and didn't pass up an opportunity to rub it in. Cambo smashed one out of the ground and straight onto the tinted windows of our dressingroom. The ball just bounced off. It's a new pavilion and the glass is reinforced. After all, Beefy and Viv Richards did play here not so long ago.

Tugga, Tub, Maysie and myself ate at Porter's wine bar and Maysie insisted on hiring a video of his favourite movie, 'Ferris Bueller's Day Off'. He is obsessed by this film and watches it twenty-five times a year. He's even been to Chicago to see what it would be like to be Ferris. Maysie said he could feel Ferris' presence in the streets. The four of us went back and watched it in the conference room of the pub. Maysie laughed at a lot of scenes we didn't find even vaguely amusing.

I rang Greg Watson, an old teammate from the University of New South Wales Cricket Club and New South Wales who played for Worcestershire. He lives in Cheltenham and said he'd try to get down to the game. I also spoke to my manager, David Collins, about the possibility of writing a column for the *Daily Telegraph* back in Sydney.

## TUESDAY, 16 MAY

We practised early, a 9 am start. It was very warm to begin with but in the middle of the session the temperature dropped seven or eight degrees in ten minutes. Everyone practised well including Dean 'the Legend' Jones who wore a helmet even during a light catching session. His face is still swollen but the specialist has said the break in the cheek-bone is too close to the optic nerve to operate. It will be wait and see with that one.

Tugga convinced Heals (Ian Healy) and myself to go on a sightseeing trip to the beach resort of Minehead. After playing for Somerset last season, he considers the resort to be his territory. I suspect he wanted to go back there to have another crack at the mini golf and, from the way he coped today, he'll have to go back next time. However, I doubt if Heals and I will return; it was 10°C and deserted and the attractions of the place eluded me.

Back at the pub we had a fines meeting — a traditional way to let off steam by being a little silly and fining just about everybody for any misdemeanour. Of course Legend cops the most fines.

We also discussed the proposed trip to Holland and Denmark at the end of the series. We're not impressed by the news that we will have to pay for our wives. This differs from the information we received before the tour.

### WEDNESDAY, 17 MAY

Today was the first day of the game against Somerset at the Taunton ground which is quite pleasant, the obligatory cathedral nearby and the River Tone behind. Clem and I both sat this one out — as did the local captain, Vic Marks, whose father died suddenly last night. Chris Tavare has taken over.

Another hot, sunny day — amazing weather. We lost the toss and were sent in on an uneven track. They bowled with plenty of spirit, especially Adrian Jones who's a fiery character with plenty to say. He appeals for absolutely everything, argues the point then is able to find something to laugh about with the batsman at his end. We ended up 8–339 at stumps which was a good effort on that wicket. Tub made 97, Boonie 61, Ziggy 48 and AB was out caught off bat and pad for 0 off the young New Zealand off-spinner, Paul Unwin, who replaced Marks.

Tub was edgy early on, his feet not moving too well. He's obviously been worried about his form, especially as he knows the selectors would probably prefer to have him open in the Tests with Swampy and keep Boonie at three. He's also got some competition from big Tom Moody. I've roomed with Tub quite often and although he

31

has been a little touchy, he is never difficult to get on with — which is a fair achievement when he has to put up with me. Today was typical of cricket. You have a bit of luck early, the feet don't move — but you survive. After a couple of hours at the crease the feet get going and the game changes. It all seems simple again. Tub was certainly relieved, not so much by the score but by the fact that he was playing well.

The day's play ended in dramatic fashion. When Merv went out to bat, the boys suggested he hit the last ball of the day for six. He obliged, smashing Unwin over mid-off and into the River Tone. Locals say it was one of the biggest hits they've seen here.

Dyso (John Dyson), who is on holiday visiting his brother, came into the rooms today. When he arrived he announced, very tongue in cheek, that he didn't have the South African contracts with him just yet. He got a few laughs with that one.

I rang Julie from the bus — it has a fax, phone, facilities for three credit cards, kitchen, bar and in-house movies. I also rang Reebok for more gear. We pay for the calls and the rate is not cheap, but I suppose it is convenient.

AUSTRALIA 8-339

## THURSDAY, 18 MAY

Very warm again. I heard today that Hick had declined the offer to play for New South Wales. Graham Thomas, the Carphone director from Brisbane who had sponsored Botham to play for Queensland and had negotiated to bring Hick out, was quoted as having said that you can't deal with someone who keeps moving the goalposts. Jim Woodward, who's covering the tour for Sydney's *Daily Telegraph* was definitely not impressed with Hick's reaction when he asked him for a comment at Worcester the other day.

We bowled Somerset out for 140. Mocca looked very

good. He worked up some pace early and got a couple to really fly. His second spell wasn't as good but it looks like his knee might be coming good. He's the quickest of us and it would be great to see him show his best for a full Test series. Mayhem (Tim May) bowled okay though his spinning finger looks terrible. We're 3–144 at stumps. Tub got another 50 and seems to have turned the corner now. Swampy also made 50. Mocca, who went in as nightwatchman, hit a full toss from Unwin which ricocheted off his pad and onto the backside of a close fielder, landing gently in Peter Roebuck's hands at silly mid-off. It's always a laugh watching Mocca bat.

I went to a XXXX appearance at the Brandninch Sports Club, about forty-five minutes out of town, with Tugga, Heals and Ziggy who has become a XXXX regular, mainly through lack of cricket which is always the lot of the second keeper on a tour. The locals, who did us easily at skittles, were a great lot and we had a typically lively English night.

AUSTRALIA 8-339 DECLARED AND 3-144, SOMERSET 140

## FRIDAY, 19 MAY

Somerset batted all day for a draw with Roebuck making a very boring but valuable hundred. The South African, Jimmy Cook, looked good in getting 50-odd and Tavare made 43 in quick time. Contrary to what Australians remember of him, he can slog well and often does so in county cricket. If he'd stayed in they might even have won.

We bowled without luck though I thought Maysie should have taken more wickets on what was a dusty turner. He bowled reasonably well but without a lot of variety. Maybe he was trying too hard. I went for a run with Clem who insisted he knew his way around Taunton from his county experience. He managed to get us lost and turn a half hour run into something more like a marathon. Still, we returned via the river at the back of the ground — very pleasant.

Before hurriedly packing our bags I swapped a sun hat for a Somerset sweater off one of their players. I'm trying to collect a sweater from every county. Then it was off on the three-hour trip back to London. We ate on the bus again and it was terrible. Still if we had to stop somewhere to eat they'd be very long days.

I've got a new roomie at the Westbury, this time another blue bagger in Tugga Waugh. He's seen a specialist about his long-standing shin problem and won't be playing the next three-dayer against Middlesex. The specialist will be doing more tests as I think Tug really wants to get to the bottom of the problem.

Rooming with Tugga should be interesting, he's not the tidiest of men. He can turn a sparklingly clean hotel room into a bomb site in ten minutes. I've never seen anyone pack so much gear into a suitcase or spread it around a room so quickly. Of course I'm super clean, even folding my socks and putting them in the corner — well almost.

I'm back in room 314 at the Westbury. It looks like it might be mine for the duration. Makes you feel at home I suppose. The verdict is that the Westbury is better than the Waldorf where we stayed in 1985. The rooms are air conditioned and have showers, and the hotel is in an excellent location, near both Oxford and Regent Streets, Soho, the West End theatres and Covent Garden. The situation couldn't be better.

AUSTRALIA 8-339 DECLARED AND 3-144 DECLARED, SOMERSET 140 AND 3-235

## SATURDAY, 20 MAY

The sun streamed in through the curtains this morning. There is talk among the Poms about the possibility of this summer being the best since the last great one, in 1976.

I received a great postcard from Julie who is staying at her sister's farm near a little village in Suffolk called Wissett. We're in the same country but she still writes.

Gatt won the toss for Middlesex and we fielded. They were all out for 245 and we were 0 for 30-something at the close. Gatt made 65. He's having a very good look at us. Mocca took 4 for and I managed 2 for about 50. I bowled 22 overs before tea so I'm very fit for this early in the summer. I beat the bat a lot and seemed to be doing it easy though not in top gear yet.

I took Tub down for a feed at one of our favourite restaurants from 1981 and 1985, the Ristorante Aroura, a good twenty-five minute walk from the Westbury. As soon as we walked in the manager recognised me and sat us next to the signed photo of the 1985 side. Don't you hate it when people older than you call you 'Mr...'. We ate well and at the right price and had a few drinks in Covent Garden on the way home. We're batting tomorrow so there is no rush to get to bed early. Tub might have been not out overnight, but he's also a lot younger.

MIDDLESEX 245, AUSTRALIA 0-37

## SUNDAY, 21 MAY

Dave Gallup, aka Morgan, a colleague from the University of New South Wales Cricket Club, rang me to organise a ticket for today's play. I spoke to Tim Mullins, sports editor at the *Daily Telegraph*, about the possibility of writing a column for the paper.

We suffered another injury this morning when Maysie found himself the predictable but very unlucky centre of a fluke accident. He was practising catching about 50 metres from the nets when he heard a call to look out. His first reaction was to turn to see what was going on and just as he did a big hit from Tom bounced straight into his face. It made a nasty mess of his mouth and he needed stitches. You could hardly say it was Maysie's fault, but he's so accident-prone it was no surprise he was the one who copped it....

We declared behind their score which is a common ploy in three day games. Swampy hit his third hundred of the tour; big Tom got 60 not out and hit the ball very well.

*Maysie's first mishap: Errol takes Tim May off for stitches to a split mouth caused by a fluke accident at the Lord's nets.*

Middlesex finished on 3-157 and the game looks set for either a set-up declaration and run chase or a boring draw.

Gatt finished on 78 not out in the second dig. By the look of him it could be a long summer bowling in his direction. He is very determined to make runs against us even in these games. At best it will set up a psychological advantage for him; at worst give him some good practice against us.

I spotted Dave Bartholomew, also from the University of New South Wales Cricket Club, while I was fielding on the boundary. He's been here nearly a year now and looked like he had survived the winter fairly well.

I had dinner in Hamstead at the home of my French optometrist mate, Michel Guillon and his wife Leslie. She is from Headingley, home of the Test ground, in Leeds, and he is a rare bird — a Frenchman with a good understanding of cricket. He's a regular at Lord's having lived in London for years now. While there I organised for Michel to check Deano's eyes.

**MIDDLESEX 245 AND 3-157, AUSTRALIA 2-233 DECLARED**

## MONDAY, 22 MAY

The England team selected for the first one-dayer on Thursday was announced in the papers this morning. No great surprises. Beefy is being tried in the one-day game to see if he's worth playing in the Tests.

We started the day looking for a declaration from Gatt, but ended up bowling them out for 227. I took 5-48 off 19 and bowled Gatt in the first over of the day. I was very pleased and he was very unhappy. He was obviously looking for a hundred and then more. We needed 240-odd to win and got them with three wickets and three balls to spare. We mucked it up a little at the end by changing the batting order but we were always going to get there. I smashed the winning runs over slips which is typical of my very ordinary batting at present. I definitely have to do some work in the nets. AB and Boonie played well and Angus Fraser took four wickets for Middlesex in a good display. He's very tall and bowls a tight line. He played for Western Suburbs in Sydney last season and I ran into him at the Sydney Cricket Ground practice nets. There is already talk of him playing for England this year and that may well happen.

I won the player of the match award which was a bit of a shock as I never win them. Still, the prize was a small stereo which will come in handy for the rest of the tour.

Again we had to pack up quickly and head north to Leeds, a long trip of some four hours. We're playing Yorkshire in a one-dayer tomorrow which means an early start. Could be a tough one.

MIDDLESEX 245 AND 227, AUSTRALIA 2-233 DECLARED AND 7-243

## TUESDAY, 23 MAY

As this was our seventh playing day in a row, the boys weren't too keen on playing today. Still, it was a fine sunny May day in Yorkshire so none of us had reason to complain, especially me because I was given the day off.

The Headingley wicket is always a precarious proposition, but it was an absolute belter today. Boonie proved it by making 172 off 157 balls. I don't think anyone could possibly have hit the ball better. Paul Jarvis, a Test hopeful, copped a fearful hammering though he wasn't the only one. Boonie has now made 619 runs in five hits for an average of 123.

Legend made 89 not out in his first dig since injuring his cheekbone at Hove. He had to wear a helmet with full visor but once he got used to it he hit the ball well. It should do a lot for his confidence with the One-Day Internationals coming up. He's probably our best one-day batsman now and we'd like to have him out there. The guys bowled well and we won easily. While all this mayhem was going on I spent the day in the sun, reading the papers and chatting to some Sydney cricketers who are over here playing in the leagues. All in all a very pleasant day, only improved by the fact that I wasn't playing.

After the match we left for the short drive to Manchester for the first One-Day International on Thursday. We'll be staying at the brand new Copthorne Hotel which will be a vast improvement on some of the old pubs we stayed in on previous trips. I'm to room with Tub again.

I rang radio station 2GB in Sydney about doing reports for all the one-dayers. Something to keep me off the streets at night I suppose.

AUSTRALIA 3-297, YORKSHIRE 188

## WEDNESDAY, 24 MAY

The papers were full of Beefy this morning. He's been given the all-clear by a magistrate on some old assault charge and won't have to appear in court on the first morning of the first Test. I think we'll see him in the papers all summer no matter what he's doing on the cricket field. The tabloids can't survive without him.

We practised at Old Trafford this morning in very humid conditions. It was a hard session, no doubt to remind us that in the morning we would be playing England not a county side. Naturally enough, the emphasis was on fielding because of the extra work we all have to do in one-day games.

After practice I went shopping for some clothes with Heals, who is in the rag trade, as adviser. The humidity of the morning turned into a thunderstorm in the afternoon which caught the two of us in downtown Manchester. Strange weather this, more like Brisbane than the grey drizzle you associate with this part of England.

We had our usual team meeting at 7 pm at the Copthorne. It was strange because the selectors (Simmo, the Colonel, AB and Swampy) did not announce the side, not even a squad of thirteen. This surprised a few of us because you really like to know the night before whether you're playing or not. It makes quite a difference to your mental preparation and even to how you sleep. But for no apparent reason we were all left in a state of uncertainty. If the selectors aren't sure who to play then they could say so. Swampy and Boonie will probably open but even that's not official. As for who will bat in the middle order or who the fifth bowler will be, we'll have to wait and see.

The main topic of discussion at the meeting was how important it is to get away to a good start this summer. Even though winning the Test series is the main objective we still want to win the one-day games and put early pressure on England. After all, we are the world champions and we've had a good record against England in recent years. One encouraging thing is that everyone is fit and available. Perhaps that is what's making the selectors' job so difficult. We discussed the England side but there are no real surprises there and nothing special to consider.

My roommate, Tub Taylor, spent the night out with his former teammates from Greenmount. He's unlikely to play tomorrow so a lateish night won't worry him. Besides he has youth on his side. I had a quiet one, writing a few letters and relaxing.

# ONE-DAY
# INTERNATIONALS

As we hit breakfast this morning, we were less than amused to see *The Sun*'s description of our pace attack. There were pictures of Clem, Mocca and myself, and Tony Greig's byline. The captions read: 'Terry Alderman... very determined but won't make mayhem. Carl Rackemann... a real trier, but won't skittle side. Geoff Lawson... he has great experience, but doesn't roar in.' We weren't impressed, even if it was only *The Sun*. Greig's comment

## BORDER'S PUSSYCATS
*The Sun, London, 25 May.*

that England's batsmen could sleep easy in their beds this summer raised some hackles at the breakfast table. Merv suggested that the quicks get t-shirts printed with 'Border's Pussycats' on the front and our names on the back. I just hope at the end of the summer it's Tony Greig having a bowl of milk and not us.

Back to reality. The first international of the season and the first cold, windy day. This is more like it. The team wasn't announced until forty minutes before play and that upset everyone. I have no idea why we weren't told, but it definitely made preparation very difficult. Tub missed out for Wag and Big Tom played as the extra all-rounder. He bowled pretty well too. The wicket wasn't all that good, a sort of slow turner, like Sydney really. We lost comfortably, bowling, fielding and batting pretty poorly.

41

*Border's Pussycats in a playful mood: Tony Greig's assessment of us in the London press caused quite a different reaction.*

In a minor surprise, Gower opened the batting and, although we were not unhappy as it gets him in early when the ball is moving, he did get them away to a quick start. He certainly looked in good nick, timing it well and playing with all the fluency and carefree attitude that typify his batting. I didn't make it too difficult for him at the start by bowling badly in my first spell. Thankfully Mocca tightened things up when he replaced me. My second spell was much better and I ended up with 3–48.

We chased 231 but never looked like getting it. Boonie went for a big drive too early and was bowled by DeFreitas; AB got a great one from Neil Foster that nipped back and took his off-stump and, as we slumped to 3–17, Swampy got bogged down. We didn't recover from that start.

I visited my old Lancashire League club, Haslingden, after the game and copped a fair serve when I walked in. Shouts of 'one-nil' and 'quack quack' for my brief duck. It was great to see everyone again, especially as we had won the championship last year, but nothing had changed — still the same blokes in the bar drinking pints of bitter.

*The lame leading the lame: Rackemann, whose knee is still not completely right from his fall at Hove, helps Healy off the field at the end of the tie at Trent Bridge.*

I began the day with a preview to 2GB radio at 8.30 am. and finished it with a postmortem at 10.30 pm. There's not much good news for the folks back home just yet.

**ENGLAND 9-231, AUSTRALIA 136**

## TEDDY BOYS PICNIC

*The Sun*, London, 26 May.

'Dex hails Gower,' cries *The Sun* this morning. Dex?

Back on the road again — an eleven o'clock leave for Nottingham this time, but it's not far and the weather is pleasant.

We practised in the afternoon at Trent Bridge and Clem immediately had the Dukes ball swinging Irish. The Dukes is the less controversial ball with a more standard seam than the Reader and swinging Irish means it swings towards the shiny side not away from it once the other side has been roughed up. It may be something to work on. Clem, Cambo and myself at least had some fun in our net fiddling with the swing and comparing results.

There was one moment of excitement in the other net. Tugga went in to bat with two brand new Gunn and Moore blades, never touched before, and proceeded to smash a few balls over the heads of the bowlers, legitimate practice for a one-dayer. As AB walked back from delivering a ball, Tugga belted a full toss from Cracka (Trevor Hohns) straight back down the wicket at waist height right into AB's backside. AB had no time to get out of the way and collapsed in a screaming heap. Merv, who was also bowling in that net, hurried down from the end of his run-up to give the skipper a consoling hug. However, he found AB far from welcoming and was told in less than polite terms to immediately leave the scene of the accident.

At the team meeting tonight Simmo was a little negative, dwelling on our poor performance at Old Trafford. The rest of us concentrated on our previous good performances in one-day cricket and spoke about repeating them in tomorrow's game. At least the wicket looks a lot better, with more pace likely than at Manchester.

After the meeting I went up to my room and watched Arsenal win the league from Liverpool in the last thirty seconds of the championship. A great climax to the soccer season I saw start here last summer. I'm rooming with Wag (Mike Veletta) who's good value, making you cups of tea at night, after practice or whenever. At present he's studying for his accountancy exams so while I quietly watched the soccer, he was hard at the books. I can sympathise with him there as I had to study a lot early in my career. I went to bed very keen for tomorrow's match.

## SATURDAY, 27 MAY

The lovely Trent Bridge ground, home of Harold Larwood, was bathed in warm sunshine when we arrived. A perfect setting which enhanced the air of expectation for both the players and the spectators. We are getting into the real stuff now.

AB lost the toss and we bowled on another slow turner, much like the last one. Maysie, who came in for Wag to bolster the bowling, did a good job taking 2–35 off his 11 overs. My stint was reasonable, nothing more. Allan Lamb made a great hundred on a wicket that was difficult to play because of the lack of pace. He hit the ball really well and scored nearly half the total.

Legend caused some consternation when he was bowled by Embers (John Emburey) trying his offside poke shot. We weren't particularly impressed as he'd been specifically told not to play the shot at last night's team meeting and he was playing well before he attempted it. Heals twisted his knee and eventually asked for a runner. Legend came on but from the first ball Heals instinctively sprinted off for a two which prompted Lubo (David Gower) to suggest to the umpires that there was no need for a runner. They agreed and Legend had to leave the field. AB was not too happy but Heals survived. It seems that England are going to play it hard this summer. There won't be any favours.

We chased 226 and made it, but only just. We had to get seven off the last over from Daffy (Phil DeFreitas) with three wickets left and in the end Heals and Mocca had to run

*Warriors from way back: AB watches as Botham makes a fine stop off his own bowling during our successful run-chase in the Lord's one-day international.*

a two off the last ball for a win. Mocca missed it and they managed a bye to tie the game.

Despite the drama at the end, we felt no elation as we all thought we should have won. After we folded in the first game I'm sure England were a little surprised that we were able to come back and, despite a slow start, bat well enough to tie. Of the top seven, only one did not reach 25 and Tugga topscored with 43. If any one of them had gone on with it we would have won. My batting improved infinitely. I made one before holing out to Graham Gooch in the outfield.

According to the rules, this game is a tie at the moment. If we win the next one at Lord's on Monday and therefore level the series, this game will be decided on who lost fewer wickets. In other words, England, who lost five to our eight, cannot lose the series even if the final scoreline is one win each and a tie. That's one-day cricket for you.

ENGLAND 5-226, AUSTRALIA 8-226.


## SUNDAY, 28 MAY

Most of the lads had a big one last night so the 11 am leave was a bonus. A Sunday sleep-in for a change. But we practised at Lord's as soon as we arrived in London and I must confess I'm feeling pretty weary tonight after all the cricket and travelling of the past few days. There's no doubt that once you get to the international games you're far more drained. The one-day matches take more out of you and the programme over the last week has been very intense.

It looks like Wag will have to keep tomorrow because of Heals' bad knee. Ziggy is still recovering from a similar injury and has little hope of being fit in the morning. Also, Tugga's shin is playing up so there might be more than one change to our side. The pace seems to be getting to us.

I ate Greek tonight then went with Clem and AB to the Clarence Hotel, a pub owned by an Australian who refused to let us pay. I watched some golf on television and crashed out fairly early again.


## MONDAY, 29 MAY

Another fine and sunny day and a full house at Lord's. It's a beautiful sight and the new Mound Stand and the electronic scoreboard haven't ruined the atmosphere of the old ground. I hoped we could do justice to the crowd.

AB lost the toss again. He can't seem to win one against

Gower. England batted and Gooch was given not out in a run out although replays showed him well short of his ground. He was on 37 and went on to make another 99. Gower made 61. Clem bowled very well and I finished with 0–48 which was not too bad in a high-scoring game. I haven't got the control I'd like, but it's still early in the tour. One highlight was a good catch by Wag behind the stumps off Tom.

We needed 279, a large total but the wicket was very good for batting and we did it easily, losing only four wickets. Swampy made a hundred, AB a very quick 50 and Tugga 35 off only 32 balls. Towards the end we were going well with wickets in hand, but it was still reasonably close, 21 needed off the last 18 balls. Then Tugga effortlessly clipped Foster off his toes for two consecutive sixes into the Mound Stand. They were great shots and put the game beyond England. Swampy won the man of the match award and Tugga our man of the series.

Our spirits were very high after the game. We levelled the series even though the trophy went to England on a technicality. That we finished with a good win was important with the first Test only eight days away. We've really turned things around from Old Trafford. As for England, Gooch, Lamb and Gower look good but that's no surprise.

We didn't leave the ground until 11 pm after drinks in the rooms with the Australian golfers, Rodger Davis, Bob Shearer, Noel Ratcliffe, Peter McWhinney and Wayne Riley. It was good to have a win and to have plenty of Australians there to see it.

ENGLAND 7-278, AUSTRALIA 4-279.

## TUESDAY, 30 MAY

We left for Birmingham at 10 am but were forced to detour because of a bad smash on the M1. It took us four and a half hours to get to the Burton-on-Trent brewery where we were to have lunch. This is where the English version of XXXX is brewed. After an excellent lunch and a look at the brewery operation, we rejoined the M1 and finally got to the Albany in Birmingham at 5.30 pm.

I went for an Italian with a few of the journos — Mark Ray, Martin Blake, John Coomber and Neville Oliver. Tugga came as well, along with Brad McNamara, a young Sydney batsman who's playing for local club Smethwick. During the meal Tugga said he'd heard that Curtly Ambrose, who is playing for Northamptonshire, is after him. He just shrugged his shoulders in resigned acceptance, as if to say: what's new? Hopefully Curtly has finished with me.

## WEDNESDAY, 31 MAY

It was much colder today for the start of the Warwickshire game. Luckily we won the toss and batted as most of us were very tired. Boonie must have been feeling the pinch a bit as he padded up to the first ball of the innings and was out leg before. He wasn't too happy, especially as he then had to sit the day out watching Legend and Tom belting them all over the park. The boundary on one side was only about 45 metres and it copped an awful bombardment during the day. At lunch Tom came into the rooms wearing an even broader smile than usual and said that batting out there with Deano today was like being a beggar who's been invited to lunch by a millionaire.

Legend certainly played like a millionaire and was out just after tea for 248. It was absolute carnage. He smashed them mercilessly, hitting them not only over that short boundary but over the grandstand behind it as well. He would have made 300 easily but got out slogging wildly just

49

before we declared. Tom made 144 not out and we closed at 3–444. It was pretty fair going, we made the total in about five hours and could easily have made 500 in the day if we'd wanted to.

It was very cold as we went out to field for the last hour and disaster struck when Maysie pulled a hamstring chasing the first ball of the innings. We all had a bit of a laugh as he trudged off because if anyone was going to get injured it was Maysie. I don't think he thought it was too funny. Pulled hamstrings never are.

After play I had a few Perriers with all the lads at the Albany. It was quite a lively night with several 'working women' eventually being escorted from the bar by the constabulary after complaints from the management.

AUSTRALIA 3-444 DECLARED, WARWICKSHIRE 2-28.

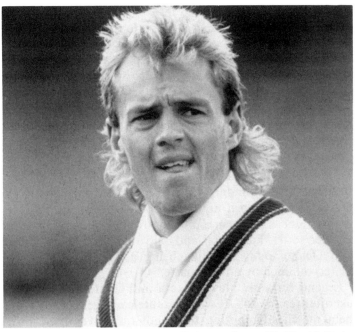

*The apprentice Pussycat: Greg Campbell, during a fine spell in Warwickshire's first innings.*

## THURSDAY, 1 JUNE

It was very cold today and the ranks were severely depleted. Clem, Mocca and Swampy were off somewhere in the hire cars. Maysie's hamstring is not too good and he also has a painful back; Heals' knee is still sore; Tugga was away having his shin treated and Boonie and Wag were back in the hotel suffering from a virus. At one stage we were so short we had Brad McNamara, their twelfth man and a Ghanian from the county staff all subbing at once. We still managed to bowl them out for 230-odd and finished on 1–112. Cambo took three wickets, bowling a good line. Cracka also had a long spell and kept things tight.

Tonight we had a free meal at a casino with the Warwickshire lads and a flutter on the roulette wheel. I was happy with a profit of fifty quid but I'm told Moody and Zoehrer fared much better.

AUSTRALIA 3-444 DECLARED AND 1-112, WARWICKSHIRE 235.

## FRIDAY, 2 JUNE

We batted on till just before lunch for practice before closing and I don't think I've ever played in worse light. It was incredibly dark, but being county cricket they stayed on and waited for it to pass and it eventually did. However the game was finally called off two hours after lunch when Warwickshire were 3–105. Thank God we were bowling.

After the game it was straight to Derby, near Nottingham, for a function at our hotel to raise money for the county club. Fred Trueman was the guest speaker at what was, because of his reputation for lively language I suppose, an all male do. We play Derbyshire tomorrow, our sixth day of play in a row, before heading north to Leeds for the first Test next Thursday. Merv and I have got the cars this time with Mocca and Clem back in harness.

AUSTRALIA 3-444 DECLARED AND 4-195 DECLARED, WARWICKSHIRE 235 AND 3-105.

51

I went to the ground this morning to watch the first session of the Derbyshire game before leaving for Suffolk to see Julie. It's wicket was very interesting—plenty of grass and an uneven surface, and the same colour as the rest of the field. I was glad I wouldn't have to bat on that minefield.

By lunch we were 6–120 and Devon Malcolm had bowled quite a few bouncers — he was born in the West Indies after all. The Derbyshire blokes looked a cocky bunch, especially their captain, Kim Barnett, so it should be a lively encounter. Let's hope we don't suffer any injuries.

After lunch I headed off in the Rover for the quiet of the Suffolk countryside. My wife's sister and her English husband live in Brook Hall, a three storey house some of which dates back to the fourteenth century. The drive along the narrow country lanes was very relaxing, real English countryside this. With the Test coming up soon, it was great to have a day or so to relax away from the cricket.

AUSTRALIA 200, DERBYSHIRE 4-153

## SUNDAY, 4 JUNE

We went to Dunwich Castle and the nearby beach for lunch today. The weather was horrendous — windy, rainy and cold — but the place was packed. You can always count on the Poms to turn up at the beach no matter what the weather is like. Back at Brook Hall I settled in to watch the afternoon sports show, 'Grandstand'. I noticed the scores from Derby on the teletext. At stumps, the locals were 5–63 after leading us on the first innings by 28 and dismissing us in the second for 180. Twenty-one wickets fell so the track played true to its looks. They need another 90 tomorrow with five wickets left so it should be an interesting finish.

The England squad of thirteen for next Thursday was announced today. Graham Dilley was not considered because of injury so the attack will come from Foster, Jarvis, Derek Pringle, Phil Newport, Beefy and Embers.

AUSTRALIA 200 AND 180, DERBYSHIRE 228 and 5-63.

52

The news this morning is that Gatt broke his thumb yesterday trying to take a catch and is in doubt for Headingley. Can't help bad luck.

I got back to the ground about 12.30 pm with the game still very much in the balance, but after the break Clem lifted himself a gear and we bowled them out for 141 to win by 11 runs. Clem ended with four wickets and Cambo and Mocca both took three. Derbyshire weren't too happy at losing. They'd prepared a green wicket with their strong pace attack of Ole Mortensen, Simon Base, Malcolm and Ian Bishop in mind. In fact, Malcolm was so upset at being the last man out that he threw his bat away in disgust, a little strange for someone with no pretensions to batsmanship.

Big Mocca didn't look like he was moving too well. His knee must still be worrying him. Apart from that, winning a close game on a bad wicket was good for the side with the start of the Test series two days away. Though it wasn't the best preparation for a Test, especially for the batsmen, I suspect a few of them expect a similar wicket at Headingley anyway so maybe this game might turn out to be better practice than it seemed.

I took Cambo to Leeds in the Rover. We're staying at Bramhope on the rural outskirts, about ten miles out of the city, luckily on the Headingley side. It's still a bit of a hike into town every day.

I'm rooming with Tub again which suits me fine. It would be even better if this turned out to be his first Test against England. It should as he's been batting pretty well and I think the selectors are keen to have a left and a right hander opening with Boonie at three, AB at four and Legend at five.

AUSTRALIA 200 AND 180, DERBYSHIRE 228 AND 141.

# TUESDAY, 6 JUNE

More bad news for England. Beefy was hit in the face yesterday trying to hook a bouncer on that dodgy Worcester wicket. He hasn't been officially ruled out yet but

I can't see him fit in two days. Gatt will come up for practice tomorrow and they'll decide then on his fitness.

We trained at 9.30 am in typical Yorkshire weather — cold and windy. I felt quite stiff at the start and was obviously in need of a workout. It was a good session even though we were all swathed in sweaters and tracksuit tops.

Tugga and I took in a film in the afternoon before fronting at a social club meeting in the evening. When you're on a long trip like this you need something to break up the routine and this is why social and fines committees are formed. The fines committee consists of chairman Boon, May and Veletta all of whom can fine each other as well as the rest of us. Moody, May and Zoehrer make up the social committee which is responsible for organising restaurants for team dinners, movies to watch on the bus and any form of entertainment deemed necessary.

I was fined twenty pence for wearing a watch onto the field when serving as twelfth man and fifty pence for bowling no-balls in the nets, something I always do. I offered to pay twenty quid in advance for the rest of the tour, but I wasn't going to get out of a weekly grilling that easily. As expected, Dean Jones received the highest number of financial penalties.


## WEDNESDAY, 7 JUNE

Beefy is definitely out and judging by the photo in this morning's paper, it's a nasty injury. He has a fractured cheekbone similar to Legend's and no one knows how long he'll be out. Barnett has come in for Beefy, and after his performance in the Derby game, this is good news.

It was freezing at the ground this morning and everyone wore thermal underwear. What a lovely summer it was.

Mocca, who would have been in the side as the third paceman, bowled for a long time in the nets but was forced to admit his knee was not up to it. He'll have an arthroscopy tonight at a local hospital and could be out for a month. A bad blow.

The wicket received more than the usual attention from media people and players from both sides. It certainly looked very good, but we won't know what it will do until the game is well under way.

We had our usual team meeting at 7 pm. Mocca had rung to say he'd had his operation and was sitting up in bed being looked after by several nurses. As Errol (our physio.) said, Mocca was lapping it up.

The twelve was announced with all our available fast bowlers named. Maysie missed out mainly because Headingley usually favours seam rather than spin. Tom looks like being twelfth man. The main news is that Cambo will play his first Test. He looked a little stunned by the news but I've no doubt he won't let us down.

After the side was announced we talked about being positive and not letting anything put us off our game. If when we bat the wicket doesn't play well, we've still got to show plenty of discipline. If we can get a good start anything is possible.

The Headingley 'hoodoo', as it has come to be known after what Beefy and Bob Willis did to us here in 1981, was not mentioned. Admittedly it was in the back of the minds of Clem, AB and myself who'd played in that match and though don't like to admit it, still carry a scar on the psyche from it. We would dearly love to win here to get over those bad memories and will probably benefit from Beefy's absence more than the rest of the team. It will be easier for us mentally without him there. I must admit that a lot of the other guys, particularly Tub and Swampy, aren't worried about Beefy or Headingley at all. They haven't played much against him nor have they played on this ground before and simply want to go out there tomorrow and play well. Hopefully it will be that simple.

I think I'll sleep well enough though I'm not sure about Tub. Tomorrow the real tour begins.

*Our final warm-up: stretching exercises on the first morning of the first Test. In the background Ted Dexter in suit and running shoes and the terrace houses and grey clouds of Headingley.*

# THE FIRST TEST

Ladbrokes this morning were quoting 11–4 against us winning this Test. Not bad odds for a two horse race. It was cold again and the ground was damp from light rain when we arrived.

My column for the *Daily Telegraph* today was about the start of the 'real' cricket this morning. Enough of the one-day games and the county matches, today we began what we came here for — the Ashes series.

You could really feel the buzz in the dressingroom before play. Plenty of nerves around. It'd been a while since I'd played a Test and I was as nervous as anyone, with the possible exception of Cambo I suppose. I was feeling reasonably happy with my bowling, was in good physical shape and was really looking forward to the game. I just hoped the wicket didn't do too much and we got the worst of it. The weather affects the wicket at Headingley more than at most grounds and today's cloud cover meant the ball was bound to move around a bit. Nevertheless, AB had decided to bat if he won the toss, a decision that would have surprised a lot of people. His thinking was that the wicket looked very good for batting and he was prepared to trust it. It was also in line with our plan to be as positive as we could.

Before the toss the captains agreed to use the Dukes ball not the Reader, no doubt both were worried that if the pitch played up at all the Reader could be devastating for the batsmen and spoil the balance of the game. The light rain and wet ground delayed the toss for twenty minutes which increased the tension in the rooms. All you want to do at that stage is find out whether you're batting or bowling and start the match. AB called wrongly again and Gower sent us in. Gatt was ruled out so both Robin Smith and Kim Barnett are playing. Embers is their twelfth man, so like us they were obviously expecting it to be a seamer's track.

We started slowly with the ball moving around quite a lot. Swampy and Boonie were both gone with the score in the 50s and at that stage anything could have happened, but the skipper walked out and went straight on the attack. AB made 66 quite quickly and it was that innings that really turned things in our favour. He took a few risks against some loose bowling and it paid off. It was a perfect example of a captain leading by example.

At the other end Tub worked his way towards an undefeated 96. He played extremely well, especially after lunch when the clouds lifted and the wicket settled down a little. He might have been lucky to play and miss early on, but you need that to survive on a wicket that is doing a bit. His job was to stay there and provide a foundation for tomorrow and he did it perfectly. His only major blemish came when Gower dropped him at slip on 89. It was a classic opener's innings on the first day of a series. To top it off, his parents were there to see every ball.

I saw Tub make his first ever hundred at school in Wagga, so I was delighted to be there to see him get to within four runs of a debut Ashes century. He's worked very hard on his game and so, after a slow start to the tour, today was just reward. His great strengths are his tight, correct technique, which helped him survive today when things were sticky early on, and his even temperament. He never worries about being beaten, the state of the wicket or who's bowling. He just plays every ball as it comes at him. That's the way we're all taught to bat, but doing it is not that easy, especially if it's your first Test against England — and at the dreaded Headingley ground as well. Most English people know very little about Tub, except of course for the few who saw him in the Bolton League last year. In Australia, anyone who saw him make any of the 1,200 runs that took him to the top of the run-making list last season won't be too surprised by today's innings.

*A classic opener's innings: Mark Taylor lays a solid foundation with his 96 not out on the first day.*

So, 3–207 at stumps on day one. A good start for us on a less than ideal track, but really it's still fairly evenly balanced. If we lose a few early wickets in the morning the game could swing around. There's plenty of work left yet.

AUSTRALIA 3-207.

## FRIDAY, 9 JUNE

Tub continued on to his maiden Test century, a little tickle down the leg side bringing three figures up and all of us on the balcony to our feet to applaud a great Test innings. After about an hour's play he pulled across the line at one that wasn't all that short and was lbw for 136. In walked Tugga to join Legend and the fun really started. They added 140 in quick time.

Tugga continued in the great touch he's been in all tour and quickly passed Legend who was playing the supporting role to perfection — a job that doesn't come naturally to him. Lege's running between the wickets was generous to his partner and devastating to England. Tugga was simply brilliant, playing one of the best Test innings I've ever seen.

He was nervous in the 90s after having been out there twice last season against the West Indies, but this time there was no mistake. A typical backfoot square drive to the point boundary brought up his maiden Test hundred off only 124 balls. The great thing was that Tugga didn't let the relief of finally reaching 100 get to him. He just put his head down and kept belting them, playing some of the best shots I've ever seen. The Poms were very dejected by this stage. With no spinner, Gower couldn't vary his attack and our blokes just pounded away as if it was a one-day game.

Deano went for 79 and Heals followed soon after, but then Merv settled in for a decent stay. Throughout all this Tugga kept pasting them, totally in control and never hitting the ball in the air. After he'd reached 100 Gower had Barnett on the deep point rope to try to stop those powerful square drives. Barnett was just below our balcony and it was like watching someone trying to catch bullets in a shooting

*The floodgates open: Steve Waugh plays one of his glorious square drives during his brilliant 174 not out.*

gallery. Occasionally he'd get his hand on one and knock it down inside the rope but more often than not he couldn't move quickly enough to get near them.

It was sensational stuff and we all felt lucky to be there to see it. I can understand how Bradman must have felt when he asked his players to come out onto the balcony at Trent Bridge in 1938 to see Stan McCabe make his famous 232. It was a similar sort of thing today. You just didn't want to look away for one ball. You'd either be in the dressingroom watching the television or on the balcony. The crowd was the same. The Yorkshire people know their cricket and they applauded generously, while saving some stick for their own blokes.

Tugga was still there on 174 at the finish and to top it all off Swerv was with him on 63. Apart from a couple of swishes, it was an impressive batsmanlike display from Swervyn. Six for 580 was the total, a scoreline we didn't dream of this morning. We added 373 in the day, a rare feat in these times of relatively slow over rates.

When Tugga came into the dressingroom everyone shook his hand and said what a great dig it had been. He was as quiet as usual, but obviously delighted and thanked the Colonel for sticking with him for so long.

A happy camp tonight. Tomorrow the hard work begins: the wicket will be just as good and they've got a few lads who can bat a little.

Tub dined with his parents tonight which must have been a great pleasure for the three of them. I had a quiet drink in town and an ugly ranch burger on the way home with Tugga. He was still pretty quiet, just pleased to have got to three figures though I think he could sense that bigger things were to come.

AUSTRALIA 6-580.

SATURDAY, 10 JUNE

7-601! — Australia's highest Test score at Headingley.

We batted on this morning to reach that nice round figure of 600 — 'Turning the screw' AB called it. Merv was out for 71 and I contributed a very tasty 10 not out. Ten runs and a half a dozen bouncers — they certainly like to bowl short. Anyone would think I'd bowled them a few over the years or I'd had my jaw broken recently by a short one.

Only one team can win after a first innings of 7–601 and England began their first dig knowing they had to bat for three days with their sole purpose survival.

......................................................................

## Lawson dismisses Newport taking his 150th Test Wicket.

....................

The wicket played slowly but quite well and they finished on 4–284 with Lambie (Allan Lamb) 103 not out. Barnett made 80 and although his technique and footwork are unusual he certainly likes to give it a whack. Two more wickets would have been nice, but it was always going to be tough bowling them out on that track. Lambie played some great shots, especially through the off-side. If we don't get him quickly on Monday morning we could be struggling to force a win.

Clem got Gooch leg before in exactly the same way he did here in 1981: caught in front playing across the line towards the on-side. I can remember watching that one from fine leg with Clem bowling from the same end. Same shot, same decision. Merv's leg break, which doesn't get anyone out in the nets, completely fooled Chris Broad and bowled him off-stump. Merv went over the top when he saw it hit, very entertaining stuff.

I had Gower caught flicking down the leg-side, but apart from that bowled poorly. I ended up with 1–74 off 22 overs but those figures are flattering. The Gower dismissal was interesting. He'd been flicking at a few outside leg stump, either missing, or hitting them in the air wide of Heals. He never looked like letting them go which meant he was quite happy to play with the bat well outside his body, a risky ploy. Once or twice he even flicked one-handed at them. After a while we decided to go for Plan B which is to move one of the gullies to leg slip and bring a fine leg squarer in case the batsman hit a few in the middle, and, lo and behold, he nicked one to Heals. We might be trying that one again.

Cambo was obviously nervous in his first outing and bowled eight overs for 39. He bowled a few good balls in

*Trapped in front: Alderman takes one of his five first innings wickets. Kim Barnett's front foot prod is a dangerous technical flaw typical of most English batsmen these days.*

there but generally was a little full and was probably trying too hard which is understandable. Plus, bowling to Lambie in full flight is never easy. Still, Cambo is through his first day and I'm sure he'll settle down tomorrow.

So far this Headingley track has produced 883 runs for eleven wickets, but at least we are the only side who can win.

**AUSTRALIA 7-601 DECLARED, ENGLAND 4-284.**

## SUNDAY, 11 JUNE

The rest day, so I slept in until 10 am then went for a run, had a spa and did a few stretches to loosen up after yesterday. A golf day had been organised by XXXX and fortunately it was an easy walk around. Legend and his team won — and so he should with all the private tuition he gets from Ian Stanley. The handicap system is being run very rigorously so no one can get away with anything. Tub Taylor reckons he'll never win playing off six.

I was weary after golf and went to bed about 8.30 pm and watched television for a while before sleeping.

## MONDAY, 12 JUNE

Warm and sunny. We bowled them out for 430 just before tea, but they passed the follow-on. Clem got five and bowled particularly well. I got three but it wasn't a great display, no rhythm at all. The run-ups didn't help, they're very uneven, down hill and up dale. Cambo had a lot of runs scored through the slips which ruined his figures but he finally got his first Test wicket. He wasn't impressed with his first innings in Test cricket, but we assured him things would improve.

Robin Smith made 66 and hit the ball very hard. He looks like a player to watch.

We finished on 3–158 which gave us a lead of 329. Tub made another 60 just to prove the point, but Swampy

*The end is nigh: Marsh catches Phil Newport off Alderman during England's collapse on the last day.*

missed out again. Boonie made 40-odd and looked good before being given out leg before to Daffy. He was not impressed with the decision.

There was some controversy when the umpires called off play with three overs left because of rain—even though it wasn't raining. AB and Legend had earlier refused two light appeals offered when a large, dark cloud appeared behind the ground, but then the umpires called it off. The Poms did not look too interested at this stage with AB and Legend smashing them, and it cost us both valuable runs today and extra time that we would need tomorrow to bowl them out. It wasn't raining and eventually only did so very lightly for a minute or so. AB was upset, staying on the ground for a while arguing with the umpires and finally leaving very reluctantly.

Tonight we all went to Harry Ramsden's, the biggest fish and chip shop in the world, for a free feed. Leeds is famous for having the best fish and chips in Britain and Harry Ramsden's had rung the Colonel to invite us along. People contact our manager quite often with these sorts of invitations, but we can only accept about one in twenty.

AUSTRALIA 7-601 DECLARED AND 3-158, ENGLAND 430.


# TUESDAY, 13 JUNE

We batted on for three-quarters of an hour this morning and left them 402 to win. After taking only one wicket before lunch I felt a draw was inevitable even though there would be plenty of pressure on them during the afternoon. The wicket was still good and I thought we'd struggle to bowl them out. In the end, they lost six wickets in the second session and were all out for 191 with an hour and a half left. Gooch made 68 and Clem took another five. First blood to us by 210 runs.

I was both elated and surprised, as were most of the blokes. The wicket had been good all day and I really thought they'd see it out. I was certainly surprised to see their middle order collapse. It was just a matter of us

66

keeping the pressure on and them not playing well when it really counted. They just cannot believe they have been beaten, but you can already see the self doubt beginning to show.

Clem won the man of the match award for a great display. I haven't bowled as badly for years even though I got Gower, accidentally-on-purpose down the leg-side again, and Smith for a duck. Basically we played five days of very professional cricket, taking our catches and batting with discipline. The thing is we can still improve even though most people over here don't know it.

As the dressingroom was being flooded with champagne, Clem, AB and myself couldn't help feeling we had taken revenge for what had happened to us here in 1981. However we didn't have much time for private reflection as Merv began spraying everybody with champagne and beer. AB was in the middle of a television interview on the balcony when he was drenched with a can of XXXX. Tub said he had now played three Tests for two wins and a draw and he couldn't understand why everyone says Test cricket is so hard. The only problem with the celebrations was that we had to pack up and leave for Manchester to start a three-day county game tomorrow.

The bus trip across to Lancashire was lively to say the least, with Merv leading us all in singing 'one nil, one nil' and 'Allan Border walks on water'. There's nothing like a sporting team in high spirits.

We arrived at the Copthorne in Manchester at about 9.30 pm and headed straight for Pier 6, a bar and bistro behind the pub. The celebrations continued in great style, much to the bewilderment of the local clientele. To a continuing background chant of 'one nil, one nil' from Swerv, Boonie and Tom decided to test out the top shelf of the bar and after some hours reported that none of the alcohol had gone off. Boonie and Tom had, however. Boonie, who always reminds me of a bomb about to explode, had obviously forgotten that he might have to face Patrick Patterson and Wasim Akram in the morning. Heals performed brilliantly. His impressions of Clem's and Maysie's bowling actions were the best I'd seen. His 'Maysie' started just outside the door to the beer garden, stuttered in and around people's tables, stretched into full rhythm across the length of the bar and ended up delivering the ball right in front of the door to the ladies toilet. Great stuff.

I had to leave all this to ring a match report through to radio station 2GB at 10.30 pm. Peter 'Zorba' Peters voiced his suspicion that I'd been drinking. I told him he should have known better, but that I'd have a few when we won the Ashes. I went to bed relatively early as I'm in tomorrow's side and I'm older than Boon and Moody. Fancy having to front up for a county match the day after a Test. It's like being a county player, something I've never much wanted to be.

AUSTRALIA 7-601 DECLARED AND 3-230 DECLARED, ENGLAND 430 AND 191.

## DEXTER WASN'T EVEN THERE

The Sun, London, 14 June.

I was probably one of the few able to read the papers this morning and already the knives are out for Gower and Dexter. 'England slaughtered in Headingley horror and . . . DEXTER WASN'T EVEN THERE' moaned *The Sun*. This referred to the fact that Dexter had returned to London on the weekend instead of staying in Leeds to see the end of the game. Did they expect him to walk his lads out to the wicket? In other headlines, England's loss was described as a 'Lily-livered limp-wristed surrender' and the England team as 'Gower's Goons'. Australian papers are never that bad.

There was much trepidation in the rooms this morning when acting captain, Geoff Marsh, went out to toss. A quiet day's batting was what we wanted, with the exception of Boonie of course. No such luck. Much to Boonie's relief Swampy lost the toss and we had to put in another day in the field.

At precisely 11.13 am Boonie dropped the easiest catch in the history of cricket: Cambo was bowling and the batsman edged one off the top of his bat and into the air about six feet above Boonie at short leg. DB looked up, tried to move back but instead fell forward onto all fours where it looked like he might have stayed. But no, his cricketing instincts prevailed and he managed to lift his arms off the ground, and look up to see the ball falling gently towards his hands. It hit him half way up the forearm and both he and the ball fell to the ground. Boonie looked apologetically down to Cambo who burst out laughing, followed by the rest of us.

Next over Swampy dropped the second easiest catch in the history of cricket, a gentle nick to first slip off me. At the end of the over he came over to explain that he had so many tears in his eyes from laughing at Boonie that he didn't see his catch too well. Apology accepted.

We managed to bowl them out for 184 on a good wicket

and only dropped five catches in the process. Not bad considering. Then we lost 2 for 1 in Patterson's first over before Tom and Legend saw us through to 3–140-odd. Patterson, just back from injury and keen to do well, bowled quite sharply and with plenty of short stuff on the fastest and bounciest wicket we've played on so far. Normally counties are only allowed to play one international in any one game, but, this being a tour match, that rule did not apply and both Akram and Patterson were selected. They were both trying hard to impress the Lancashire selectors to win the one spot in the side and our boys copped some solid stuff from both ends. As Boonie said after play, it was lucky we fielded first otherwise he might well have been killed this morning.

LANCASHIRE 184, AUSTRALIA 3-137

# THURSDAY, 15 JUNE

We made 288 and had them 8–172 at stumps. It was an uneventful day's play, but very pleasant out in the hot sunshine. My batting form continued — a second ball duck to Akram. My bowling was also very poor although I took some wickets which is a small consolation. I don't seem to have any rhythm. It's very much like a golfer's swing. If you haven't got any rhythm things don't come out in the right place and everything is a struggle. My run-up feels alright but I'm losing a lot of control: the out-swinger is swinging in, I'm bowling too full and at leg stump most of the time. As usual, the harder I try the worse it gets. There's no substitute for plenty of work in the middle so I'll just have to bowl myself out of this bad patch.

Before my duck I read a Geoff Boycott interview in the *Daily Mirror*, headlined 'Why Gower should GO!'. We have only played one Test haven't we?

I went to see 'Working Girl' tonight with a few of the lads at the theatre complex next door to the Copthorne.

LANCASHIRE 184 AND 8-172, AUSTRALIA 288

## FRIDAY, 16 JUNE

Last day of the Lancashire game. We rolled them early and won by nine wickets. Patterson and Akram managed to bowl five bouncers an over even though we only had to make 80.

After the early finish we headed off to Northampton for tomorrow's three-dayer and yes, I'm playing. I know I need the bowling but this will make it eleven days play in the last twelve. Don't they know I'm an old man?

We had a team meeting on arrival, just some general information from the Colonel and a bit of a chat. Someone mentioned the rule about players' wives not being allowed in the same hotel as the team until 15 August. AB was very strong on this point so it looks like we'll have to live with it. Some of the senior players — Boon, Alderman and myself — were not too happy.

LANCASHIRE 184 AND 185, AUSTRALIA 288 AND 1-84.

## SATURDAY, 17 JUNE

The hotel here seems to have improved since 1985, but then I was ill during that stay. The main drawback now is that the weather is very warm and there's no airconditioning. The rooms are stifling and you get hit by a wall of heat when you leave the foyer area and enter the residential section.

I ricked my neck this morning during the first ten paces of the warm-up and had to pull out. It was very painful and I laid down all day with an icepack on it. Maysie had a fitness test this morning and just managed to get through it. He said he was alright but you could see he still wasn't moving too well. The selectors are keen for him to be fit for the second Test next week and he was under pressure to play in this game.

Tugga had some good news when we heard that Curtly Ambrose had pulled out with the flu. In fact four others from their senior side have withdrawn in what has become a common practice when county sides play the tourists.

AB plundered a hundred in quick time and Boonie made 50. Swamp got into the 30s but would have loved a longer stay in the middle. We made over 300 and had them 1 for not many at stumps. Lambie left the field during our innings after getting a knock on his hand trying to take a catch, but he should be right for Lord's on Thursday.

My neck felt okay after the ice treatment so I went with some of the lads to a XXXX appearance at Milton Keynes, a half an hour away. We didn't get back until midnight and by then my neck was aching again.

AUSTRALIA 329, NORTHAMPTONSHIRE 1-28


### SUNDAY, 18 JUNE

We knocked them over for 180 with Wayne Larkins making a good 84 in his usual hard-hitting way. Merv took five wickets and looked sharp. We finished on 3-182 with Tub batting very well for 69. He's in great touch now, but his opening partner, Swampy, didn't reach double figures. He's beginning to worry about his form and just can't seem to get the time in the middle he needs.

My neck seems to be slowly improving.

Before play, Clem and I had a chat with Dennis Lillee who's coaching Northants. He congratulated us on the win at Leeds and made the point that some of the English batsmen seemed to be playing across the line. His advice was that if we kept bowling wicket to wicket, we should continue to give them problems.

The England side for the second Test was announced today with quite a few changes to the bowling. Newport, Pringle and DeFreitas are gone with Angus Fraser and Graham Dilley coming in to the squad of thirteen. Gatt is back as well. Apparently Embers injured a hand yesterday and considers himself only 50-50 for the Test. Also Lambie is in doubt and Lubo (David Gower) is still recovering from a minor shoulder operation he had yesterday.

AUSTRALIA 329 AND 3-182, NORTHAMPTONSHIRE 180.

# MONDAY, 19 JUNE

We finished the game by 2.30 pm, bowling them out for 106. Even though Lambie did not bat again, their performance was atrocious and the whole day was like playing third grade in Sydney.

As we half expected, Maysie struggled to get through the day. He strained his hamstring again this morning during Simmo's warm-up exercises and there is a lot of blood behind his right knee, suggesting the tear is quite serious. No Test for Mayhem just yet.

During the day I went over to the nets, bowled one ball and thought my head was going to fall off. The neck is not good and I'll have to see a chiropractor in London first thing in the morning.

The day at Northampton ended well with a charity match between Eric Clapton's XI and Alan Lamb's XI with half a dozen of us playing. The game started at 6 pm so we had a few hours on the balcony after our match to enjoy the sun and meet a few of the celebrities. EC's team shared our rooms and he, David Essex and Dennis Waterman seemed like very nice blokes. Merv stole the show in front of 3,000 people by bowling to David Essex's son with seven slips and two gulleys. EC's side won off the last ball from Merv with an all-run seven fielded by the bowler.

We didn't get to the Westbury until 11 pm and I'm back in room 314 with Tub. We all decided after Headingley that for good luck we would stick with the roomies we had for that Test.

**AUSTRALIA 329 AND 5-229 DECLARED, NORTHAMPTONSHIRE 180 AND 106.**

# TUESDAY, 20 JUNE

No practice today after the cricket of the past twelve days. As I was about to set off to the chiropractor in London, Noel Pattison, my chiropractor from Perth, rang. Talk about fate, he's the genius who got me through my back problems in 1985–86, and he's in London. He said he'd come over in the afternoon to work on my neck.

The team went to a lunch organised by Bob Willis at the Cafe Royale, a short walk from the Westbury down Regent Street. Kate Fitzpatrick was one of several Australians there.

Noel came round at 3 pm to give my neck a crunch and it felt better immediately. At 3.30 pm I met Julie to go and see the new James Bond movie, 'Licensed To Kill'. Outside the theatre we ran into Peter Doohan, the Australian tennis player, who is in town preparing for Wimbledon.

*The perfectionist at work: Waugh rehearses his out-swinger during our pre-Test session at the Nursery nets at Lord's.*

# THE SECOND TEST

We had another team photo this morning before practice. I told the boys that the 1985 side had their photo taken on the field in front of the pavilion and that we should look for another spot. Of course the blokes who hadn't been on an Ashes tour before did not agree and, as they're very much in the majority, they had their way.

England were due to practise after lunch but Gooch and Gatt were already in the nets when we got there, the former working on playing straight and the latter getting in as much batting as possible after having been out with his injured hand. I bowled off a shortened run and the neck was stiff but not too painful. Noel gave it another crunch this afternoon and I've been given until the morning to decide whether I'm fit to play. I'm no better than 50-50 at this stage. The way it feels now it would be a struggle to get through the five days of a Test match. The other worry is that I haven't really bowled a ball off the full run since the Lancashire game.

We all worked well in the nets with Tugga hitting the ball beautifully. One square drive off a ball of perfect line and length from me was truly memorable. He also spent quite a deal of time with Clem trying to improve his bowling. He may be in great form but he's still working hard at his game. Tugga varies his training. At times he works very hard when he thinks he needs it, at other times he will cruise if everything is going well. But even when he's cruising there is something of the perfectionist about him. He sets himself high standards and is annoyed if he can't maintain them.

75

There is a good feeling in the camp about this Test. Australia's record here is very good although Headingley showed that you can never rely on history. Still, we beat Middlesex here in a one-dayer and a three-dayer, the MCC in a one-dayer and England in the one-day international. It's no wonder it's good to be back at Lord's, my favourite English ground, especially when it looks as magnificent as it did today. The sun was shining; the outfield looked perfect; all the marquees were up in the Nursery. If the warm, sunny weather holds it should be a great occasion.

Team meeting at the Westbury at 7 pm as usual. Maysie is not fit so Cracka is in the twelve. Otherwise, it's the same team as at Headingley with Cambo the likely twelfth man. We're obviously happy with our game. The batting was excellent at Headingley and we know we can improve our bowling. There's no reason we can't keep our winning record at headquarters. And that means two nil.

After the meeting we went for a team dinner at a Mexican restaurant off Regent Street which had been booked by the social committee. Either holes in the walls were real bullet holes or this is the most authentically decorated Mexican restaurant in Europe.

## THURSDAY, 22 JUNE

Overcast and cool this morning. One paper described this game as the 'Anxiety Test' for England and the widespread doubts about their batting won't hurt our cause at all.

The guys were a little tense at breakfast which is quite normal on the first morning of a Test. Still, Merv managed to consume several tonnes of food, all very nutritional he assured me. I had my usual grapefruit and orange juice, plenty of it though. We left for Lord's at 8.45 am and there was already a large crowd gathering when we arrived. The first day of a Test is always special with a strong sense of anticipation running through the place. Who'll win the toss? Will he bat or bowl? Who'll be the twelfth men? When you arrive and see hundreds of people lining up at ticket

*Searching for rhythm: I bowled 27 overs on the first day, took two important wickets but was still nowhere near my best. Dickie Bird looks on.*

77

windows or waiting near the nets to watch the warm-up, you always feel a buzz up your spine.

Cambo was our twelfth man and Fraser theirs, so each side had added a spinner. Lambie was ruled out and my neck had improved enough for me to be a starter. AB lost the toss to Gower for the fifth time this summer and England batted on what looked like a very good wicket. Yet by lunch we had Broad, Gatting and Barnett out and at 3–88 they were in trouble again. It might have been 4 for at lunch had Legend caught Gower for 11 at deep fine leg off me.

The second session was one of the most amazing I've seen in Test cricket with England scoring at better than a run a minute but losing five wickets in the process. It didn't seem like Test cricket at all. They never tried to consolidate or build partnerships. It was all helter-skelter shot-making with Gower, in particular, batting with abandon. His was what we call a numbers innings where the batsman decides to defend, e.g., two balls and hit the third for four, irrespective of the merits of the individual deliveries. He made 57 and Gooch was steady in getting 60, but at 7–191 we looked like knocking them over for just over 200. Then Jack Russell, showing great improvement with the bat since Headingley, led a fightback by the tail that took them to 286. Even so, we were delighted at bowling them out for that total on such a good track.

Clem again bowled well early but Merv was probably the best. He got both Barnett and Gatt in the first session, the latter caught at bat-pad for a first ball duck. Merv tends to take a while to warm up in a spell, but this morning he was accurate and fast from the start. I bowled Gower when he tried to cut one that was too full, a mistake he makes quite often. That's three out of three for me against Gower and I must say it's a special pleasure to dismiss him as he's taken me for a few runs over the years. I bowled 27 overs which, given that we bowled them out before stumps, was a high work-rate. I was still nowhere near my best, but again I took a couple of important wickets.

ENGLAND 286, AUSTRALIA 0-4.

Swampy went early to a good ball from Graham Dilley, but Boonie and Tub put on more than 140 to steady things.

During that partnership the dressingroom was invaded by half the Australian cabinet. Gareth Evans, John Button and Kim Beazley were in there chatting to AB who was padded up to go in next. A few of us wondered who was running the country while all these guys were at Lord's. When I put that question to Gareth Evans, he quipped they were over here having a love affair with Maggie. After a while AB looked a little on edge and began pacing around, so I went over to the politicians and reminded them of the importance of the game and suggested they let the skipper sit down and concentrate on the play. They agreed and left the rooms immediately, but soon after the Prime Minister arrived and joined AB on the balcony for the compulsory photo opportunity. In fact I took that opportunity as well. Mr Hawke left when Tub got out and AB was required out in the middle. To his credit, the distractions did not seem to affect him and he played well for 35.

*A meeting of legends: Dean 'The Legend' Jones offers some advice to an amused PM on the balcony at Lord's. AB looks worried about what Deano will say next.*

*On the attack: as in the first Test, the good form of the other batsmen encourages AB to go for his shots.*

AB got off the mark by dancing down to Embers and driving him through the covers. He was as aggressive today as he'd been at Headingley. I think he has so much more confidence in the batsmen around him on this tour that he is prepared to attack more. Boon, Jones, Waugh and himself can either play carefully or flamboyantly according to the situation. It's that adaptability that is encouraging AB to attack as often as possible. Also I think he realises that we were too defensive against England's spinners in 1985 and so he is keen to assert himself early and offer a positive example to the others. From the start of the tour his plan has been to be more positive about everything and if it doesn't come off at least we'll go down trying. Besides, AB has had to play so many defensive innings in his career that he is probably just keen to play a few shots when he knows he can rely on the others to defend when necessary.

Boonie's 94 was very patient, very disciplined. With Swampy out with the score on 6, he and Tub settled in against some good, tight bowling and built a very good foundation. Boonie was upset with himself for getting out so close to his first century in England, and at Lord's at that. He had struggled on the 1985 tour and is very determined not only for himself to do well but also for the side to win the series. He's a very determined character and after playing such a controlled innings the wayward dab he played outside off-stump to get out was unexpected. He was annoyed when he came into the rooms, a little throw of the bat and a few choice words.

Had AB and Deano gone on from their starts we could really have buried them today. As it was we ended on 6–276, ten runs short of their total. Tugga is not out 35 and looking in control again. If we can stick with him in the morning we can still reach a big total.

England's bowling showed a lot of improvement on their effort at Headingley. Foster and Dilley bowled well and Embers was more like his old miserly self. It was certainly more like what you expect of Test cricket: bowlers giving little away and batsmen working hard to build their innings. In the end a fairly even day's play.

We went to Australia House tonight for a do with the Prime Minister who told us a few stories about his days as permanent twelfth man for Oxford. We feasted on freshly imported lobsters, prawns and Sydney rock oysters — a fine gesture from the taxpayer. After the function I drove Boonie and Tugga to a hotel to meet up with their wives who'd just arrived in England.

ENGLAND 286, AUSTRALIA 6-276

## SATURDAY, 24 JUNE

Hot, sunny and a full house again. Our last four wickets added another 252. Swerv got 30, Cracka 20 and me 74! Oh yes, Tugga made 152 not out. An extraordinary day.

After some very good batting by Merv and Cracka I came in just before lunch with the score on 8-381. I faced five balls before lunch and played a cover drive, three sweeps and a swipe through mid-wicket. I missed all of them and went into lunch 0 not out. Tugga was on 92 I think.

During the break the boys intimated that it might be wise if I just supported Tugga who, after all, was hitting them pretty well. So I went back out with the best of intentions to stay with Tugga until he got his hundred and maybe a few more. But they kept bowling me the odd half volley or wide one outside off-stump and I kept taking a swipe at them, hitting a good shot here and there and getting away with a few inside edges.

By this stage Tugga had reached his second successive hundred and England were quite happy to give him a single and me the strike. After I reached 30, Tugga came down to me and said he was happy for me to take the strike they were offering as I was hitting a four an over. And that was how we went on for a while until I looked up at the board and to my amazement saw I'd made 50. I looked across to the Q Stand and spotted Julie. She was easy to see, she was the only one giving me a standing ovation.

A few mutterings reached my ears from some of the Poms who were less than impressed with the sight of G. Lawson

*The budding all-rounder: Merv on his way to a good 30 in his first Test at Lord's.*

making Test runs. But Tugga and I carried on in the same way for a while longer until, when I'd reached 74, he came down for yet another mid-wicket conference and told me I could get a hundred myself. 'When is the last time someone got a Test hundred in a session at Lord's?' I asked, somewhat inspired. And that was it. Next ball I holed out to deep mid-on. I still maintain it wasn't a slog, I just mishit the one I'd been lifting Embers over the infield with. Still, we'd added 130 in 107 minutes and put the game out of England's reach. Apparently that was a record for an Australian ninth wicket stand in England and not far off an all-time record.

It was a marvellous experience to put my helmet under my arm and walk off Lord's to a standing ovation, and to walk through the Long Room after making runs in a Test. You can smell the history in that room. It wasn't until I sat down in the dressingroom that I realised what might have happened. I said to Tub: 'I'll never get a better chance to score a Test hundred will I?' If I had've got three figures, I think it would have qualified for what the boys back at my club, University of New South Wales Cricket Club, call a 'MOG' — making a mockery of the game. The main thing is that, while my bowling is still below par, I might have contributed to a win with my bat.

Tugga was again magnificent and the members rose as one for him. Not out 152 and two undefeated hundreds in as many digs. Most of us thought that that first ton at Headingley would open the floodgates and we were certainly right. He's now made 329 without being dismissed and is proving that those of us who thought he would be a great cricketer were right.

Tugga is an interesting character. For someone so compact and ordered on the field, he is amazingly untidy off it. He's forever losing things, wallet or keys in his hotel room, batting gloves, socks and shirts in dressingrooms. His kit is so messy that when he's packing it after a game, he has to stand on it while someone clips it shut. One day early in the tour he even left his suitcase in a hotel room. He's a keen reader of the British tabloids, with a special fondness for the 'Sunday Sport'. He also loves the movies and he and I are regulars at the flicks on tour.

Waughie is quiet and self-effacing off the field, but once he walks through the gate, look out. He's one of the most competitive people I've met. It doesn't matter who's at the other end batting or bowling, he'll back his ability against

*A rare moment: walking off to a standing ovation from the members at Lord's after scoring a career-best 74.*

theirs. Those three bouncers he bowled at Viv Richards in Brisbane last season or the two he gave Beefy at Worcester at the start of this tour were good examples of that attitude. He's making plenty of runs on this tour, but he'd also love to be taking more wickets.

Tugga comes across as a shrewd character who doesn't

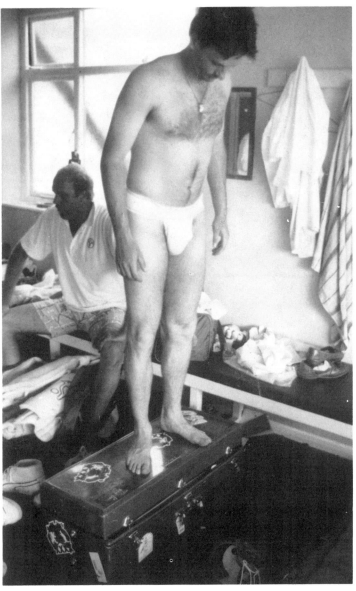

*The other Waugh: compact and ordered on the field, Tugga is chronically untidy off it. Here he tries to control the mess in his kitbag.*

give much away. He's cautious when dealing with people he doesn't know well, but once established as a friend he is very loyal. He also has a very good cricket brain. Early in his career he was reluctant to speak up on the field but last season I found him very useful when I captained New South Wales. He would be great captaincy material.

At the moment Waughie just wants to keep scoring runs in this series. It took him forty-two Test innings to reach three figures and he is now determined to make up for lost time. The Englishmen have not seen the last of Tugga.

As if all those runs weren't enough fun for one day, we had them 3–58 at stumps and well and truly in a hole. Clem got Gooch again, leg before for a duck; I bowled Broad with one that cut back up the famous Lord's slope; Clem picked up Barnett as well.

Such a great day's play was hard to follow, but we did so by accepting Tim Rice's invitation to see his production of Cole Porter's 'Anything Goes'. We went with a few of the Poms, David Gower, Robin Smith and Neil Foster. After

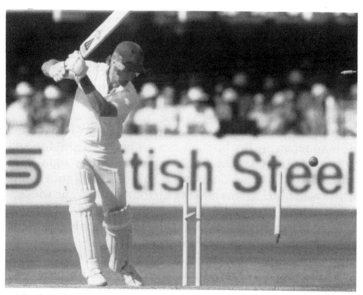

*A lovely sight: Chris Broad loses his off-stump to one I managed to cut back up the Lord's slope.*

87

the show we went backstage to have a few drinks with the cast and then walked back through Soho to the Westbury. A great day — and a rest day tomorrow — life can be good.

ENGLAND 286 AND 3-58, AUSTRALIA 528.

## SUNDAY, 25 JUNE

I slept in this morning and lashed out with croissants for breakfast. Surely I deserved a little self-indulgence after my career-best innings yesterday. When I looked at the papers I realised why David Gower was so early to the show last night. He'd walked out of the official Saturday night press conference, apparently because of repeated questions about how he allegedly bowled Foster from the wrong end. It's amazing how former players, including his recent teammate, Phil Edmonds, can get stuck right in. It must be tough being a captain. You not only have to bat, bowl, field and run the show when your side is bowling but you've got to answer to the press every day of the week. I do feel some sympathy for him, but I'll feel a lot more when the series is over.

I picked up Julie and John Rogers, my captain from my early days in Sydney, and his wife Ros and went down to Camden Town markets for lunch. It was very hot, very crowded and very interesting — all varieties of food and of people.

After dinner at a restaurant in Hampstead I spent the evening repairing my boots. I use a mixture of araldite and cotton wool to coat the front of the toe on my right boot which I drag when I deliver the ball. I always ruin a few ashtrays in hotel rooms making up the mixture. The wickets aren't as hard here as they are in Australia so I don't have to do it as often, but the drawback is that English araldite is not as strong as the Australian version.

Some of the guys played golf with Rodger Davis today. AB, Boonie and Swampy never miss their golf on a rest day, but as far as I'm concerned rest days are for resting. In fact you rarely see bowlers playing golf on a rest day.

*A captain under siege: David Gower faces the press. Minutes later he was to walk out and head off to the theatre.*

## MONDAY, 26 JUNE

As I expected, it was a long, hard day. Typical Test cricket. Gower was missed off me in the third over. It looked a fair catch by Swampy in the gully and Lubo was well on his way before the honest farmer called him back. Given the pressure Lubo is under at the moment it was a lucky break for him. At that stage he was on 26 and England were 158 behind with seven wickets left. We dropped a couple more catches during the day but four wickets in the last session meant we had them 9–322 at stumps, only 80 ahead.

Gower went on to 106 but AB reckons he had him leg before off the first ball he bowled. It was very close and AB was quite upset at the decision. Gower played his usual number of shots and gave a few chances but none of them quite went to hand. Robin Smith supported him well with 96. He and Merv continued their duel with Swerv sending down plenty of short ones. Smith didn't handle them all that well and was forced to take quite a few on the body, but he's a tough character and stood his ground, returning every glare with a determined one of his own. I think they're both enjoying their little duel. While Merv couldn't get Smith out he made it hard for him and got the reward of Lubo's wicket when Gower spooned a short one around the corner for an easy catch.

Russell again played well, making 29 to go with his 64 not out in the first innings. We're not quite sure where to bowl to him. Usually you can just bowl across the left-handers to the slips, but he doesn't have the normal weakness there and can counter that tactic with some good attacking shots off the back foot through the covers. We'll have to have another think about him.

........................................................

## Alderman dismisses Gooch, reaching 100 Test wickets.

.....................

Clem finished the day with 6–111, bringing his tally to 19. He keeps bowling a perfect line and length, moving the ball either way just enough to cause problems. He denied Smith a well deserved 100 with a real jaffa that pitched leg and hit off. As we say in the trade, even Braddles (Don Bradman) wouldn't have hit that one. I bowled the best I have bowled all series though I only finished with 2–89. At least it feels like I'm improving.

At the tea break, we were presented to the Queen and Prince Phillip. Merv, Clem and I were standing together chatting away as usual when the Duke came up, shook hands with Clem, got to Merv and looked across to me: 'So that's why you chaps bowl so well,' he said. We all looked at each other wondering what he was talking about. 'You never shave,' he explained. Following a long tradition, we don't shave during a Test and by now were looking fairly untidy, though Merv would look untidy in a dinner suit.

As the Royals left the field, most of us sat down for a short rest or stood around in groups chatting. AB walked around to all of us, waving his arms and telling us to get our minds back on the job. The score was 5–235 and a few

*All for one: the slips shout an appeal. From left, Taylor, Alderman and Border.*

wickets would seal the game. 'Come on, think about it again,' AB was saying. 'If we pick up a few in this session we'll be certain of going two up tomorrow. We can win the Test in this session.' AB lost his cool a little towards the end of the day's play when we couldn't get rid of the tail, but, barring torrential rain tomorrow, we should go two up. Rain is forecast, of course.

**ENGLAND 286 AND 9–322, AUSTRALIA 528.**

## TUESDAY, 27 JUNE

There were a few showers about as we were having breakfast and we were all worried that this Pommy weather would turn bad at the wrong time.

It took us nearly an hour to get the last man out. Swampy dropped Embers off a fairly easy one but we got Dilley out soon after. We needed 118 to win, but as we came off at the end of their innings it was very dark with a lot of thunder

91

about. After a delayed start due to poor light, we were 1–20 at lunch as the rain started.

Tub was out at 51, then AB and Deano went and put us in a little trouble at 4–67. AB, Clem and myself were very tense at this stage. We'd played at Headingley in 1981 where we'd needed 130 in the fourth innings to win and had only made 111. Some of the younger guys didn't seem particularly worried though. AB decided to relieve the tension and his anger at hitting one straight down fine leg's throat by having a shower. Boonie and Tugga were going along slowly but reasonably well, though Broad had dropped Tugga in the gully off Jarvis when the score was 4–91, so we decided not to let AB back into the rooms to watch. It is a cricket superstition that it is bad luck to change your position during a tense session. I hadn't moved since the start of the innings and while AB was in the shower we hadn't lost a wicket. Nor, despite the black clouds and thunder, had it rained. AB came back when we had about 15 runs to get, but we sent him out for another shave or shampoo or whatever. Eventually, with two to get, we let him back onto the balcony to watch Waughie crack a four off the back foot through point to take us to a two-nil lead.

I must confess that I shed a few tears on the balcony as Boonie and Tugga ran off. There was great jubilation, but the three of us from 1981 were again a little subdued. We knew this was more than just a Test win; it was a big step towards regaining the Ashes, and having been involved in two losing series here, we weren't going to celebrate properly until we'd tied up the series. At 4–70 things could so easily have turned, but Boonie and Tugga played very well. Boonie, solid and determined, ended on 58 not out to give him a total of 152 for the match for once out. He couldn't stop smiling in the rooms after the game. Although Boonie was here in 1985 and has his own point to prove, he doesn't have the same concerns as we three older blokes. Waughie, like all the younger players, doesn't have those inhibitions either and that's a good thing for the team. It makes us very confident about the future of the side.

There were many Australians at the ground today and

after the end they gathered below our balcony and called for us to come out — as we did willingly. Merv managed to douse most of them with champagne, as he had Rodger Davis who was in our dressingroom.

Once again England can't believe they've lost. They think that because they took us through to near the end of the fifth day that they've done well, but the point is that we won by nine wickets and, despite some tense moments, did it quite comfortably. After we bowled them out on the first day, they were never in the game. Apparently Gower has said that he thinks Tugga is lucky. They are blaming bad luck and missing out on a few close umpiring decisions for having lost. Yet we won by *nine* wickets. If their attitude doesn't change, their performance won't improve because they'll blame circumstances and won't realise they have to lift their game.

Boonie again led us in the team song — twice in two games! Rod Marsh was Boonie's predecessor in this tradition and had handed the honour down to him. It was pretty wild in the dressingroom, with Roy Orbison's 'Anything

*Two nil: Boonie leads us in our victory song after the win at Lord's.*

you want, you got it...' playing loudly and repeatedly. It has become our theme for the tour.

There was an interesting incident during the day. Boonie tried to bring his baby daughter, Georgina, up to the dressingroom, but was not allowed. Women are not permitted in the pavilion at Lord's and the staff here take great delight in enforcing every little rule they know. Boonie was not impressed.

I dined with Julie and the Guillons and then joined the lads at a nightspot near the Westbury for a few drinks. We have a one-dayer at Oxford tomorrow, but I'm not playing. There might be a few extra memories to worry about, but there are advantages to being a senior player.

What d'ya know? Two nil!

**ENGLAND 286 AND 359, AUSTRALIA 528 AND 4-119.**

## WEDNESDAY, 28 JUNE

I rang Mum and Dad in Wagga this morning. They were more than a little upset at not getting the cricket on television down there, especially Mum who gets nervous when I'm playing. It was great to talk to them, they are very happy with the way we're going.

The local press still have not given us due credit for the way we've played, instead they're concentrating on bagging their own blokes. Yesterday Foster bowled 18 overs in a row from the pavilion end and took 3–39. That seemed to prove the point that Gower did not mess up the ends on Saturday as some of the press alleged, but I didn't see any apologies in the papers this morning.

The lads headed off to Oxford at about 7.30 am, no doubt a few of them feeling less than 100 per cent.

It rained most of the day so they had a pretty ordinary time. They started their innings once, went off for rain, abandoned that match and started another 30-over innings. Swampy, who has been struggling for runs in the Tests so far, and Wag were happy because they got some batting in.

I went shopping in the morning with Julie, but I started feeling a bit off and spent the afternoon in bed resting. I went for a pizza for tea, the traditional food of fast bowlers, and took things easy for the rest of the night.

AUSTRALIA 5-215, COMBINED UNIVERSITIES 4-116.


## THURSDAY, 29 JUNE

'Australian cricket team and drugs' — well I never. There was a big story in the papers today about Jamie Astaphan, Ben Johnson's doctor, who said that he once prescribed steroids to the Australian cricket team. I never thought the Ben Johnson affair would have repercussions on us. The lads had a good laugh about it and the ACB issued a statement to the effect that Australian cricketers never have used and never will use steroids. I suppose if you looked at Merv's body and all that hair growing out of it you might

*High on steroids or just enthusiastic? Merv practises his grimace during a training session.*

think he was on some kind of steroid, but his is a natural one.

We all had a great time at Wimbledon today. Our wives came on the bus with us and, with the tennis starting late because of rain, we spent most of the day in the players' bar talking with any number of Australians who were there. The officials welcomed us by putting our names up on the match draw board: AB was drawn to play B. Becker; Clem got I. Lendl; I got M. Mecir and, appropriately, Legend was paired with I. Nastase. Ziggy was drawn to play S. Graf which did not please him too much.

## FRIDAY, 30 JUNE

A free day for me today which I spent with Julie in Oxford Street at the summer sales. Most of the guys left for Neath in Wales for the three-day game against Glamorgan which starts tomorrow. Cambo and I are the only ones left in London.

## SATURDAY, 1 JULY

I got up at 6 am to watch Australia play the Lions, live from Sydney. A great victory for the Wallabies — 30–12. The Poms won't enjoy that one too much, nor will the Welsh for that matter. Cambo and I were thinking about going down to Neath to do some work in the nets, but one of the lads rang to warn us that the hotel there was a bit basic, so we decided to stay in London. The two of us went to Picadilly Circus to see 'Indiana Jones and the Last Crusade' and tonight I doubled up to see 'Paris By Night' with Dave Gallup.

AUSTRALIA 4-373.

## SUNDAY, 2 JULY

I slept in till 11 am this morning, for the first time on tour, and lay around resting for most of the day, writing a few letters and watching television. It was good to read in the paper that Wag got a hundred yesterday. We made 4–373 declared and the teletext tonight says that after bowling them out for 301 we're 0–56 in the second dig.

Cambo and I went to John Emburey's for dinner tonight. Embers was late getting back from a one-dayer at Lord's because his pushbike had a flat tyre. He was riding a bike because he's temporarily lost his driver's licence due to some indiscretion. He's a good bloke Embers, especially for a Pom; he always tells you what he thinks—it must be the influence of his Australian wife, Suzie. The conversation was interesting, Embers' comments on the England captaincy being quite illuminating.

It was great to be able to have such a decent rest as we are off to Birmingham tomorrow to meet up with the other guys and prepare for the third Test which starts next Thursday.

AUSTRALIA 4-373 DECLARED AND 0-56, GLAMORGAN 301.

## MONDAY, 3 JULY

Cambo and I had a fairly pleasant drive to Birmingham, arriving about the same time as the bus. The game at Neath ended in a draw, but the boys said the locals were very hospitable and the food at the ground was the best they'd had on any tour. High praise indeed. Wag made 80-odd in the second dig and won the man of the match award, so he was pretty happy.

AUSTRALIA 4-373 DECLARED AND 5-216 DECLARED, GLAMORGAN 301 AND 5-135.

## TUESDAY, 4 JULY

Back to business today. We practised at 9.15 am in very warm conditions. I bowled for one and three quarter hours, off the full run most of the time, and we all worked very hard despite the amount of cricket recently.

The Australian golfer, Noel Ratcliffe, came to practice looking for some treatment for his back. He'll be around for physiotherapy and some cricket-watching over the next few days as will Ian Stanley who is due in town soon.

There were plenty of takers for golf this afternoon. Swa, playing off a ridiculous handicap (he must have slipped through the system somehow), and I scored a brilliant 4 and 3 victory over Border and Marsh who were so disappointed they didn't speak on the twenty-five minute drive back to the Albany.

## WEDNESDAY, 5 JULY

*The Sun* was a treat today. 'Botham Brawl' on the front page with a picture of John McEnroe, his back to the photographer, dropping his shorts on centre court at Wimbledon on the back. They did admit that the picture was a composite, but only at the end of the story. Beefy has been accused of jobbing some bloke in a Northampton carpark. It reminds me of the story that did the rounds in 1985 when he was on a similar charge. His defence counsel: 'My Lord, I conclude by submitting that my client could not have struck the complainant with a series of forceful, accurate blows'. To which the judge asked: 'Well, why not?' 'Because he is a member of the English cricket team, M'lud,' was the reply.

Practice at 9 am. My body felt terrible today, so bad that I slept for three hours in the afternoon.

We had our team meeting at 7 pm as usual. It looks like we'll play the same eleven. However, England have got more injury problems. They dropped Broad, and Barnett was going to open, but when Robin Smith pulled out they brought in Tim Curtis who is a specialist opener. Lambie was in the thirteen, but as in the first Test but has had to pull out again, this time with a shoulder injury. At least he'll benefit from the personal insurance policy some of their players have that means they get paid the Test fee if they are

*Growing in confidence: Cracka Hohns is back scoring runs and that is adding confidence to his bowling.*

forced out through injury less than forty-eight hours before a game. Foster did not bowl in the nets this afternoon because of a blister on one of his bowling fingers and is in doubt. Paul Jarvis is on standby for him.

The biggest blow to England came late this afternoon when Gatt rang home to check on the condition of his sick mother-in-law only to find she had just died. He went straight back to London and Chris Tavare has been called in for him. Good to see the Poms going for some youth for a change.

The main thing for us is that Beefy is back. AB stressed to us that we should treat him like any other player and play his bowling as well as it deserves. From what we've seen in the one-dayers and in the game at Worcester, he's not bowling too well, and he hasn't been scoring many runs either. AB said we were not to talk to Botham out on the field. He likes to do that; it makes him feel more comfortable. As AB said, we're ahead in this series, we're playing from in front so we should make him feel like he's on the losing side. That way we lessen the chance of his mental attitude as well as his physical presence lifting England. Beefy is likely to do anything with the bat. He'll come out and try to be aggressive so it's important for us to bowl tightly and try to get on top of him from the start. There will be an enormous amount of pressure on him. He'll have all of England riding on his back when he walks out there and we must try to make sure he feels it.

The ABC television blokes are covering this game because Channel Nine has opted to cover Wimbledon instead. At least the folks back home out in the country will get to see some cricket.

After our team dinner Tub and I retired to watch some tennis. It's very hot tonight and, because there is no airconditioning in the hotel, we've both windows wide open. The noise from downtown Birmingham directly below us is deafening.

# THE THIRD TEST

The forecast was for 27° C and some humidity which suited us more than England. Foster had withdrawn.

AB won the toss for a change and we batted. Swamp and Tub put on 88 on a wicket that seamed and spun a little. Swamp looked a lot better today but was eventually leg before to Botham while Tub was stumped by Russell off Emburey. We then lost AB to a strange dismissal. He let one from Embers go behind his legs only to hear it hit the leg stick. I think it surprised Embers more than anyone. At that stage we were 3–105, but Boonie and Legend put on 96 before Jarvis got a finger to a straight drive by Legend and Boonie was run out backing up for 38. A little good luck for the Poms at last. Boonie was not too happy when he came in, and when Simmo noted that he was carrying his bat in his right hand rather than his left, which meant he had to turn a full 360° to get his bat back in the crease, Boonie grunted: 'Been doing it all my life'.

When bad light, followed by a wild rainstorm, stopped play at 5 pm, Legend was not out on 71 and Tugga 17. Merv had been padded up as nightwatchman and for the third time was not needed. He says he's doing a great job.

Fraser was the pick of their bowlers although he didn't take a wicket. Still, not a bad start to a Test career. Beefy was steady. You could hear the buzz around the ground when he came on to bowl — it was his first Test in two years. And he almost had Tub leg before off his first ball, only it swung too far. The crowd roared along with Beefy and the game came alive. He certainly gave England the lift we thought he would bring to their game. They seemed more competitive and better organised. You could see today what they lacked in the first two Tests, but we'll have to wait and see if it lasts.

During the day there were a few rumours floating around about the impending English tour to South Africa. There'll be more news soon, we're told.

I dined at Gino's Italian, around the corner from the Albany, for the forty-second time this decade. Still as good as it was four years ago.

**AUSTRALIA 4-232.**

## F R I D A Y ,  7  J U L Y

It was absolutely hosing down as we gathered for breakfast and it continued like that for most of the day. We sat in the dressingroom until 5 pm when play resumed. We played 15

Waugh 393 before dismissal — most runs scored in a Test series without being dismissed.

overs and finished on 6–294 with Tugga bowled by Fraser after a total of thirteen hours batting — finally losing his wicket for the first time in the series. He is now averaging 393! He wasn't too happy when he came into the rooms which shows the kind of competitive spirit the man has. Heals missed out again and doesn't look like getting a run at the moment. Legend reached his hundred before stumps and a very good innings it was too. Some of his driving through mid-wicket was brilliant. When he's in that sort of touch, he's very difficult to bowl to.

Most of today was spent sitting around the dressingroom waiting for the rain to stop — and there is nothing worse! The dressingroom at Edgbaston is fairly small and we had 17 players, a coach, a manager and a physio. all packed in together. AB and I were stuck in one corner, virtually in each other's lap. Luckily my shoes are bigger than his and we don't mix them up before we go out onto the field. It does happen with some blokes.

I wrote ten letters and with Clem did the *Daily Telegraph* crossword — a regular past-time for the two of us. Mostly it was a typically boring, rainy day in the dressingroom. Some guys even had a sleep which is generally not allowed during playing hours, especially if Simmo is anywhere in the vicinity. Merv, Clem, Mocca and Ziggy played 500 until it was coming out of their ears. They'll play anywhere, anytime on any surface. I can't believe how seriously they take it, and they're not even playing for money. Swampy spent most of his time checking his bats, which I suppose is understandable as he seems to have about forty of them. I think he even takes his favourite three or four to bed with him. Waughie did his usual quick read of the tabloids and retold his favourite *Sunday Sport* story about the World War II bomber found on the moon. Legend checked the Deloittes ratings to make sure they were accurate. He is still number 12 in the world and is not happy.

Another bad thing about rainy days is that you can't go to the nets to loosen up. During a Test, the indoor facilities are usually converted to dining areas for sponsors so there is nowhere to go to escape the dressingroom. Some guys will play a few shadow shots for a while or go through their bowling actions, work on new grips or just generally fiddle with bat or ball, but it's never satisfying. If you spend all day sitting around doing very little you end just as stiff and tired as you would if you'd been in the field all day.

After two days we are 6–294 and shouldn't really lose from here. A draw is already looking the most likely result.

**AUSTRALIA 6-294.**

## SATURDAY, 8 JULY

Same again today. This time we managed only two hours play, but they were quite valuable to us. We finished on 7–391 with Cracka making a very good 40. It was his highest Test score and he hit some fine shots through the covers.

*Who'll stop the rain? Deano waiting in the dressingroom during one of the several rain breaks that interrupted his first century of the series.*

Deano is 141 not out and is batting as well as I've ever seen him play. He had a terrific duel with Embers, using his feet to attack as often as possible. His driving was again of the highest class, using the slow pace of the wicket to hit balls on off-stump through mid-wicket with complete safety. He's now made 359 and been out only once in his last two innings — more than I make in three years.

It looks like England have dropped their bundle. They were alright when they got Merv out early, but they struggled once Cracka held them up. Even Beefy seemed to lose inspiration.

During the day, Ian Stanley and Noel Ratcliffe came into the rooms to watch some of the play with us. Stan said he thought cricket as a team sport was so totally different to the solitary, essentially isolated game of golf. Watching us comment on Deano's batting was a revelation to him. Legend was out there scoring a hundred for his country and, while we were obviously appreciative, we spent most of our time making jokes about his batting or his antics. 'Are you blokes like this all the time?' Stan asked me. 'Only when we're in front,' I said. I told him we were always full of fun and frivolity when the game was going well for us but as soon as we lost a wicket, no matter what the score, the dressingroom would go quiet until, after a while, the noise would gradually build again.

**AUSTRALIA 7-391.**

## SUNDAY, 9 JULY

The second Rugby Test against the Lions was on at 6 am this morning, but this time I only managed to see the second half. Australia blew it right at the end. Andy Slack, who was commentating, sent a cheerio to Mocca and me as he said he was sure we'd be watching. How right he was.

More rain again today so the rest day was very quiet.

There's no way we can lose from here and on Monday England will have to bat well to save the game. Of course, we have three wickets left and may still add more runs.

I made 12 very ordinary runs this morning, had my middle stump removed by a Fraser no-ball and was then legally bowled. We finished with 424 all out with Legend out last for 157.

England batted badly and were 7–185 at the close. Gooch was leg before again, to me this time, from one that kept low. Tavare, Barnett and Gower all played ordinary shots although Gower did cop a beautiful couple of overs from Clem before he half-played at one that swung back in from outside off and was also out leg before. It was the best bowling spell of the series so far and by the end of it Gower looked all but gone. He made 8 in forty minutes and was hardly the free flowing player we're used to seeing.

At least Clem's new aerodynamically designed haircut hasn't affected his form. When he came into the bar with it the other night, the reaction was the same as with any new haircut, a chorus of 'what's that?'.

Tim Curtis batted for two hours for 41 without looking totally convincing. It seemed strange seeing him out there opening for England instead of Chris Broad who we thought should have been retained.

Beefy and Russell held us up. Russell played well and we still aren't sure which plan to use to him. At present we're having a bit each way. Maybe it's just that he's playing well. Cracka eventually got him today trying to cut one against the spin. Perhaps Cracka is the one to worry him.

Beefy made 46 in 154 minutes which was not a typical innings for him. But he looked good, his feet were moving much better than most of his teammates and he played according to the circumstances. It was very strange to see him with a helmet on, no doubt he is under doctor's orders to protect the cheekbone he fractured a few weeks ago. He was uncomfortable in the helmet and took it off as often as possible. When Cracka was bowling, Beefy gave his helmet to Russell to mind for him. So there was Russell with his own helmet on, his bat in one hand and Beefy's helmet in the other. None of us had ever seen that one before. I saw Beefy

*A wicket at last: Tugga Waugh shows delight at taking Barnett's wicket, only his second wicket of the series.*

108

after stumps to get one of his t-shirts which has a great picture of him in 1985 hitting AB back over his head for six on it.

Although ten hours have been lost to rain, we still have a chance of winning. They are 40 behind the follow-on with only three wickets left. It will be an interesting morning and there'll certainly be a lot of gas flying around the England dressingroom during that first hour.

AUSTRALIA 424, ENGLAND 7-185.

## TUESDAY, 11 JULY

# ENGLAND DROWN IN A SEA OF MEDIOCRITY

*The Guardian*, 11 July.

There's nothing like the quality broadsheets getting stuck in as well. Warm and sweaty again today.

We ran Fraser out in the first over and then Swampy dropped Embers in the gully off me. That would have made them 9–215, still 10 short of the follow-on. They eventually passed that mark when Jarvis hit me over mid-off for four. Jarvis is the sort of player to bowl to just short of a length on or just outside off-stump, hopefully going away to slip. The one he hit to pass the follow-on was the in-swinger. As soon as I bowled it I knew it was the wrong ball and he knew it was the one to go after. We were very disappointed with that as it put the game out of our reach. We thought that if we could have enforced the follow-on we would have had a chance of winning.

One good thing from today was Cracka's bowling. He had figures of 1–18 off 16 overs and looks like he might cause some problems in the rest of the series. I think his 40 runs in our first innings helped his confidence a great deal.

The rest of the day became batting practice for us. Swampy made 40-odd, Tub another half-century and Heals 33 in a valuable spell at the crease. I went out behind the nets and sat in the sun reading a book for a couple of hours.

109

Less time lost to the weather and we would probably have won this Test. But you've got to expect some rain in England and at two-nil with three to play we're looking very good.

Before dinner at a local restaurant, I wrote my *Daily Telegraph* article on Merv. No shortage of material there. Later on, I joined the lads for drinks at a nightclub and then at the hotel. Heals and Maysie were in their usual post-match condition. A few drinks and they're away. I succumbed to some late night hunger and had a serve of fish and chips on the way home from the nightclub with Brad McNamara and Scott Hookey, another New South Wales cricketer. Hope I don't suffer for it in the morning.

**AUSTRALIA 424 AND 2-158, ENGLAND 242.**

## WEDNESDAY, 12 JULY

We left the hotel at 9 am this morning for Birmingham airport and the flight to Glasgow. Quite a few of the lads were seedy and were not happy when the flight was delayed. They were desperate to get the travelling over with as quickly as possible. Maysie, in particular, did not look well.

We landed in Glasgow at 3 pm and headed straight for Haggs Castle Golf Club for a round that had been organised beforehand. They used to play the Scottish Open there so it's quite a good course though it's always a drag playing with Mocca as he takes so much time over every shot. After the golf I had a quick pizza and went to bed. I was tired and need to be at my best for tomorrow's round at St Andrews.

## THURSDAY, 13 JULY

An 8 am leave this morning as St Andrews is an hour and a half from Glasgow and we were due to hit off at 11 am. Mocca had organised this with the club secretary whom he had met in the Foster's tent during the Lord's Test.

Before hit-off we got a guided tour of the club house and saw all the old trophies and the current British Open trophy as well as glass-fronted cases full of old clubs and memorabilia. It was windy out on the course, but I played the outward nine in two over. During the early holes I noticed a couple of guys playing behind us, who were watching us closely. Eventually I thought I should introduce myself and they turned out to be two young Australian professionals, Bradley Hughes and Steve Earl.

I didn't play so well on the way home. I took three to escape from 'Hell Bunker' and missed three birdie putts on the last three holes. Still, I finished with a 79 and you've got to be happy with that. In fact it turned out to be the best score of the day. Simmo had 82. It's always good to beat him at golf.

Back on the bus (Austin had driven it up on his own), Mocca was given a huge vote of thanks for organising such a great day and then everyone slept until we got back to Glasgow. Cricketers certainly become adept at catching some sleep whenever and wherever they can.

This morning we went to Culreach Castle, about an hour out of Glasgow, for a day of Highland Games. It was mainly organised for Scottish XXXX reps and was quite an enjoyable day. I ended up with rope burn and a sore shoulder from the tug-o'-war, but the two highlights were the sight of Boon, Moody and Rackemann in kilts and Tom setting a new world record for haggis throwing. Tom and Mocca looked fairly presentable in their kilts. Being tall and fair-haired the outfits seemed suitable enough on them, but Boonie looked outrageous. The fact that he is short made him look funny for a start, but he also wore a dark sports-coat and black sunglasses and had a cigarette in his mouth most of the day. He looked like the Mafia's undercover man in the local clan.

The haggis is about eight inches long and shaped like a pear. It's kept in cold storage before the event to prevent it from going mushy. You stand on a cut-off barrel, no run-up allowed, and throw it with a spiral action like a gridiron football. Most of us managed about 180–190 feet, but Tom, who I think holds the record in Australia for throwing a cricket ball, nearly put the thing into the North Sea. He threw his more than 230 feet, past the designated area and into a group of people eating lunch on the grass. The Scots were not too happy with an Australian breaking the record but Tom assured them that he had Scottish ancestry and reminded them that he had broken the record while wearing a kilt. We're told he'll make the next edition of the *Guinness Book of Records*.

We actually had some haggis as an entree for lunch and it wasn't too bad. Georgina Boon found it very appetising — and a fun toy as well.

Tonight we went to a reception given by the Lord Provis (the Mayor in our language) at the impressive Town Hall.

*'McBoon the Outrageous': the kilted Tasmanian takes part in the XXXX Highland Games at Culreach Castle near Glasgow.*

## SATURDAY, 15 JULY

We played Scotland today at the headquarters of the West-ern Scotland Cricket Club which is home for the season to my New South Wales teammate, Trevor Bayliss. It was probably the hottest day of the summer today and there'll be some red and raw Scottish bodies around for the next few days. I wasn't playing, so after watching the first hour in which we made heaps of runs, I went off for another round of golf up in the hills above the city.

Apparently Boonie took a wicket today. He befriended a group of boisterous characters on the fence who were quick to spot one of the clowns in the side. They continually pestered AB to give Boonie a bowl and AB finally succumbed. Boonie promptly got hit for six. However he recovered brilliantly to take a wicket and immediately turned to his mates in the outer and raised his arms in triumph. They roared their approval. We'll be hearing about that one for quite some time though it was pointed out to him that it was not a first class match. 'Still a wicket,' he grunted.

Cricket in Scotland is basically an upper class sport; the working class plays soccer. But the crowd today was typical of any at a cricket match in Australia — eskys full and by mid-afternoon the lads were in good voice. The local officials were delighted with how well we're playing. Here, as in Wales and Ireland, they don't support the Poms too much.

AUSTRALIA 7-307, SCOTLAND 9-210.


## SUNDAY, 16 JULY

We flew back to Heathrow today while poor old Aussie (Austin Grundy) drove the bus all the way down from Glasgow. We met up with him in London and headed straight to Bath in Somerset for tomorrow's match against Minor Counties at Trowbridge.

It was very warm in the early afternoon when we arrived in Bath, an old Roman city. It's a beautiful place in the worst weather, today it looked stunning — clean streets and the old stone buildings in perfect nick. I went for a stroll around the shops and settled in for a sunbake and a read in the park opposite our hotel. Mark Ray and Blakie wandered over looking totally wasted. The hot weather, the travelling, not to mention the journalists' lifestyle, seem to be getting to them.

114

Tugga, who is back in his county cricket territory, took me to eat at the Bathampton Mill House where we sat outside on a terrace and ate in the evening sun, very pleasant. The shock came when we got back to the hotel. There is no airconditioning and the rooms are like saunas. I might not get much sleep tonight.

The four days in Scotland were the longest break from serious cricket we will get on tour. Tomorrow is a one-day friendly and we are back on the county circuit at Southampton on Wednesday.

Many people think that going on a cricket tour to anywhere, especially England, is like being on a paid holiday. In truth, you rarely get to see the monuments or the scenery or whatever it is that interests you. Life on tour is basically spent on the playing fields, in the dressingrooms, on the team bus and in hotels — and occasionally on golf courses. I have to admit though that most us find golf a good way of taking our minds off cricket. I know that's why AB rarely misses a round.

A cricket tour is very much a business trip except that we love the business we're in: practice in the morning, and sometimes in the afternoon too when there is no game; playing; packing suitcases and 'coffins'; travelling on the bus at night then checking into the next hotel; unpacking; sleeping; practising or playing the next day. In the first hundred days of the tour, we have only four days when we don't play, practice or travel. When you're not playing you seem to spend most of your time and energy keeping your clothes in order and your bats or bowling boots in running repair. As the tour progresses your suitcase gets harder and harder to close as you pick up things along the way. At night you head off to one restaurant or another. There is no home cooking or the relaxing atmosphere of a place you usually call home.

After touring off and on for ten years, I've accustomed myself to it fairly well, but you never get completely used to it. Some guys, particularly the younger ones, suffer quite badly from homesickness. Cambo is a classic example — calling his girlfriend back in Hobart almost every day. (We

*A day off for AB: playing golf is the most popular relaxation for us on such a long tour.*

pay our own phone bills, by the way.) Homesickness can also eat into team morale and badly affect performance and I've seen that happen on other tours. Blokes with families a long way away find the touring hardest, but I suppose it's better than being a golfer or a tennis player. As Ian Stanley pointed out, they've only really got themselves when things aren't going well. We've got twenty others with whom to share the joys and sorrows. As well as homesickness and injuries, there can be the worry about form, especially for the less established players who are trying to do well to break into the team. There is always someone a little depressed and anxious about why he isn't taking wickets or making runs.

If you're winning most of the time and the weather is good, you can put up with all the bad things. On the two previous tours to England I'd been on, both our cricket and the weather was ordinary and a lot of us suffered from boredom and depression. This time around it's much better and that is a real bonus for me. I very much want my last Ashes tour to provide me with better memories than the others. The same goes for AB and Clem.

Living in each other's back pockets can cause the occasional spat, but so far on this tour I can't remember one faintly unpleasant moment — and that is quite remarkable. Even on minor things like what to put on the bus video or what music to listen to we seem to come to an amicable agreement. Of course success does tend to put you in a good frame of mind. The cigarette smoke on the bus does annoy me somewhat but when the captain and the physio. both smoke there is very little chance of stopping it.

The bus trips are spent watching videos — Roy Orbison (at least once every trip), Aussie Rules or Rugby League replays and various movies. There's always a card game going on up the back, usually with Rackemann, Alderman, Moody, Hughes and Zoehrer. It's not easy to sleep on the bus and necks and backs suffer when you try. Meals are served from the kitchen at the rear from pre-cooked packages. The menu is more impressive than the food — Spinach Florentine and Florida Cocktail are among ten or so starters; Pork Marsala or Chicken Breast with Leek are among a dozen or so main courses. The chicken curry on the way to Worcester has been the lowest culinary point so far, I think.

Austin Grundy our driver is from Littleborough, a Central Lancashire league club, is the driver of what he calls the coach. Anyone who calls his coach a 'bus' cops a serve. Aussie is very safe but has no idea of direction. He can even get lost using directions mapped out by a computer. He is a terrific bloke who gives as much as he gets — which is plenty. He always has drinks ready for us or a cigarette lighter handy when we come off the field. A genuine Lancastrian, Aussie is always there celebrating a win or consoling us after a loss.

The bus becomes very much a part of your routine on tour. You change hotels constantly (eighteen different ones on this trip) but the bus is always the same. People mostly sit in the same seats — the Colonel, Simmo, Walshie (Mike Walsh, the team scorer) down the front; AB, Swamp, Swerv, Mocca, Ziggy and Clem up the back; Tugga where he can see the television. As the tour progresses, the bus fills with assorted gear — bats, blazers, magazines, training gear and XXXX paraphenalia. A home away from home. The toilet is just about big enough to accommodate a small jockey so Tom Moody and other large lads find it quite an adventure when natures calls, especially on the bumpier back roads. Doing the county circuit and having to drive all over England season after season must be horrendous. The traffic in England increases every time I go back. No wonder so many English cricketers have car accidents.

Despite the grind of touring you never really get sick of the cricket. Even professional cricketers love the game. If you really enjoy and appreciate it then you never tire of it. But sometimes a slightly longer rest between matches would be appreciated. Naturally you want to be at a peak for the Tests so you often go easy in county games, especially if you're carrying a nagging injury like a thigh or a groin strain, both of which are quite common. But, the body willing, you try to give 95–100 per cent in county games. It is first class cricket after all. On this tour the good weather is making life on the road much easier to handle. Playing in the cold and wet is not my idea of fun. Injuries occur more often and take longer to heal. As well, I tend to suffer from bronchial problems, as I did in 1985 for the whole four months.

One of the regular tourists and an important member of the entourage is the baggage man, Tony Smith. Smithy has been doing cricket tours in England for every visiting country since 1972. He also does other sports and last year looked after the Australian Rugby Union team. His main job is to transport all our luggage, especially our cricket gear, and of course the cartons of XXXX. He travels separately, towing a van chock full of the gear. But Smithy's duties really cover a wide variety of fiddly jobs — posting letters, delivering tickets and buying anything from glue to notepads, postcards, tape etc.

In many ways Smithy is a typical prim and proper Englishman, polite to the point of irritation (to some of us anyway). I've always found him likeable and helpful beyond the job description. He's been on so many tours and has never uttered a word out of order to the press. This tour he will do 10,000 miles around Britain in his sedate, safe way. Smithy knows everyone on the county circuit, particularly the women in the kitchens which is important for keeping us happy with extra helpings of lunch, cakes and cups of tea. After all these years he has his working system well organised and usually gets some young lads at each ground to do the carrying and loading after a match, paying them with autograph sheets. When he's not working he loves to sit in the sun and watch the cricket. He also enjoys the fringe benefits — meeting celebrities and going to functions.

As well as Smithy, there is the scorer, Walshie, from the Essendon club in Melbourne. This is Walshie's first tour and he's having a great time. As well as scoring, he, like Smithy, acts as a general dogsbody. He is an accountant by trade and helps Lawrie a great deal with hotel accounts and the general day to day running of the tour. He's a chain smoker but that doesn't dissuade me from asking him for various statistics for my newspaper articles and radio reports. I haven't heard Walshie utter a cross word yet.

The touring entourage also includes eight Australian press people who follow us around in hire cars and stay at the same hotels. There is one radio reporter, the ABC's Neville Oliver, photographer Phil Brown, and seven news-paper reporters: old hands Jim Woodward, Rod Nicholson, Terry Brindle and John Coomber, Peter Bills (an English-man filling in for one of the Sydney papers), Martin Blake and Mark Ray. The last two regularly offer their services as net bowlers which we welcome as it eases the workload on us a little. At various times, the party is joined by any number of people with various functions. There can be up to thirty people in the dressingroom after a game, especially if it's been a big win. Aussie, his relief driver and the bus owner, Ian Craig, Mike Walsh, Smithy, the Colonel, Simmo, Errol, various medical people, Gunna Wilkins and associates from the hotel chain, Nick Potter and a few of his colleagues from XXXX in England. As well, we often gets visits from other sportspeople, like Australian tennis play-ers and golfers who are around at the time or from the occasional pop star or cricket-loving celebrity. All this and Merv as well.

## MONDAY, 17 JULY

Another gloriously hot day, a pleasant ground and good crowd for our game against the Minor Counties in Trow-bridge. We struggled to 230 with one disaster along the way. Wag had his finger broken by the only ball all day that did something strange off the wicket. He has been frustrated by not playing much cricket on the tour and will be very unhappy at this. Wag works hard on his game and would love to establish himself in the side. When he has played he's done well, but now he'll have to sit and watch even more than he has already.

The dressingroom was just big enough for the Seven Dwarves, and half of us had to get changed outside. At one

*Disaster strikes: Veletta flinches after being hit on the hand during the match against the Minor Counties. The hand is broken and Wag will be out for a few weeks at least.*

stage they could have won the game, but we bowled well enough to dismiss them for 202. After play we jumped straight back on the bus and drove to Southampton where we play Hampshire on Wednesday.

We had a Chinese meal at a restaurant near the hotel during which Boonie showed us one of his party tricks, how to stick cucumber to the walls. We left in a hurry.

We're staying at the Polygon, or the 'Dead Parrot', as it's known on the county circuit. The rooms double as saunas here as well. It's a nice old-style English hotel but again no airconditioning. I suppose you can't blame English hotels for not forking out the money for airconditioning as a summer like this only comes around every twelve or thirteen years, but it's not making life easy at present.

**AUSTRALIA 4-229, MINOR COUNTIES 202.**

## TUESDAY, 18 JULY

A free day today — no practice, no game, no travelling. Yes, I played golf again, this time with Maysie and Tub at a course that was more like the Sahara Desert than an English golf club. Maysie was very funny during the round, sending himself and the game up mercilessly. He has a very funny, quick wit and could become a comedian when he retires. His golf was mixed, but luckily when a local television crew came along he hit his best shot of the day.

One of the good things about the Dead Parrot is that there are half a dozen restaurants within walking distance. I ate Italian tonight at a restaurant I'd been to in 1985 and thought I recognised the waiter from that visit. I took in a half an hour of jazz with Mark Ray in a wine bar near the hotel then retired for a sauna. I'm rooming with Cambo who seems to sleep most of the time. Alan Crompton rang to keep me informed about what is happening at the New South Wales Cricket Association. Being a lawyer, he took forty-five minutes to tell me what should have taken three minutes.

## WEDNESDAY, 19 JULY

Hot and dry for the first day of the Hampshire game. We are at the height of summer right now.

We closed with 340-odd on the board, made on a very good wicket and a lightning fast outfield. Boonie and Tugga both made a hundred while I spent most of the day in the sun perusing the large crowd.

I'm not feeling all that well tonight. I think it's the poor quality of the sleep I've been getting. It's just so hot in the rooms. You open all the windows but you still don't get much air. As well, I haven't bowled a full day in a first class match for about two weeks. We needed and enjoyed that break in Scotland, but a lot of us seem to have lost our momentum and are struggling to return to the rhythm of full scale touring.

AUSTRALIA 6-343 DECLARED, HAMPSHIRE 0-33.

## THURSDAY, 20 JULY

Hampshire, one of the stronger counties, declared after tea at 6-275 with Mark Nicholas scoring a good hundred. We may see him in the Tests before too long.

Maysie should really have bowled them out on that track. It wasn't a bad wicket, but it had pace and spin and was ideal for the slow bowlers. His spinning finger was giving him trouble, as it has since the start of the last Shield season. It seems like he doesn't really want to play. He's homesick which doesn't help. He and his wife had a baby last summer and he no doubt misses them very much. Maysie is a man of highs and lows and little in between, but I still think a more positive attitude would improve his game a great deal. And playing well can make the homesickness easier to bear rather than it working the other way 'round.

Mocca bowled a great first spell, taking the wicket of Robin Smith caught behind off a real jaffa, but his knee then began to trouble him and he ended up going for four runs an over. We ended on 2–63, Swampy missing out again.

Merv, Legend and I were invited to a local cinema to see the premiere of 'Lethal Weapon 2'. Plenty of death and destruction in this one. It reminded us of playing the West Indies last season.

AUSTRALIA 6-343 DECLARED AND 2-63, HAMPSHIRE 6-275 DECLARED.

# FRIDAY, 21 JULY

We were in a spot of bother early and could have been bowled out cheaply enough to lose the game, but Tugga rescued us with an amazing 67 in forty-five minutes. He hit some fantastic shots, one a cut behind point off a medium-pacer for six over a long boundary. You don't see that too often. Another came when he went back to a short-of-a length ball from yet another county medium-pacer. He didn't look like he was going to go for it at all until at the last split second he seemed to think, 'Oh well, might as well put this away'. It bounced just inside the rope at deep extra cover. I was sitting with some of the Hampshire coaches and officials and they were absolutely amazed at his shot-making. Just how good is he?

By the time we had saved our innings, Swampy did not want to set them a target as their batting was very good, the wicket still hard and true and the outfield as fast as any I've ever seen. Nicholas, their captain, was a little miffed at this and they batted the rest of the day out in a minor protest for a score of 0–81. Despite that it was an enjoyable game of better than normal standard.

We packed up quickly and reached Bristol at 11 pm. I went straight to bed. I was below par in the Hampshire game and wouldn't mind a rest from this next match.

AUSTRALIA 6-343 DECLARED AND 246, HAMPSHIRE 6-275 DECLARED AND 0-81.

The rooms are quite good at this pub, but again there is no airconditioning. I don't think I've ever slept as badly as I did last night. We've got a lovely view of the cathedral next door, but the trouble is they light it up at night and, with the curtains open to get some air into the room, it's as bright as Picadilly Circus in here. The last fortnight has been uncomfortably hot and humid, but it can't last much longer.

We lost the toss this morning and, bugger me, we're in the field and I'm playing. Mocca said his knee was a bit sore and he had to withdraw. What about me? I'm suffering from a sore shoulder, a strained neck, a bad ankle and a suspect back. Then again I am thirty-one. Not surprisingly, I bowled very poorly, but luckily they were all out for 200, thanks mainly to Clem.

Their innings finished at tea time, so Merv stayed on the field at the end furthest from the dressingroom to sign autographs. He was still there twenty minutes later with a huge line in front of him as Tub and Swamp came out to start our innings. Merv moved over the rope and finished signing every piece of paper that was offered, 200 at least. When he finished he got a generous round of applause from that side of the ground. Nice PR, Merv.

Wayne Grady is leading the British Open at present so interest amongst the team is at a peak. AB said we will have to bat all day tomorrow, not only to ensure the safety of the match, but to make sure we get to watch the whole day's golf.

GLOUCESTERSHIRE 200, AUSTRALIA 3-142.

More carnage. We made 438 by tea. Tub made 141 and Legend 167. Towards the end Tub was running down the wicket to the spinners and driving down field. In the press this would probably be described as aggressive use of the feet to the slow bowlers. We call it slogging.

Legend was in awesome form, hitting quite a few balls onto the tops of sponsors' tents. He is counting the sixes he hits because one of the magazines or papers is running a contest for the most sixes hit this season. If he reaches twenty he automatically wins 1,000 pounds. While I was batting with him they were naturally giving him a single to long-on and long-off, so he would dance down to the spinners or medium-pacers, smack it along the ground to those fieldsmen, tuck his bat under his arm and stroll down the pitch for the single. Arrogance? You must be joking.

At the end of his innings Deano informed us that he is now on top of the first class batting list with an average of 105.366 recurring. Deano is fascinated with statistics. The Deloittes ratings have him particularly enthralled. He always knows his average to the fourth decimal point and his teammates are forever taking the mickey out of him for it. He does get on some people's nerves at times because he has so much energy and is a constant chatterer. He doesn't have a strong sense of the tactful time to say or not to say things, but he's always good for some entertainment. He also occasionally says a less than tactful thing to the press, like: 'Terry Alderman bowls only slightly quicker than me' or 'Geoff Lawson is only Tony Dodemaide's pace'.

On the field Deano oozes arrogance and confidence. When he came back out to rejoin Tugga after having his cheekbone fractured at Hove, he was on 10 and Tugga 71. Tugga walked straight up to him and said: 'You shouldn't be out here Deano. I don't care about making a century.' Legend replied: 'Don't worry about me. I'll beat you to 100.' He hit the next ball from Tony Dodemaide for six! Angus Fraser said to me after Legend's century at Edgbaston that The Lege had an air of arrogance about him while batting and he does like to chat to the bowlers out in the middle: 'You can't bowl there to me and get away with it' and 'no need to run for that one'. It can be very annoying, especially when he's in the form he's in on this tour.

As a batsman, Legend is technically correct, but he can also improvise very well. On his day he can be virtually impossible to bowl to. The main thing with Deano as a bloke is that he is consistent; you know where you stand with him and what to expect of him. The important thing is not to take him seriously.

AB was upset that we'd been bowled out; he'd settled in for an afternoon's golf viewing and, with Grady and Greg Norman in the lead, didn't want to spend time on a cricket field. We did the right thing by the skipper and bowled them out for 92 in only 29 overs. When we walked out to bowl Grady was going down the ninth fairway and when we came in at the end of the game, we were in time to see the last four holes of the play-off. During Gloucestershire's innings Mocca was on the balcony sending the golf scores out to us with hand signals. This didn't help me too much as I was either bowling or fielding at the far end of the ground, but the Australian journos were settled in front of a television in a quiet bar near the fine leg boundary and occasionally relayed scores to me.

Although most of my attention was on golf rather than cricket I managed to take 6–30 and find some genuine form with the ball. Today I just tried to bowl the same ball all day and get it right. I think I've been bowling with too much variety up to now. My rhythm was certainly the best it's been so far on tour and the body felt good, though the fact that I was in the right frame of mind for a decent bowl was crucial. It shows you can't perform at your best all the time when you're playing this amount of cricket which is the reason I've never been keen on playing county cricket. With the fourth Test only four days away, I'm very happy with things right now.

When the tenth wicket fell, everyone rushed from the ground to get back to the golf. I was 200 yards away at fine leg and by the time I made it to the dressingroom, all the best viewing spots were taken. Huddled around the set we lived every shot with Grady and Norman, hoping that Calcavecchia would stumble. The only one happy with Calcavecchia's win was Tim Zoehrer who'd put some money on him with an English bookmaker weeks ago. For the rest of us it was like losing a Test match.

So, a first class match on a good wicket completed in two days. An extra free day for us which should ease the tour weariness somewhat, but I don't think Gloucestershire will be doing too well in the county championship this year.

GLOUCESTERSHIRE 200 AND 92, AUSTRALIA 438.

## MONDAY, 24 JULY

We left for Manchester at 9 am this morning rather than at 7 pm or 8 pm tonight as it would have been had the Gloucester game gone the distance. I asked permission to travel with Mark Ray so we could visit Greg Watson, an old clubmate of ours from Sydney who played Shield cricket for New South Wales and Western Australia and county cricket for Worcestershire. He lives at Cheltenham, on the way to Lancashire, but we must either travel in the bus or in our own hire cars. Mark managed to have lunch with Greg and reported that he is in good spirits. Strange to see someone from Gulgong, in the mid-west of New South Wales, living in Cheltenham, England.

Golf was organised for the afternoon at the Chalton Golf Club in Manchester after which I went out to Heyward where I had played league cricket ten years ago.

## TUESDAY, 25 JULY

This morning's practice nets were set up out the back of the ground rather than on the oval itself and the wickets were very poor. Legend spat the dummy after a dozen or so balls when a yorker from Mocca hit him on the foot. He began slogging everything and was soon called out by Simmo. AB and I had a slight run-in over the ball I was using. He wanted me to use an older ball; I maintained that the batsmen were getting themselves out and it was not the ball's fault. A typical batsman-bowler argument, but he is the skipper and I accepted his decision.

We found out today that the Test wicket has not ever been played on! It's one of the tracks that has been relaid and so far this one has not been tested at all. Amazing. England have picked Nick Cook as a second spinner to Embers and all the talk is that this wicket will turn. As Clem said, it has very little grass on it which makes it quite different to ones they've had here in recent weeks and to the one we played on against Lancashire. The recent Worcester-Lancs game here was over in two days with the quicks causing mayhem. Graham Dilley said it was the fastest wicket he'd ever played on, but I can't see the Test track being like that from the way it looks. The groundsman, Peter Marron, admitted he has not watered it for eight days. Besides, even if it does spin, we are not worried about Cook. He got five wickets against us for Northants but we were going for our shots at the time. Embers might be a problem on a track that helps him, but so might Cracka who is bowling well at the moment. Our major concern is that if the wicket starts to go through the top it won't be a true test of skill as there'll be a lot of luck involved.

Waggy was an interesting study today. He couldn't bat at all with his finger broken so he spent most of the morning walking around with a bat in his left hand swinging it up and down, up and down thousands of times. The guy loves practice more than a good feed. And naturally enough everyone had a go at him: 'Come on Wag, do another hundred sit-ups and a few more laps.' 'Wag, put that bat down and do something.'

After training we had a general information meeting. It looks like Hooter (Errol Alcott) will have to go home on Thursday morning for business reasons. Lawrie has organised for Pat Farhart, an Australian physio. who is playing league cricket in Lancaster, to fill in for him. The management were keen to get an Australian to replace Errol. Pat plays first grade for St George in Sydney and should fit in easily. Another net bowler at this stage of the tour is a bonus.

I met Julie after practice and we ate out with some friends of ours, the Grimshaws, who are putting her up for the Test.

## WEDNESDAY, 26 JULY

Today we practised on the wickets on the main ground and they were better, though a touch green and seaming which always offers the batsmen a decent challenge. They like a very flat wicket for practice but they forget that bowlers need to enjoy practice as well as have their confidence boosted. Waggy, bored again, was leaning on a roller watching the session and got the idea of seeing what would happen if he pushed the roller over a full can of Coke. A minor explosion and a mess. You can tell he's bored when he does things like that.

After practice Julie and I drove up to a little shop called Collectors' Corner, in a village called Barnoldswick up near the Pennines. Tugga found it last year and put us on to it. You can buy authentic old cricket cards quite cheaply as well as signed Elvis Presley posters, a great range of kitsch plastic toys like the Thunderbirds spaceship and even a signed Bradman program from the 1948 tour.

Team meeting at 7 pm. England have dropped Tavare after his brief appearance at Edgbaston. Why pick him in the first place? Tim Robinson is in for him. Gatt has been overlooked and has announced he won't be touring the West Indies early next year. Dilley's knee is playing up again and it looks like he will pull out to make room for Cook. Again, we will play the same side. No reason to change.

We're all well aware that this Test could be it. A win here and it's all over.

# THE FOURTH
# TEST

Gower won both tosses this morning. Yes, we had two — one to decide what ball to use and the other to decide who would use it first. It's not usual to toss to decide on the ball. AB wanted the Dukes again — we used it in the first three Tests — and Gower wanted to change to the Reader with the higher seam. Obviously Gower thinks he needs an extra advantage to try to bowl us out. Of course that means we get the advantage as well, but that is a risk he feels he has to take. Who knows how many we might bowl them out for with a Reader?

AB only found out about their change of preference for the ball when he went over to get Gower for the toss. He was taken aback but didn't care about losing on the ball issue. We weren't worried about the ball and in the end they used last year's model of the Reader which didn't look any different to a Duke. What he did mind was losing the second toss and not being able to bat first. If this wicket is dry it may well crumble towards the end of the game and batting in the fourth innings might be difficult.

Robin Smith saved England from total collapse. We had them 7–158 but he and Foster added 66 for the eighth wicket. They ended on 7–224 with Smith undefeated for half that total. It was a well deserved maiden Test hundred and, as usual, he hit the ball very hard. He does have a tendency, like many English batsmen at present, to prop too early onto the front foot, but he has a very good eye which helps him get away with it.

Cracka bowled very well, taking 3–59. Two of those wickets were top shelf — Gower and Botham. He got Gower with a flipper which Lubo tried to pull but it was on him too quickly and he was out leg before. Beefy tried to lift Cracka over the top to put him off his length but completely missed and was clean bowled. Cracka doesn't normally show much emotion when he takes a wicket, but at the sight of Beefy's scattered stumps, he ran down the wicket and crash-tackled Deano. It was a big psychological win for us and was no doubt depressing for them. The wicket did move around a little, but nothing untoward for the first day of a Test. It was simply another case of them not batting well enough. Clem didn't take a wicket today for a change, though he was tight all day. I took four and the rhythm was back, really just following on from the Gloucester game where it came together. I'm feeling much happier tonight.

*Asking the question: I'd dived to stop one off my own bowling which clipped a finger and hit the stumps at my end. The appeal for run out was refused.*

I saw Embers in the nets before play and he assured me that all would be revealed about the South African tour very soon. Sounds like there will be an announcement during this game. Also sounds like there's a fair chance he's going.

After stumps, AB said he'd seen some of the Australian journos and they were not looking too well. They told him that yesterday a number of them ate with the English press at a nearby pub before the English practice session and went down a few hours later with food poisoning. It was not surprising as there is a phenomenal number of salmonella cases being reported at the moment. The English fridges aren't set low enough to handle the hot weather and the food is going off at a great rate.

Julie and I took the risk and ate at a restaurant at Berry with Trevor Bayliss and his wife and then visited some friends at Haslingden. I got home to the pub just in time to catch the highlights of the day's play. A minor shock seemed to run through the television when Cracka got Gower with that flipper. I've never heard Richie Benaud so excited.

ENGLAND 7-224.

## FRIDAY, 28 JULY

We finished them off for 260 in an hour. I ended up with my first haul of six wickets in a Test for some time. I nearly missed one of them when AB almost dropped Foster. He'd brought himself in to a short extra cover and I obliged him by bowling the slower ball. Fossie obliged me by hitting it in the air straight to AB who spilled it, then dived full length to hold onto it.

Swampy and Tub put on 135 before a minor collapse had us 3–154. AB settled things and we finished on 3–219. We were all pleased to see Swamp get 47 though he was very annoyed at getting out after such a good start. Tub just continued on in his own way, accumulating 85 in comfortable fashion. AB took a long time for his 19 not out and looks very determined to make a big one tomorrow. Legend is on 49 and they don't seem to be able to tie him down at all.

The wicket was very slow and it might be hard going trying to bowl them out in the second dig. England were on the defensive for most of our innings which I suppose is understandable given the dominance of our batsmen, but they are the ones who have to win a Test pretty soon. A typical example came at the end of the day when Cook was bowling to Legend with five on the leg side — a long-on, a deep square leg and a ring of three saving one. Cook was bowling outside leg stump when you'd have thought he'd be trying anything to get a wicket so late in the day. Legend kept picking him off for singles with drives down the ground or sweeps to deep square. A hard one to work out, that one.

We found out today that Beefy has been receiving death threats. Hopefully he has been able to laugh them off. We did wonder whether this followed on from 1985 when there was a bomb threat in the Old Trafford scoreboard. At that stage we were hoping it was fair dinkum so we could get out of the Test with a draw.

A large group of us went to a restaurant at Oldham to celebrate Linda Veletta's birthday. It was a pleasant meal but you needed a cut lunch for the journey. Luckily Swampy's farmer's sense of direction got us there and back.

ENGLAND 260, AUSTRALIA 3-219.

## SATURDAY, 29 JULY

A day of grinding Test cricket. They bowled well and we batted steadily. AB battled away for 80 trying to ensure a big enough total to allow us to turn the screws on them in the second dig. We ended on 9-441 with Legend making 69 and Tugga 92.

Tugga showed a lot of patience against Beefy, treating him with respect and not playing any shots that weren't definitely on, especially after Legend had been bowled playing across the line to an in-swinger. I was out there when Tugger got out, hooking at Fraser. You don't see him play that shot very often, but it was a good piece of thinking from Angus. He knew Waughie would be looking for runs

134

*No luck for England: Waugh plays his textbook forward defence while
Gower dives in hope. Tugga failed by 8 runs to score his third
hundred of the series.*

with only the tail to stay with him for his hundred and
sensibly gave him the chance to hit a four, but not with the
sort of shot he likes to play. Just before he got out, Tugga
was averaging 460 for the series. Them's not bad numbers.

I called by Ramsbottom Cricket Club to watch the
Haslingden Second XI win a thrilling cup final in the dark. I
had a leave pass from the hotel and spent the night with
Julie at the Grimshaw's.

**ENGLAND 260, AUSTRALIA 9-441.**

## SUNDAY, 30 JULY

You wouldn't believe it, Haslingden is the same as last
summer — cold and raining. I slept in, went to the White-
horse Hotel at Hamshore for the usual excellent lunch and
then on to Bent Gate to watch Haslingden do battle. Simon

O'Donnell, who's proing for them this year, made 65 and the home side won easily. As always after a win, there was plenty of good cheer at the clubhouse. Then it was back to the Copthorne for an early night in preparation for tomorrow's play.

## MONDAY, 31 JULY

It was cold and miserable today. I got out in the second over, bowled by Fraser yet again. We finished with 447, a lead of 187. And to our great shock, they went in to lunch at 5–53. Russell and Embers held us up and the last session was lost through rain, otherwise it could have been over today. They are 6–123 and while the two that are still in could offer some resistance tomorrow, they can't escape. We should have the Ashes sometime tomorrow afternoon, barring a washout of course.

England's batting collapses have been absolutely astonishing. Today the wicket was playing well, but they just got out. In fact today's effort was the worst of the lot. They were 5–53 at lunch and we hadn't even bowled for the full session. Some of their defensive technique was way below Test standard. It's strange. We keep expecting them to put up a fight and give us a hard day in the field, but they just keep folding. It doesn't really seem like Test cricket when you keep knocking over the top order so easily.

More rumours about South Africa.

**ENGLAND 260 AND 6-123, AUSTRALIA 447.**

## TUESDAY, 1 AUGUST

Today we won the Ashes. I didn't sleep too well last night. The feeling of anticipation was very high and I was too keyed up to sleep soundly. I never expected to know this early that we would win the series, but it's taken only four Tests.

It wasn't an easy day. Russell and Embers played really well, the latter making a stubborn 64 in what will be his last innings for England and the former making his first Test century and a very good one at that. We've a lot of respect for Russell. He's obviously a keeper of the highest class, but he's shown great determination and pride with his batting. He'll be annoying us for a few years yet. Clem finished with five wickets in the second dig and I took three.

The English side to South Africa was announced this morning with Gatt, Embers, Jarvis, Foster, Dilley, DeFreitas, Barnett, Robinson and Broad among them. What a day for Gower.

## Win No. 100 for Australia against England; Win No. 200 in all Tests.

It was a pity AB couldn't hit the winning runs. We suggested he go out at three instead of Boonie, but he wouldn't have it. He said he was happy to sit on the balcony and watch the victory from there. I thought I would shed a few tears when the moment came and I didn't let myself down, but I wasn't the only one with moist eyes on that balcony.

As the champagne and beer flowed and the flash guns of the press photographers popped, Clem and I sat in a corner of the dressingroom, each holding a bottle of champers, and watched it all happen around us. We agreed that this was much better than 1981 and 1985. As Clem said, it was probably the last time either of us would tour here so we should enjoy this one to the maximum. We'd worked very hard for this win and it was an enormously satisfying feeling to sit back quietly in a corner with an old teammate like Clem and drink in the atmosphere.

After Boonie led us in a brilliant rendition of 'Underneath the Southern Cross', our victory song, AB made a great little speech thanking everyone for all their hard work and

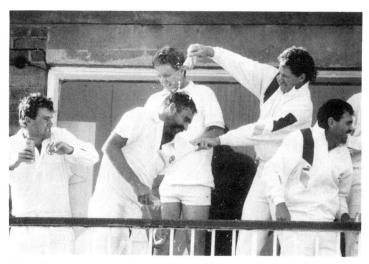

*The Ashes are ours: Deano douses Merv with XXXX on the Old Trafford balcony as the celebrations begin.*

saying how proud he was to be an Australian. I felt particularly happy for him. He'd carried the team many times in the past few years and had really set himself to win this series. He'd left his wife and kids at home and made us accept his rule that there'd be no wives staying with us until we won the Ashes. I think he's been smoking more on this tour, but today it was all worthwhile.

Once these informal formalities had been attended to, a few visitors came in. Gower, Embers, Russell, Fraser, Beefy and Smith came in briefly to congratulate us. Angus gave me a stump as a souvenir for my man of the match award which was very good of him. He was the pick of their bowlers in this match and, like Russell and Smith, will be around in Test cricket for quite a while. A few of the Australian press guys came in for a drink and were obviously delighted. Pretty soon they were wet as well. Merv and Ziggy were spraying everyone in the room with iced water, beer or champagne. No one was exempt. David

Frith, the Australian who edits *Wisden Cricket Monthly*, brought in one of only two exact replicas of the Ashes urn and he and Patrick Eagar took AB and a few of the boys out onto the baclony for some pictures.

A few of us went out the back of the stand to the lunch room to see our families (no women allowed in the pavilion here either) and it was a wonderful scene out there with our wives, girlfriends and children all very excited. Swampy brought his young son, Shaun, into the rooms and he was immediately into the thick of things. Swamp was having a little trouble stopping him from throwing ice cubes at people, but you can't expect a six-year-old to behave calmly when all around him grown men are carrying on like five-year-olds. Merv wasn't exactly setting a good example.

After all this, AB, Clem and I were in the large shower room having a tub when Boonie, who had already showered and dressed, came in and spontaneously started the team song again. Within seconds the whole side was in there, many of them under the showers. Boonie climbed onto a tiled wall about four feet high that runs along the room and led the whole lot of us in the best rendition of the team song I've ever heard. The acoustics in there were brilliant and I've never been involved in such a spontaneous celebration. Wonderful stuff.

So, the short but intense celebrations ended by 8.30 pm as the boys had to drive to Nottingham for another three-dayer starting tomorrow. I'm not playing, and the same, naturally, goes for AB and Clem. AB never plays the game after a Test and Clem has become known as 'TMO' — Test Matches Only. That's a little unfair as he has played in quite a few county matches, but he prefers not to if he can avoid it. I feel sorry for the boys who are playing. They'll be in an awful state at the warm-up in the morning and the stand-in skipper, Swampy, will again have one of the toughest jobs on tour.

As I had the game off I thought I'd stay in Haslingden and relax with another round of golf. I made a few calls to organise the golf and then went to the Haslingden clubrooms to rub it in a little. I felt in a wonderful mood and gladly accepted the locals' grudging congratulations. I stayed up till 2 am writing my *Daily Telegraph* article. I may never have another chance like this.

**ENGLAND 260 AND 264, AUSTRALIA 447 AND 1-81.**

*Explaining away the Ashes: Gower looks on as Ted Dexter tries to find something positive to say about English cricket to the local press.*

I had to get up at 8.30 am to ring the folks back home. I'm never much good on less than five hours sleep, but I sparked up after hearing how delighted the people back home are. I usually do a two-minute call with Peter Peters on 2GB but this time he kept me talking for twenty-five minutes. I didn't mind though, not when the subject is so pleasant. It sounded like a lot of people back home stayed up to watch the end of the game and then did some celebrating of their own.

The champagne had not totally agreed with me. I was feeling very weary but played golf anyway at Royal Rosendale with Brian Knowles. After 12 holes I was completely shagged out.

The media concentrated on the South African business and reports about England losing the Ashes were hidden on the inside pages of the papers. Again the emphasis was on how badly England had played not on how well we had played. 'Gutless England are laid to rest' was what *The Sun* said. As well it had the scoreboard set in a tombstone with 'RIP — 31 July 1989' engraved on the top. Not bad. The byline on the story was: 'Ian Todd mourns at Old Trafford'. It does annoy you when all they can say is that our opposition is hopeless. They weren't considered hopeless before the series started.

We were a little surprised at some of the names on the list for South Africa, but it obviously didn't affect the way some of them played in this game. Embers hit his highest Test score and Fossie (Foster) certainly didn't play like a man who knew it was to be his last Test. With so many top players going, England's strength may be down, but it might also allow some younger players or a few that have been mysteriously overlooked to come through.

The teletext tells me that Boonie and Deano were in good enough shape to make runs today. Swampy must have won the toss which might just have saved his neck.

AUSTRALIA 284, NOTTINGHAMSHIRE 0-21.

# THURSDAY, 3 AUGUST

Diabolical weather in Haslingden today. It took me five hours to drive down to Suffolk to see Julie.

The papers are full of the South African issue: former players in support, politicians moralising, black athletes criticising.

The word from Nottingham is that a few injuries were sustained on the dance floor at Madisons. Apparently Clem is claiming he has a six-weeker (an injury that will keep him out of action for six weeks). Some of the lads had a run-in with some vandal-proof paint on a railing in the middle of the road near the hotel. There was a sign on it warning of the paint but no doubt none of them could read at the time.

Merv took five wickets today and we are about 240 ahead with eight wickets left and one day to go.

**AUSTRALIA 284 AND 2-158, NOTTINGHAMSHIRE 195.**

# FRIDAY, 4 AUGUST

I left Suffolk at 10 am and arrived at Trent Bridge at 1.30 pm, just in time for lunch. Well planned I thought.

The lads bowled Notts out for 148 with Mocca taking five and Maysie four. Mocca got a few to lift past the eyeballs, but it still amazes me how these county sides keep collapsing.

After play we made the forty-five minute drive to Leicester for another game tomorrow. The body is still recovering from the Test and now my left knee is sore. I hope we bat tomorrow.

This is the second time we have had to play six days in a row immediately after a Test — eleven days play in twelve. We do it again after the fifth Test. This sort of thing wears you down, and, in this case, keeps the celebrations to a minimum. As for county cricketers, who have to keep to a similar program all summer, it must be soul-destroying playing day in, day out, especially when the weather is cold and wet and there are only a handful of spectators present.

You really have to wonder how competitive the cricket is. It is the opposite of the Sheffield Shield competition where games are played on a less regular basis but with as much intensity as a Test match. I suppose Australian cricketers would like to play slightly more first class cricket and English cricketers significantly less.

I don't know how Clem can cope with a Shield season and then a full county program. I suppose he has an economical run-up and has learned to minimise the stress to his body. Tugga says as a batsman county cricket is alright because it gives you constant time in the middle, and, unless you're having one of the worst slumps in history, a good score is never too far away. Perhaps that explains the injury to his side that kept him away from the bowling crease at Somerset last season.

In England the demands of sponsorship and the financial needs of the county clubs are dictating the amount and type of cricket played, but while that might be keeping the clubs financially healthy it doesn't seem to be doing much for England's standing at an international level.

There is constant criticism here that the excessive amount of one-day cricket has ruined English batting technique. I think the problem lies in the way they play their three-day cricket. Two or sometimes three declarations are needed to obtain a result — that is when the wickets are good. When they're not, the game can be over in two days with some very ordinary bowlers getting bags of wickets. Look at our game against Worcestershire — twenty-four wickets fell on the first day.

Overall, the drop in the standard of county cricket since our 1985 tour has been astounding. We have bowled out a number of teams in 40 overs on good wickets and this just does not feel like first class cricket. Perhaps they need to abandon the idea of three-day county matches altogether and play 16 four-day games. In the end that is their problem, but it is certain that playing cricket at less than full competitiveness does not prepare a cricketer for the move up to Test cricket.

AUSTRALIA 284 AND 4-255 DECLARED, NOTTINGHAMSHIRE 195 AND 148.

## SATURDAY, 5 AUGUST

AB lost the toss to Gower yet again and we bowled. Fortunately it wasn't a long day in the field. They were all out for 157 by tea and we ended on 3–105. There was another good crowd at the game — the crowds on this tour are definitely better than on the last two tours.

I bowled pretty well but the body is protesting. In fact I felt some sharp pains in my left knee, something I've never suffered before. A worry really. Gower was dropped first ball off me. We'd put in the leg slip and he nicked it straight into and out of Swampy's hands. If caught it would have maintained my rather large psychological advantage over Gower, but he went soon after, caught in the gully. He seems to always be caught either in the gully or at leg slip and generally when I'm bowling. He also seems to play with even more flair in these games than he does in the Tests.

**LEICESTERSHIRE 157, AUSTRALIA 3–105.**

## SUNDAY, 6 AUGUST

Cracka missed his third first class hundred by five runs today. He's grown in confidence as the tour has progressed and is now playing very well. Heals also made 70-odd which is a relief as he's struggled with the bat for most of the tour. Tub picked up a tidy little 70 just to keep warm. We finished on 305 and they're 2–133. I made a significant duck — significant because I was the third man in a hat-trick by Winston Benjamin, clean bowled. Cracka did tell me later that it was a very good ball which made me feel much better. It's not the first hat-trick I've been involved in. I followed Marsh and Yardley in 1982 in Pakistan, I was bowled that time as well.

Benjamin took 7–54 and bowled with plenty of pace. Some of the county players might take it easy against us but the young West Indians see these games as a chance to impress their national selectors and go at us quite hard.

A heavy fog of lethargy has descended on everyone.

We're worn out from all the cricket and travelling. We've been on the road now for thirteen weeks and we're beginning to start the usual countdown for home. The abnormally hot weather has also taken its toll, and it has made sleeping difficult. The nerves are on edge a touch.

David Gower invited AB, Swamp and myself to his place for a barbecue tonight with his girlfriend Vicki and a few of his friends. It was a very good night with Lubo running us through a few party tricks. He tried to show AB how to take the top clean off a bottle of champagne with an axe, but it went slightly wrong and resulted in a small cut on AB's arm that bled profusely. Lubo also let me send a fax to my mates at the Cornea and Contact Lens Research Unit at the University of New South Wales in Sydney. I told them what a pleasure it was to have won the Ashes and to be able to send the message from David Gower's private fax machine. It's good to see that he has managed to retain his sense of humour while all about him crumbles. The sense of humour extended to the toilet where he had some very good reading material: copies of the satirical cricket magazine, *Sticky Wicket*.

The highlight of the night was golf off the cobblestones in his driveway at 11.30 pm. Lubo plays right-handed so AB struggled a little with the right-handed sand iron, but the rest of us were in good touch. A few of the neighbours in suburban Leicester must have wondered what was going on as it started raining golf balls. Or maybe they are used to it by now.

We got back to the hotel at 1.30 am, a late but relaxing night.

LEICESTERSHIRE 157 AND 2-133, AUSTRALIA 305.

## MONDAY, 7 AUGUST

I took a wicket with my warm-up ball this morning, D. Gower's in fact. He didn't look too interested today and you could hardly blame him. We took 8-110 in the first session and made the 96 for victory for the loss of Tom's wicket.

We're now 6 for 7 against the counties. They just keep folding in front of us.

We left in the afternoon for Nottingham to prepare for the next Test which starts on Thursday. Some of the guys played golf at 5.30 pm but I was too knackered. Has golf become a drug of addiction on this tour?

LEICESTERSHIRE 157 AND 243, AUSTRALIA 305 AND 1-99.

## TUESDAY, 8 AUGUST

No practice! Only our fourth full day off of the tour and we've earned it.

In this morning's *Today*, Leicestershire's fast bowler, Jonathon Agnew, has written a column in which he says what a pleasure it was to play against a touring side for a change. These games have degenerated quite a lot over the years mainly because the tourists have treated them merely as opportunities for batting practice and the counties have responded by resting most of their leading players. We always play these games properly even though we are bowling them out quite easily. We also make a point of having a drink and a chat with the county players at the end of the day, especially as the warm evenings made an hour or so sitting around on a pavilion balcony a delightful way to wind down. It was good to read that although we are beating everybody, we are also making friends.

Jonathon's article reminded me of a story the boys told me about the Notts game. Merv was bowling a fiery spell and followed each delivery with a few comments: 'What sort of f... shot was that?' and 'The next one will take your f... head off.' Just the normal sort of verbal intercourse between intelligent, sensitive cricketers. This went on for a few overs until, at the end of one over, the umpire went to hand Merv his jumper and with a smile said: 'And that, gentleman, is the end of another f... over.'

Tub didn't get out of bed until 4.30 pm. How many overs has he bowled in the past week?

I walked around the shops for a while and then sat in the

grounds of the castle to read and take in some sun. Our hotel is only 61 metres from Nottingham Castle where Robin Hood argued the toss with the Sheriff of Nottingham back in the days when spinners opened the bowling.

I dined at the Pizza Hut and then retired for an early one. I'm still very weary. How about some rain?

## WEDNESDAY, 9 AUGUST

There may be some rain on the way, in fact they are predicting a hurricane. We can only hope.

We practised this morning after which I went straight back to the pub for a rest. I thought I'd have an easy afternoon dozing in my room, but I think they're building another channel crossing underneath the hotel. Pneumatic drills were going all afternoon and it was deafening; you couldn't make a phonecall. It was as though the drill was boring in at the wall next to my pillow. If this goes on much longer we might have to forfeit. They seem to be doing up one half of each floor while people are staying in the other half. Either that or they're pulling the place down, which wouldn't hurt. I need my rest. Let's hope we bat tomorrow and make a big score.

Team meeting at 7 pm. The message is about not slackening off, and instead really trying to bury them. AB and Simmo pushed this point — don't give them any chance whatsoever. It's so easy when you're this far in front to let your game drop. I'd be surprised if we let things slip too far. We are playing very well and enjoying it, so I don't think we'd risk losing form. I must admit that with the Ashes in the bag there is not the same pressure. There is not the same tension in the air tonight as there had been earlier in the series. This could work to our advantage too, as you tend to play more freely when the pressure has eased.

Maysie has come into the twelve in case we decide in the morning that the wicket will spin, but I think we'll stick with the same side. England will play two spinners again. This time it will be Cook and Eddie Hemmings, who's replaced

Embers. It's good to see the Poms going for youth again. I think Eddie's only just turned forty. Gooch has pulled out saying that he wants to find form in county cricket. I can't believe that. I'd be amazed if an Australian player ever even considered that option. Still, AB has said that Gooch prefers playing for Essex to playing for England. Perhaps that is symptomatic of the way cricket is going over here.

We discussed the other new caps — Mike Atherton, Martyn Moxon, Greg Thomas and Devon Malcolm — and AB, Tugga and Clem all knew something about them. But for us the main point is that it doesn't matter who's in their side, we just have to keep going the way we have all along.

The team meetings on this tour have usually been very constructive though I suppose if most of our tactical ideas were failing in the middle, I might not think so. Lawrie, Simmo and AB had obviously thought very deeply about the whole tour before the team was even chosen. From the start, AB's determination to do everything possible to win was clear to us all. His county experience was invaluable as was that of Clem and Tugga. We had some idea of how the wicket might play at most grounds and of the strengths and weaknesses of most players we came across in the international games. This gave the team meetings a focus and made them more constructive. We actually had things to discuss and plan rather than platitudes to mouth about trying hard and concentrating. We planned in detail.

Even before any of the formal meetings for the major games were held, there were various informal tactical chats between players during that first week of training at Lord's and at pubs and restaurants in the early weeks of the tour. The meetings for the big games were held at whatever hotel we were in, either in a reception room or in the Colonel's room (sorry, the Colonel's suite). It was at these formal meetings that definite tactical plans were adopted.

Many of the tactics we used against their batsmen were settled upon at the team meeting in Manchester on the night before the first one-day international. With a few exceptions, those plans worked well from there on in.

The idea of placing an extra man in short on the on-side

to Gooch was accepted at that meeting. Clem had got Gooch leg before several times in the 1981 series when he played across the line to out-swingers. Simmo and AB in particular suggested the short mid-wicket position. AB's experience of Gooch's playing at Essex was obviously a major factor here. We thought that the extra man would either take the odd catch or put doubt in Gooch's mind. Any doubts were likely to lessen the confidence with which he would go for the shot, but we were sure he would still want to play it as it is one of his favourite 'bread and butter' shots. If Clem kept a tight line on leg stump to middle and leg swinging towards off, he could still tempt Gooch to play that favourite shot without giving him enough room to play an alternative run-maker like an off or cover drive. This tactic worked in the one-dayers so we stuck with it in the Tests.

We didn't really have to plan too much for Gower before the one-dayers. We knew a lot about him anyway and just waited to have another look in case anything suggested itself to us. From our observation of his batting in the first one-dayer, we decided to have an extra slip or gully for his off-side slash. The leg-slip theory, one that could cost runs and so was too risky for a one-day game but which could work well in the Tests, came from me with AB in strong support. I'd first used it in Brisbane in 1982–83. When Gower kept flicking at a few outside leg-stump at Headingley, we turned to this 'Plan B', moving one of the gullys or slips out to leg slip and bringing fine leg squarer in case he hit a few in the middle. We also had a mid-wicket, but no mid-on as he rarely scores through there. By bowling outside leg stump, a rare play, we forced Gower to think about his shots and footwork on both sides of the wicket. Normally a left-hander would expect an attack from a right-arm bowler to run across the angle towards the slips. That sort of ball made Plan A, the two gully trick, successful, but the Plan B attack outside leg stump was different and gave Gower much more to think about. At various stages, both tactics have worked.

At the start we hadn't seen much of Robin Smith. The

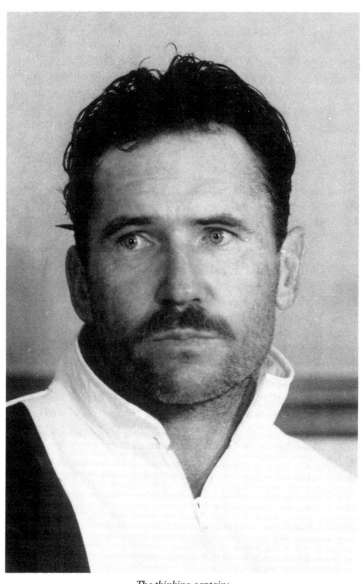

*The thinking captain:*
*in this series AB used all his years of experience to develop some*
*very shrewd tactics.*

three guys who'd played county cricket said that he liked to hook and cut and generally attack. So we knew we would have to keep things very tight to him and try to frustrate him into a bad shot. We also thought the slower ball might work because Smith is always looking to move into attacking shots. Being a South African, we thought he might respond to a little chat; they don't seem to like that too much. Merv thought this was an excellent idea and quickly took on full responsibility for it.

AB, partly because of his county experience and partly because of his growing confidence as a captain, is always full of ideas. He is keen to use attacking fielding positions — not standard ones but well-thought out specific positions for individual players. AB's thinking has not been tied to orthodox methods on this tour. He's keen for us to bowl around the wicket whenever one of their batsmen gets set. He wanted us to try this against Gower, but I thought that we'd tried it enough in the past without much success. It did work against Jack Russell, at least in tying him down if not in getting him out. After Merv unsettled him in the first Test with some short stuff, we thought we'd spotted his weakness, but he handled that sort of bowling well at Lord's and we were forced to try going around the wicket. We still haven't quite worked out his batting although Cracka worried him at Edgbaston.

Clem's main line at team meetings is about the importance of the bowlers being patient. He's that sort of bowler himself, always prepared to work away at setting a batsman up over a few overs. He often reminds me of this when we're in the nets or in the dressingroom during a break in play. Early in the tour I was trying too hard to get batsmen out and was losing control as a result. Clem spotted this and has continued to remind me to be patient.

Swampy's main line is about how important teamwork is, how we have to play as a unit, something which has been a feature of our play.

Of course, some of the newer players occasionally make good contributions. Merv often throws in some sensible thoughts: 'Okay, we bowl just outside off-stump, fairly full going away to the slips, occasionally go around the wicket and bowl just short of a good length with a bat-pad and a short cover if the wicket is slow — and if that doesn't work, WE'LL BOUNCE HIM!' This always breaks the seriousness of the meeting with everyone, except Simmo who likes to keep things serious, reduced to laughter.

Although the pressure has eased, we have developed a few ideas for this match and I think everyone is keen to assert our dominance again.

# THE FIFTH TEST

We won the toss and didn't lose a wicket.

None for 301. Tub not out 141, Swampy not out 125. It was only the ninth time two batsman have batted through a full day of a Test match and the first time two openers have done so on the first day of an Ashes match. On a day when we might have fielded and been below par because of fatigue, and the 'new-look' England side might have shown improvement, we buried them mercilessly.

The openers had some luck early, but that's life. Malcolm beat the bat with some good balls in the first session, but he also served up some loose stuff which was put away every time. Tub just continued on his merry way, totally unflustered. Swampy had to fight hard, but that's his great strength. He kept the scoreboard ticking over by pushing and prodding with the occasional great drive or cut. We were all pleased to see Tub make another hundred, but we cheered even louder when Swamp reached his. The crowd reaction was the same. Like us, they know how hard he's fought and what a great trier he is. He's struggled for most of the tour, but has been in the nets constantly, trying to find form, Swampy is always very disappointed when he doesn't make runs. mainly because he feels he's letting the side down. But even in the middle of a slump he is in the rooms encouraging and praising other guys. He's a genuinely supportive team man, never selfish.

In many ways Swamp is the archetypical Australian

*The hard work pays off: Marsh on his way to the century that ended a worrying period of poor form.*

cricketer — a no frills battler with less natural ability than some but with an enormous capacity for work. He plays to his limitations and has great patience. As everyone knows, Swampy is a farmer and he has the dry sense of humour of the cocky. If you're not careful he can slip a double entendre past you with no change of expression on his open, innocent-looking face. On this tour, he is always talking about farming with our other man from the land, Mocca. On the bus they're often looking out the windows analysing the crops as we drive through the countryside.

Swampy and Tub had to go out onto the balcony after stumps to pose for the photographers and then go upstairs for a press conference. Although they'd been batting all day in helmets, they quickly grabbed their baggy green caps for the official appearances. It was more than appropriate on such an historic day.

Of course there are disadvantages to a day like today. Boonie for instance. He claimed, and probably correctly, that he was more tired than the two batsman from sitting for six hours with the pads on, waiting and waiting. But the worst problem with a day like today is that you have to put up with a bored Merv Hughes. Merv gets bored easily and spent most of today throwing things around our small dressingroom or trying to wrestle anyone within reach. He's not known as 'The Fruitfly' (the great Australian pest) for nothing. Quite often today Merv wandered around the rooms moaning: 'I'm bored. I'm bored. Why doesn't some-one get out?'

Of course Merv is not a complete pest. He's one of the great triers in the game. Even when he's not bowling well, he's yelling encouragement to the other guys, often from way down at fine leg. He's always good for a laugh at serious moments, team meetings or at the fall of a wicket, one of ours that is, which is not normally a time for lighthearted-ness. But Merv gets away with it. He's enormously popular over here because of all the media attention he's attracted. And that has not only helped the team in its relations with the English people, but it's taken some of the attention away from his teammates and let them get on with their cricket.

Merv doesn't mind the hype too much although early on when he was trying to adapt his bowling to English conditions it began to annoy him. Basically, he has played up to the media's image of him and not taken himself or the press too seriously.

I don't drink and I suppose I lead a quieter life than a lot of the blokes and Merv is forever telling me to loosen up, to live a little. If Merv was any looser he'd fall apart.

**AUSTRALIA 0–301.**

## FRIDAY, 11 AUGUST

### Taylor/Marsh score highest opening partnership in an Australia v England Test and highest partnership in England by any Test nation.

I organised tickets for my University of New South Wales Cricket Club teammates, Dave Gallup and Jamie Baker, before leaving for the ground. Tickets are at a premium these days. Even though the series is wrapped up the games are still sold out and our share of complimentaries is kept to a strict minimum because priority is given to our sponsors.

The first wicket fell at 329, the highest ever for the first wicket in an Ashes Test, passing the 323 Jack Hobbs and Wilfred Rhodes set at Melbourne in 1911–12. History in the making.

### Taylor reaches 196 and becomes 2nd only to Bradman for runs scored in an Ashes series.

Tub went on to 219 and 720 for the series. A double century in only his seventh Test is a great achievement. When he reached 196, he also passed Arthur Morris to become second only to Bradman for runs scored in an Ashes series. It's interesting to watch the progress of new players when they come into the team. Since Tub first played for New South Wales in 1985–86 very little has changed in his cricket or in his general approach to life. His elevation to the Australian team has been no different. He's accepted success with all the nonchalance of a typical Australian and that nonchalance is one of his greatest assets as a player. Nothing flusters him. He can play and miss several times and then play the next ball on its merits. He has confidence in his own ability without being over-confident. He has a great range of shots which he is not afraid to play — that hasn't changed since he was twelve and playing for the Lake Albert Cricket Club in Wagga — but he does know when and when not to play them. A bad shot at golf will bring forth more self-criticism than a bad shot in a Test match, which probably means he's chosen the right sport. He also works hard at his game, especially his slips catching. He has a great pair of hands and rates with Greg Chappell and Rick McCosker, two of the best slippers I've played with. He might be known as 'Tub' because of his thickish build, but he is surprisingly athletic. He's a friendly, easy-going bloke though he does get a little touchy if his largish backside is mentioned too often. Tub loves a beer and a good time as much as anyone and on this tour has formed a comedy duo with Maysie, giving a lot of sharp lip to everyone.

Boonie finally got a hit after seven hours and did very well to concentrate properly and make 73. AB is still there on 46, but someone had to miss out after such a start and today it was Legend and Waughie, predictably enough, I suppose, seeing they've been making so many runs up to now. Legend made 22 before being given out caught in the gully off what was obviously his pad not his bat. Tugga made a duck which was bad news for him but not a great worry for the team as we were past 500 at the time. He hit one from Malcolm off his toes right in the meat of the bat but straight to Gower at square leg. When Tugga walked back into the rooms after his brief visit to the middle, Legend came out with one of his classic comments: 'You're only as good as your last innings'.

We finished on 5–560, but despite the gloom, Lubo showed in two incidents during the day that he still has a

*On and on: Taylor does it easily, making his first Test double century in only his seventh match.*

158

sense of humour. The first was before Swampy got out, with the score 0–300 plus. Lubo called twelfth man Greg Thomas onto the field and after a few words from the skipper, Thomas broke up laughing. We found out later that Lubo had told him to go around to the press box and ask the English cricket writers for some advice on how to take a wicket. The second incident happened at lunch when the score was still 1 for. The Poms were already at the lunch table when we arrived and the first thing I noticed was that Gower had a glass of champagne in front of him. I know it's his favourite drink but I had to ask him why he'd succumbed to the temptation at lunch in a Test match. 'I'm celebrating our wicket, Henry,' he explained.

Sitting watching your batsmen make heaps of runs is very pleasant, but it does give you time to think about what might happen when it's England's turn to bat. If it's easy for our blokes it suggests that the wicket is so good that we might be out there for two days as well trying to bowl them out. Again it was boring at times in the rooms today. The indoor nets were taken over by sponsors so there was nowhere to go for a hit to loosen up. Merv was bored again. Unfortunately his gear is right next to the phone and every time he answered it he used a different accent, never Australian. 'Allan who? No, no one here called that.' 'Steve Wo? No, I'm sorry.' 'Who? Who? Oh, it's you Simmo.' Clem and I struggled all day with the *Daily Telegraph* crossword. At one stage I even took the opportunity during a Channel Nine interview to ask if anyone back in Australia knew of a six letter word for the mouth of a river. We got some promising replies but unfortunately they were all wrong.

There was one minor disaster for England today, as if they hadn't had enough already. Boonie edged one off his glove to slip where Beefy dropped it then immediately ran from the field with a badly dislocated finger. It could well be broken. Malcolm finished the innings with 1–166 off 44 overs and a beanball to AB who was clearly not amused.

**AUSTRALIA 5-560**

159

## Australia passes 600 for the 2nd time this series, equalling the 1930 and 1946–47 record.

We closed at 6–602 and at stumps they're 9–246.

It all seems so easy. We're still expecting them to come good but they're still collapsing. There's nothing like being 2 for 1 at the end of the first over chasing 600. Clem had Moxon caught at slip by Tugga off the fourth ball of the innings, then two balls later had Atherton out leg before for a duck on debut. On the replays it just looked like he missed a straight one. Clem finished with five wickets for the fifth

*The start of another England collapse: Moxon departs as Alderman leads us in congratulating Waughie who took the catch.*

time in eight innings. A marvellous display. I got Lubo yet again, caught behind on the off-side this time. Heals spilled it at first and both of us had our hearts in our mouths for a second or two until he held it at the second grab.

Smith made a very hard-hitting 101 but it didn't matter. When he was out the score was still only 172 and they were gone anyway. Russell and he put on 80-odd in their usual determined way, but when the top order folds so easily you can't expect the middle and late order to make enough runs to save you. Beefy batted at nine because of his finger, but, on recent performances, the odds are that he wouldn't have made much difference.

We're 353 ahead with eleven wickets to take. It could be over on Monday, a day early.

I had a pizza with Mark Ray tonight before going back to the bar where it was fairly low key. I think that's because we've dominated almost every second of the three days and it just doesn't seem like a Test match. My body feels tired tonight and my Achilles tendon is sore, no doubt as a result of sitting around for two days and then bowling 21 overs in five hours this afternoon. Doesn't AB know I'm getting on?

AUSTRALIA 6-602, ENGLAND 9-246.

## SUNDAY, 13 AUGUST

I slept in until 10.30 am and just caught the end of breakfast with AB, Simmo and Lawrie. They were discussing the team for the Nehru Cup in India which is on not long after we get home from England. Lawrie asked me for my thoughts on prospective fast bowlers around Australia.

It was cold and windy today, but Mark Ray and I went for a short drive to Eastwood, an old mining village and birthplace of D.H. Lawrence a few miles out of Nottingham, and had a large, hot, traditional English lunch at a pub there. I rang Julie tonight and she is not too happy about the trip to India. Who is?

We bowled them out for 167 just after tea.

This has been the easiest Test match I've played. No, it's the only easy Test I've played. England just caved in. We bowled fairly straight as usual and held our catches, but their total lack of spirit was unbelievable. A Sydney grade side would have lasted longer today.

Earlier in the week, one of the English journos asked me whether I thought Gower was now my Bunny. I was forced to agree that my dismissing him five times out of eight meetings in the Tests and twice in the recent county match suggested fairly strongly that that was the case. In the ensuing story, it came out as if Lubo had said it not me. Before play started this morning, he came into our rooms to tell me he was thinking of wearing ears and a tail out to bat.

Gower opened in the second innings which was a positive move, something different which might have broken the pattern. He hit the first ball of the innings from Clem for four down the ground and took a single later that over. In my first over I bowled him two out-swingers (in-swingers to a right-hander) which left him towards the slips and which he played uncomfortably. Hoping that he would leave the next one on that line, I then bowled an in-swinger (outie to a right-hander) which pitched on or just outside the line of off-stump. He didn't seem to pick which way it was going to move and decided to let it go, no doubt thinking that the angle across him would take it safely past the stumps. But it held its own or moved back in a fraction and hit off-stump. The look on his face seemed to say: 'what a season this is'. It was a very satisfying wicket for me because it's not often that you plan something and it works exactly the way you want.

Atherton made quite a good 47 to top score and this time we got Smith cheaply. Merv exacted some revenge by bowling him with a great leg stump yorker. It was another instance of Merv taking a crucial wicket.

Towards the end of the day there was some controversy when Hemmings nicked one off me to Tugga at third slip. I

*Gone at the second grab: Heals holds an edge from Gower to give me his wicket for the fifth time in eight innings.*

was in the middle of a good spell and was pretty fired up as we were trying to finish them off. The catch appeared to carry and Tugga told Hemmings he'd caught it, but Hemmings just stood there looking dumbfounded at us and at the umpires. Hemmings is one of those irritating people who is chirpy and friendly when things are going his way, but not when it's the other way around. Tugga was standing quite close to him by then and I joined them telling Hemmings that if Tugga had said he'd caught it fairly then he should accept that and get off the field. AB came up and asked what was going on. Tugga told him, but Hemmings didn't budge or say anything. The umpires didn't even consult each other — just the odd glance from where they were. I asked the umpire at the bowler's end, Nigel Plews, what the decision was and he said that his colleague, David Shepherd, had given it not out. Later, Shepherd said Plews had given it not out. Our view was that if the fieldsman said he'd caught it then the batsman should accept that, espe-

*Still in the groove: the rhythm that returned at Old Trafford
is still there.*

cially as in a similar situation Swampy had done the right thing at Lord's and called Gower back. The worst of it was that a few balls later I thought I had Hemmings plumb lbw, but that appeal was also refused. Hemmings then swung the bat and made a few runs before the tea break. As I was waiting at the boundary for the batsmen, he came over towards me. Before he could say anything, I told him that he was not playing within the spirit of the game and pointed to the dressingrooms, suggesting he stop mucking about and get off the field. AB was trying to calm us down as we went through the gate and up the wooden steps. When we got into the dressingroom, AB called us all into one of the two rooms (the dressingroom here is separated by a partition) and told us the Hemmings business didn't matter as the Test was over for them. They were 7-160 with Beefy unlikely to bat. He told us to go out there and resume normal cricket. And, after tea, that's what happened. Merv cleaned them up quickly and we won the game in four days and have gone four Tests up. Hemmings was eventually out leg before to Merv to a decision that one commentator said wasn't half as clearcut as the earlier one from Lawson. Oh well, Hemmings didn't take a wicket in his return to Test cricket which probably means he'll be retained for the Oval and I'll get another crack at him there.

......................................................................

## Australia wins by an innings and 180 runs — their greatest victory margin in England.

......................................................................

It's amazing to think we have won four Tests and would have won the other had it not rained. I don't care what anyone says, this is a very good Australian team. The dressingroom was subdued after the match. There's not much of a contest left now and we have only records to play for in the last Test.

Back at the hotel it was more like a creche than a cricket team's pub. Many of our wives and children were there, and, after months living in an all-male world, it was pleasant to have them with us. It's fascinating to see your teammates at the bar with a can of XXXX one minute and feeding their baby with a bottle the next. Maysie was in fine form looking after his six-month-old daughter, Georgina. He seems much happier now that his family has joined him.

Of course, not every team member is ready for parenthood. Merv and Cracka, whose wife and children are back home in Brisbane, did a demolition job on themselves, working their way through the cocktail list with gusto. Merv was very vocal until the tenth drink when he faded rapidly and was carried up to bed by Cambo, Tom and Patrick.

There was plenty of speculation in the bar about Gower's immediate future. He certainly doesn't lead with any conviction, but you do wonder about the quality of the personnel under him. David began the summer in a blaze of publicity and is ending it the same way, but for completely opposite reasons. Apart from the occasional lapse, he has maintained his dignity and sense of humour throughout. The walkout at the press conference at Lord's was understandable when you consider how hard it must be to cope with all the personal abuse a losing England captain gets from most sections of the English media. It would wear the toughest man down. He's been pleasant to me all summer even though I'm giving him a hard time on the field.

Gower's main problem is simply that he has not captained well. He seems to have had one plan out on the field and when that hasn't worked he's been stuck for alternatives. That is the main difference between him and AB. AB did not really want the job in the first place and struggled to come to terms with it for a while. But he is a smart bloke who when he sets himself to do something works at it until he's improved enough to satisfy himself. AB has learned to be a good captain; Gower does not appear to be too interested in learning. Of course, AB has had some excellent support and advice, especially from Simmo, and that does make you wonder about those people in the England set-up close to Gower. I know that his captaincy is not highly regarded by his teammates.

Despite his gallant attempts to remain dignified and

philosophical in defeat, he has made a forlorn picture at times. I still remember that image of him at Headingley, on his knees at cover point as another Waugh square drive raced past him to the rope. It was certainly a portent of things to come.

Still, that's not our problem. We've got an extra day now before the second last county game of the tour against Kent at Canterbury on Wednesday.

**AUSTRALIA 6–602 DECLARED, ENGLAND 255 AND 167.**

## TUESDAY, 15 AUGUST

A nice late sleep-in this morning before an 11 am leave for Canterbury which is a fair hike down the eastern side of the country. Along the way the bus was pulled over by the highway patrol and we were all concerned that Austin might have been speeding. Not so. All the police wanted were some autograph sheets and we obliged, of course.

During the trip I saw today's *Sun* which has a headline on the back page: '**** OFF HEMMINGS' and 'That's what Lawson told England star'. Misquoted again. Still, I liked the use of the word 'star'. On the inside pages there was another RIP scoreboard and 'Ashes to Ashes... dust to dust... Gower's goons have turned to rust'.

We played at the Canterbury Golf Club this afternoon. The club secretary came down to the first tee to watch us hit off. 'Seeing all you chaps play off single figures you may as well play off the white tees,' he said. I proceeded to hit my first two drives straight into the trees in front of me, and Patrick hit his tee from underneath his ball. I wonder what the secretary said to his members when he got back to the clubhouse.

I'm resting from this game against Kent and so managed to improve my tee shots at the first hole this afternoon.

The papers didn't let up on England today. Micky Stewart had the boys in the nets yesterday at Trent Bridge, sensibly making use of a rare free day off in the busy program. The *Daily Mirror* headlined their story on this with 'Back To School', 'Gower gets detention' and 'Naughty boys in the nets'. I think that might have tickled Lubo's sense of humour a trifle.

There was great jubilation in the dressingroom today. T. May hit his first six in any competition — from the under-12s up. He's talked about it all tour and Deano has been offering various odds to any takers. It says something about our confidence in Maysie's hitting that it took until today before anyone laid a bet. Legend had blown the odds out to 60-1 which was quite generous as the boundary on one side was short and Kent had two spinners. Ziggy could not resist taking a slice of that and put ten quid on Maysie. At 6.28 pm, with instructions from AB, the resting captain, and Swampy, the playing captain, to bat carefully so as to be not out overnight, Maysie lifted R.P. Davis over cow corner for his maiden six. He then raced off down the wicket in celebration and nearly retore that hamstring. He then acknowledged the help and support of his teammates by pointing the bat horizontally towards the dressingroom as Legend does when he passes a milestone. Maysie was out next over, caught at long-off slogging, again. Ziggy decided to split the 600 pounds with Maysie 50-50.

Legend smashed another hundred just to keep things in perspective.

Clem is back in his old home town and he and I had a few drinks at the Maidenhead Hotel with some of his mates. We went to a fish and chip shop for a nightcap on the way home and as it was late I parked half up on the footpath next to a zebra crossing. A very ordinary park. While we were in the shop, a policeman came in and said: 'Excuse me Mr Law-

son, is that your car?' I admitted as much and waited for the
ticket. 'Well played this summer and could you move it up
twenty feet please?'

AUSTRALIA 8-353.

## THURSDAY, 17 AUGUST

It actually rained for a little while this morning and the joy
that brought was not diminished by this morning's headlines. England's Second XI, captained by Peter Roebuck,
was beaten by Holland yesterday in the first of a series of
one-day games. 'Clogged' cried the tabloids. We can afford
a chuckle but I doubt 'Dex' is smiling.

Then came the amazing news from Trent Bridge that the
wicket was so bad for the Notts-Derbyshire game that the
officials and the umpires moved it to the Test wicket in the
middle of an innings. Michael Holding, who was bowling at
the time, refused to take any further part in the game. The
captains, Tim Robinson and Kim Barnett, said they had
come under intense pressure from the Test and County
Cricket Board not to abandon the game. What is going on in
English cricket? Michael is a man who has his standards and
I agree with what he did. You wouldn't think of swapping
wickets half way through a club match in Australia, let
alone a Sheffield Shield game. And now there is talk of
Derbyshire penalising Michael. It's an absolute joke.

Jamie Baker, my clubmate from Sydney and a promising
leg-spinner who's just been chosen in the New South Wales
pre-season squad, bowled in the nets before play and had a
long chat with Cracka. I hope Jamie took some notice. He
has ability but he needs to get his head right.

With the rain well and truly gone, we bowled them out for
191 and there were then some ugly scenes in the dressingroom when acting skipper, Marsh, enforced the follow-on
with 20 overs left. The real captain would have opted for a
rest for the bowlers and some centre-wicket practice for the

batsmen. I'd even told the opposition that we would bat again. At this stage of the tour I don't think we need a full day in the field in a county match if it can be avoided.

Tub and I ate in town tonight and strolled around the beautiful streets. Canterbury is ancient, with narrow cobbled streets and a Roman city wall with four main gates which now serve as arches through which the traffic enters the city centre. The whole thing is dominated by the great cathedral. A very pleasant walk then back to my room and my roommate, Campbell, who took four wickets today and bowled very well.

AUSTRALIA 8-356 DECLARED, KENT 191 AND 1-42.

## FRIDAY, 18 AUGUST

A day in the field did not go down too well. They batted it out for a draw despite a career-best 4–30 from Big Harry Moodini (T. Moody) who was on a hat-trick at one stage. Mark Benson was the man who denied us a win with a fine hundred. Why doesn't he get a game for England?

After stumps Roy Pienaar, the South African on the Kent staff, entertained us with an excellent magic show; he had us all very confused. Danny 'the Destoyer', Kelleher, the Kent opening bowler and a good mate of Clem's, gave me one of his county jumpers to add to my collection. I had a long chat to Hartley Alleyne whom I first met in 1979 when we proed in the Lancashire League together. He's one of those high-spirited, laughing West Indians and was in great form this evening.

We left Canterbury at about 7 pm for the drive to Chelmsford and tomorrow's match against Essex, the last county match and the second last game of the tour. The end is nigh. It will be interesting to see how well Gooch and Mark Waugh play. I'll have a chat to Junior (M. Waugh) at some stage about how he's been going (obviously with a view to the coming Shield season).

AUSTRALIA 8-356 DECLARED, KENT 191 AND 9-237.

*Moody the bowler: Big Tom runs in during his career best effort of 4-30 against Kent.*

Yet another fine, warm day. It never rains in England. Chelmsford is one of the better county grounds and Essex probably the strongest team. The ground itself is compact, lined by trees and with a river at the back which all adds to the atmosphere. Today it was full and it was an impressive sight. The facilities for players and spectators are good here and Essex, judging by their success on the field and the quality of their ground, is a financially well-off club.

We won the toss and batted, declaring forty minutes after tea at 7–387. Boon 151, Moody 80, Jones 70. Another day of absolute carnage. Admittedly Essex are not playing their best attack with Foster, Pringle and Don Topley, a useful county seamer, all resting. But John Lever is still a good bowler and John Childs has been spoken of this summer as a possible candidate for one of England's spin bowling positions.

I doubt whether their best bowlers would have made much difference to Boonie today. He was in awesome form and simply hit them wherever he wanted. It's hard to imagine how Australia made 721 in one day against Essex at Southend in 1948 although I think they faced something like 140 overs in the day. That works out at about five runs an over. We faced 93 overs today which puts our scoring rate at just over four an over.

Legend hit his twentieth 6 today which earned him 1,000 pounds — or rather us 1,000 pounds. Into the team kitty, Legend.

We had them two down at stumps, both wickets going to me in successive balls. The poor nightwatchman missed a straight one on off stump.

I spent a quiet night at the hotel tonight.

Neil Foster and Paul Prichard, the Essex batsman, came into the bar for a chat. All our lads are praying for rain so we can have a day off. We're near the end of a very long tour and are feeling weary.

AUSTRALIA 7-387 DECLARED, ESSEX 2-43.

*Carnage: Boonie during his slaughter of the Essex attack at Chelmsford.*

173

Heals dropped two straightforward catches today, but at least they were from the bat of Mark Waugh. If anyone was going to get a hundred, it might as well have been an Australian against the Australians. I don't think Merv was too impressed though as both chances were off him. Junior was also dropped by another wicket keeper, Ziggy, who was at mid off. Is this a record for being dropped by different keepers in the same innings? Junior's was only the third hundred by a county player against us all summer and without it we would have bowled them out quite cheaply.

I went to dinner with Derek Pringle — nicknamed Suggs after the lead singer in Madness, his favourite band — at a village about a half an hour outside Chelmsford. Like Foster, he's not playing in this game, but is still the leading wicket-taker in county cricket this year. I've known Suggs since 1979 when we played against each other in a Lancashire versus Cambridge University match. In 1983–84 he came out to Australia to play for my club, University of New South Wales Cricket Club. He didn't do all that well, but he had a great time.

Suggs was resplendent as usual in a checked suit, 1950s sideburns and his new narrow-framed glasses that have replaced his National Health pair. This could be the look of the 1990s. Greg Matthews would have been impressed. Suggs is an interesting character, a bit of a non-conformist who likes left-wing new wave and punk rock and somewhat way-out clothes. Mark Ray was telling me he heard a great comment from someone in the crowd at Trent Bridge during the second one-day international. After Suggs had misfielded one and we'd taken a single we should not have got, this loud, annoyed voice called out: 'Come on Pringle, you commie'. In fact Suggs is forever copping a bagging from the English crowds. I suppose that's because he's never taken his success at county level to Test cricket. This season he's actually been reprimanded for giving the crowds some

174

of their own back, but tonight at the restaurant he was on his best behaviour.

Suggs lent me his car so I could get back to the pub and I'll take it to the ground tomorrow so he can pick it up.

AUSTRALIA 7-387 DECLARED, ESSEX 6-290 DECLARED AND 1-130.

## MONDAY, 21 AUGUST

The last day of the county games. Tugga spoiled AB's plan to bat till around tea and then field for a couple of hours by making a quick century. The second 50 came off 18 balls and forced us to declare before lunch. Cricket records cover most vagaries of the game, but surely this is the first time in the history of the game that twins have scored hundreds for opposing sides in a first class match.

Ziggy opened in the second innings and made 93. It was disappointing to see him miss out on a hundred on tour as he's worked hard on his game all summer despite the fact that he hasn't made it onto the park too often. Being the second wicket keeper on a long tour like this is a very difficult job, but Ziggy has handled it well. It's the first time I've had much to do with him really. His reputation from the last Ashes series in Australia was not good, but he must have matured since then. I wasn't sure what to expect but he's been an excellent member of the team, maintaining his enthusiasm despite becoming known as 'Hirem Holiday' because of his lack of on-field work.

The declaration turned out well as we bowled them out for 205 and had a good win against a top side on an excellent batting wicket. Junior made another 50 and it was probably a better innings than that of his hundred. Merv took 5-64 and unsettled Nasser Hussain with some short pitched bowling.

Hussain and his teammate, John Stevenson, were both named in the England squad for the sixth Test later this week. If Hussain plays he will know what to expect. Stevenson made three in each innings so we haven't seen much of him, but we're not exactly concerned. Gooch, who is back after presumably finding form in county cricket, was very determined to make runs today. You could see it on his face. But I managed to move one late on him and bowled him for not many. The disappointment and annoyance were obvious when he saw his castle knocked over. Still, Gooch is a class player and we'll be giving him the best we can at the Oval.

David Capel has come into the England team for Beefy which is to be expected I suppose. Capel is the next best, some cite figures and say the best, English all-rounder, but he has not produced the goods at Test level so far. With a place on the tour to the West Indies at stake, he will be feeling some pressure. Dexter and co. have retained Atherton which is fair enough after his 47 in the second innings at Trent Bridge. He was lucky to survive some close lbw appeals early on but played well after that. His technique looks better than most and at least as he is young it is worth persisting with him.

Gladstone Small has also been chosen. I know he has had injury problems this season, but if he has been fit and not been chosen it's been a mistake. He might not always make their side when all the bowlers are fit, but we rate him as a good Test bowler. DeFreitas has also been recalled after pulling out of the South African tour.

So that completes Ted Dexter's work for the series. It hasn't exactly been the revolutionary change announced five months ago and on current form it would take a miracle for these new players to turn it around at the Oval and salvage something for Dexter.

A chairman of selectors who arrives at the ground on a motorbike and wears jogging shoes with a suit, much to our amusement, is putting his credibility on the line. Presumably the plan was for Dexter to bring some consistency to selection after the debacle of the recent season against the West Indies when five captains were chosen, and players like Northants' Robert Bailey were given one Test in which they played reasonably well but not brilliantly and were then ditched. Nothing has changed this year except the names of the selectors and the players. In fact their selections have been so inconsistent and numerous that we started a competition to see who would get picked next.

England plays a total of 29 players in the Ashes series; Australia plays same 11 players in 5 consecutive Tests for a new record.

After the early statements about giving young players a chance, the players were dropped after one failure. DeFreitas is a good example. He had a bad game at Leeds, but that can happen to anyone. We regard him as one of their best bowlers and he continued to perform well in county cricket. No wonder he originally took up the South African offer. Bringing Eddie Hemmings back at the age of forty with the series three-nil our way and the Ashes lost was difficult to work out. That was a perfect time to put a young spinner in and give him some experience. It's not as if Hemmings is a world class spinner — he didn't take a wicket.

Admittedly England had a number of injuries which disrupted the teams originally chosen, but have these injuries been the result of too much cricket or a lack of motivation? And if the standard of county cricket is too far below Test cricket then you've just got to pick your most talented players and put them into the Test team where they can learn. Waugh, Boon and Jones have had to learn the hard way. The crucial thing is to be able to spot someone with the talent and temperament to come through.

Early in the tour, the English press was giving the new Dexter regime a lot of praise, yet when you look at it — Dexter, Gower and Stewart — there was little that was new. I was surprised at just how much was being attributed to them before a ball had been bowled. One captain can get more out of his players than another, but Gower's record didn't suggest that he was about to do anything outstanding in that regard.

Early on, Simmo told us that Dexter was flamboyant as a player and full of wind. Simmo obviously wasn't expecting any divine leadership to come from Lord Ted. A few of the early statements from Dexter and Gower suggested a certain smugness which not only raised our hackles but smacked of unjustified over-confidence. That might well have been one of the reasons why the England players have been so unprepared for losing to us. They've never quite come to terms with the fact that they've been completely outplayed.

Another thing that puzzles us is how Micky Stewart has escaped criticism. If he were a football coach/manager he'd be gone by now. There seems to be some confusion about his role. Simmo's is clear enough; he is involved in tactical planning, selections, running practice, handling the media and in other general organisation. As well, there is plenty of talk here about the old north-south split. Stewart and Dexter are from the south of England and northerners like Geoff Boycott, Brian Close and Ray Illingworth have been very critical and you can understand why.

I'm afraid that while this member, among others, of the Australian team has a few views on the problems confronting the opposition, none of us will be hoping for an improvement from them in the final Test. If we can win five-nil, we'll be the first side to do so in an Ashes series since Warwick Armstrong's team in 1920–21 and therefore the first to do so in England.

I seem to be catching Clem's flu so at lunch Cracka went down to the shops to get me some more garlic tablets and I'm stuffing them down my sore throat at a great rate. We left Chelmsford at about 6.30 pm for London via Aussie's scenic route — lost again. At one stage he even had us on the wrong side of the Thames: a Lancastrian with no sense of direction in the big city. He copped plenty of stick from us but returned it in full.

We're back at the Westbury for the last stretch. No more hotels after this stay, at least in England. I had my second

178

curry for the tour tonight. It was quite good, but I don't how Maysie has one every second night. Cambo and Moodini tried the raw chilli which was asking for trouble. It was very funny watching two grown men running around a restaurant with mouths full of ice cubes.

I'm sharing a small room with Moodini. The beds are pushed up against each other and with our bags in there as well, there's very little room to move, especially with Tom being 2 metres tall and me 1.9 metres tall. I've asked for another room, but at this stage they're all booked.

AUSTRALIA 7-387 DECLARED AND 2-258 DECLARED, ESSEX 6-290 DECLARED AND 205.

*The happy tourist: Ziggy Zoehrer manages to raise a smile at the end of a long tour during which he's played little cricket.*

## TUESDAY, 22 AUGUST

Our fifth completely free day on tour. Just for a change, most of us played golf at Moore Park. Clem and I beat the locals, with the ageing swing bowler (Clem, that is) playing well below his handicap. My tee shot at the first was sensational — 274 metres up the middle in full view of the 'Sixty Minutes' crew who are doing a story on AB to be shown in Australia next weekend.

I rang Julie from the Westbury. She's not too happy at present and is very keen to get to London. We ate Italian at the restaurant next to the Windmill Hotel, our local just around the corner from the Westbury. Swerv was outrageous, wearing the waiter's clothes and eventually buying his tie for ten quid. He seems to be getting crazier, if that's possible, now that the end is close. Our room is in chaos, junk everywhere. Fortunately there was some baseball on television so I took refuge in bed and watched that till midnight.

## WEDNESDAY, 23 AUGUST

We practised at 9 am at the Oval and I couldn't believe how brown and bare the outfield was. The grounds in Wagga are better than this in the middle of summer. Still, the wicket looks good, a typical Oval belter which will probably be the quickest wicket all summer. My neck was sore after practice and the Achilles tendon is not too flash either. Thankfully there's not long to go.

In the afternoon AB and I went over to Swiss Cottage to organise trunks for the boys to take home their goodies.

The last team meeting, at 7 pm at the Westbury. There have been plenty of changes in the England side. Fraser and DeFreitas have withdrawn because of injury and been replaced by D. Pringle and Kent's Alan Igglesden. Suggs and I had only said our farewells and promised to correspond two days ago and now I'll be seeing him tomorrow. Needless to say, no one picked Alan Igglesden in our selection competition. He didn't play against us in Canterbury, but Clem knows his bowling fairly well and clued in the batsmen. He is about the sixteenth fast bowler they've chosen all summer and it's not easy to win a Test match when you're down to your sixteenth best pace bowler. If it was Australia you'd be just about grabbing someone out of club cricket.

The dilemma for the English selectors was highlighted again when Greg Thomas was called up to replace Malcolm only to then tell the selectors that he had just accepted an offer to tour South Africa in place of Daffy. If the selectors are so inconsistent and so unwilling to pick players and give them a fair chance to acclimatise to Test cricket, they can't expect much loyalty in return. Players don't expect to be pampered but they do need some sort of security. English cricket is certainly in a mess at the moment.

We went through their batting order and really the only major problem is Smith. Clem suggested that we just try the patience ploy — bowl as tightly to him as we can and wait for him to lose patience and try a risky shot. Merv said the best tactic was to bounce him. The general emphasis was again on not being complacent. AB and Simmo were still very strong on this point. We have a chance of history if we can win here so there is still something to play for.

After the meeting we enjoyed a take-away meal organised by the social committee. They'd ordered about twenty family size pizzas, spare ribs, chicken and salads. Once again they'd done very well and were given a vote of thanks for their efforts over the past four months. The room was filled with all sorts of cricket paraphernalia to be signed by the team and after the meal we set to. Most of this gear is owned by the players — stuff we've collected along the way as mementoes of the tour: full-size and miniature bats, stumps, books, programs, prints, cigarette cards — you name it we've got it. As well there are another hundred bats to sign for XXXX. I've got dozens of autograph sheets, quite a few bats and programs. They're all part of cricket history and will be valuable mementoes as the years go by.

I rang 2GB tonight for my last preview. I hope there's still some interest left even though we're so far ahead.

# THE SIXTH TEST

My sister Carole rang the dressingroom this morning to remind me that it was Mum's birthday; she knows I'm pretty hopeless with dates. I made up a sign and put it over the balcony, hoping that the cameras would pick it up, but I forgot that the telecast doesn't get to Wagga. Still, it's the thought that counts.

England goes into 6th Test at odds of 11/1 — the longest ever quoted for England in England.

I was sitting next to AB in the dressingroom when Gower came in to toss. Lubo put his hand on my shoulder and said: 'H., I've got some good news and some bad news for you.' I asked for the bad news first. 'You'll have to wait a while today to get a bowl at me.' That meant he wasn't opening, so then I asked for the good news. 'You might only have to wait three balls,' he said. So at least we knew Gower was batting at five again.

Lubo continued in his lighthearted mood at the toss by acting as if he'd won it. We were watching from the room and when he went over to the television cameras first as is the usual procedure for the winner, we assumed he'd won it. We knew whoever won the toss would bat, so I had my ankle half strapped by the time AB returned to tell us we were batting. Gower even fooled the ground announcer.

182

*A great century: Deano salutes the Oval crowd after really collaring the English bowlers today.*

183

We finished on 3–325, another very good day. Tub made 71 in another impressive effort. Swamp missed out again, but Boonie made 46, AB 66 not out and Legend a superb century in quick time. It was probably his best innings of the series. He really collared them today. At one stage we were 3–149 and could have been in relative strife, but again our strong middle order came through.

Our batting was always going to be strong this summer, but it has developed and dominated more than we expected. I think having Tub open has added balance. Boonie has played a lot of his career at three, especially for Tasmania, and although he would still prefer to open he is a very good number three. AB is the steadying influence at four who can use his experience to dictate the pattern and adapt to the circumstances. After that we've got Legend and Tugga who are now two of the best attacking batsmen in the world. If the top four set things up, those two can add the icing.

The great strength of the middle order is its versatility. Each player can defend or attack depending on what is required. I think that is a carry-over from one-day cricket. The batsmen know how to handle both forms of the game and in the one-day matches they don't score runs with cross-bat slogging. Contrary to popular opinion, one-day cricket has not adversely affected the techniques of our batsmen. Simmo has always said that a good Test batsman will be a good one-day player. Geoff Boycott is a classic example of that. He was known as a very slow Test batsman but he was scoring hundreds in one-day games even at the end of his career. This is why I don't think one-day cricket is the problem with England's batting. They have technical problems because as they come through the county system they are playing on poor wickets and are not being coached properly.

Small was the best of their bowlers and Igglesden did well for his first game. He bowls straight which is half the battle. Suggs kept it tight, but Capel came in for some heavy punishment, especially from Deano.

I had a pizza for dinner with Merv followed by a few

mineral waters at the Windmill. We spent almost two hours over dinner in quite a serious philosophical discussion about the tour, about getting to know different blokes and learning to bowl consistently at Test level. We both agreed this group was a very good one to be involved with. As for Merv's bowling, I said I thought his main problem was his mental attitude. He tends to let himself down by bowling that occasional half volley on leg stump or that short one too far outside off-stump. It's just a matter of concentration. Yes, I know it's hard to believe, but this was a serious, sensible conversation between two fast bowlers.

AUSTRALIA 3-325.


# FRIDAY, 25 AUGUST

It was decidedly cooler today and it seems like summer is just about gone. Some cloud cover arrived making the ball seam around more than on the first day and this helped England's attack.

We mucked it up a little, but still managed 468. Tugga only made 14 and Deano was out for 122, so we didn't go on to something like 550 or 600. Heals hit 44 off as any balls in his best innings of the series, Cracka and Merv chipped in well, and I made 2 before being bowled by Suggs. Back in the rooms I was asked what it was I was trying to do with the bat, but I pleaded that I was just a fast bowler and couldn't be expected to explain such things.

Gladstone finished with 3–141 off 40 overs, Igglesden 2 for and Suggs 4–70 off 24 overs. A few of the lads were surprised by Suggs's figures because he has never quite performed at Test level. But his height (2 metres) meant that he could extract some awkward bounce from the hard Oval wicket.

Rain intervened in the afternoon but not before Clem got Gooch for a duck off the third ball of the innings. It was his seventeenth leg before of the series which says a lot about his accuracy. As we waited for stumps Clem and I did the *Daily Telegraph* crossword in record time, for us.

I ate on my own and then went to bed to watch some more baseball. Patrick is moving in with me as Tom has found another room with more space to stretch out.

AUSTRALIA 468, ENGLAND 1-1.

## SATURDAY, 26 AUGUST

It was very gloomy and wet today and we lost half the day's play. Still, we managed to take five more wickets to have them 6–124, 145 behind the follow-on. Gower is there on 40-odd not out and he was more sedate today, it was more like a captain's innings.

Merv was warned by Dickie Bird for bowling too many short ones at Smith and AB was incensed, having quite a lengthy discussion with Dicky about it. Naturally he came off second best. It seemed ridiculous, especially as I spent last summer watching the West Indies bowl aggressively at England without once being warned for intimidatory bowling.

Clem finished with 4–34 which brought his tally to 39. He had to leave the field at times to take oxygen, his chest was so bad. A few of the lads suggested that he ought to be fit by now and was really only pretending to be sick so he could have a rest. With Clem's oxygen cylinder on the floor next to him in the rooms, it was more like being at a gridiron game than at a cricket game.

I took just the one wicket, but it was a very satisfying one — Smith clean bowled by a quicker, fuller one that did him all ends up. I hope someone got a decent picture of those stumps splattered all over the place. Always a lovely sight.

I spent the evening in Soho showing Jamie Baker, Dave Gallup and some of their mates the sights. A sleep-in tomorrow.

AUSTRALIA 468, ENGLAND 6-124.

*A prize wicket: Robin Smith's stumps scatter after I got a quicker one through his defence.*

## SUNDAY, 27 AUGUST

I got up at 10 am and headed off to Liverpool Street station to pick up Julie who was arriving from Norwich. The station is being done up at present and it was a complete bunfight, but we eventually found each other. We spent a fairly quiet afternoon at the hotel and dined.

## MONDAY, 28 AUGUST

There was more rain today, but we still managed enough play for things to follow the by now familiar pattern. We bowled them out for 285 which was not a bad recovery from being 6–98 on Saturday. Gladstone Small made 59 and, with support from Pringle and Cook, saved them from following on. When they passed that mark, the crowd applauded as if they'd won the Test rather than reached the landmark of being 200 behind on the first innings. Gower made 79 and was again out caught behind down the leg side, this time off Clem. This gave Clem five wickets in an innings for the sixth time this series. I was happy with my three though I wouldn't have minded a bowl at the tail a little earlier.

We went in at stumps on 1–87, a lead of 270 which means we will bat on tomorrow — how long will depend on AB.

AUSTRALIA 468 AND 1-87, ENGLAND 285.

## TUESDAY, 29 AUGUST

We declared at lunch 400 ahead. This might seem a little cautious but who cares. Despite the threat of rain and the poor position England was in, the crowds were good. Either they love their cricket a great deal or they were all Australians out there. There was a funny incident when AB went out to bat this morning. When he went to mark his block his

*Man of the series: Clem celebrates his 41st wicket which makes him the first bowler to twice take more than 40 wickets in an Ashes series.*

spikes didn't make much of an impression and when he looked down to check them he saw he'd put on one spiked and one rubber-soled boot. That's what happens when gear is strewn all over a dressingroom.

................................................................

Alderman takes his 41st wicket — the 2nd time he has taken more than 40 wickets in an Ashes series (first time in 1981) — the first player to do so.

...........................

Rain cost us the whole of the last session and they ended on 5–143 with Smith top-scoring with 77 not out. Clem and I took two each, Clem finishing with forty-one wickets and me with twenty-nine. He got Gooch yet again and I took Gower's wicket for the seventh time in eleven innings, caught off his slap shot by one of the two gulleys. If it hadn't rained I think we could have bowled them out and won. The match and the series finished in something of an anticlimax, but we asserted our dominance right to the end.

During the afternoon, AB and I answered mail and signed all sorts of things for people. They ask for or send in bats, caps, autograph books — quite unbelievable. By the end, AB had a pile a metre high next to him. If the game hadn't been washed out we would never have signed everything, including another 200 or 300 official bats which arrived during the afternoon.

When the game was officially called off we all went out

................................................................

Australia takes series 4–0 equalling the record of Bradman's 1948 side.

................................................................

onto the balcony. There was still a great crowd there and they gave us a wonderful farewell. AB proudly held that little Ashes urn aloft for all of them to see. Legend won his

190

*The final farewell: all of us gather on the balcony at the Oval to say farewell to England. In the background at left, AB poses with the Ashes urn.*

second man of the match award for his fine century and Clem deservedly won our man of the series award, though Tub with a total of 839 runs for the series, cannot have been far behind him. Jack Russell was their man of the series.

Back in the rooms, the celebrations were quieter than they were earlier in the series because of the anti-climax of the finish, although Boonie led us in one last 'Underneath the Southern Cross'. We were disappointed we couldn't win here for a five-nil scoreline, but it was satisfying to play well to the end. Some people might say we don't rank with the great Australian teams of the past, but our record in the Tests and the county games is very good and that's what I'll be reminding people of in twenty or thirty years time. Let's just hope we don't get beaten in Denmark or Holland.

Gower, Russell, Pringle and Cook came in for a drink and Gower told AB he was happy for him as he deserved success after all he'd been through. They are close friends and do feel a lot for each other. I didn't feel any sympathy for Gower or the Englishmen during the series because I wanted to win so badly, but I felt some today. After all, we're only playing cricket.

I don't think I could extend that sympathy to Ted Dexter. Apparently he said at the press conference that he was not aware of having made any mistakes during the summer. An amazing statement.

I swapped my Australian jumper for Jack Russell's England one as I still hadn't got one of those. I thought it was a good swap too with Russell being their man of the series though I doubt I'll ever be able to fit into it. As I packed up all my gear for the last time in a Test series in England, I decided to leave all my boots behind. They'd seen a lot of wear and tear and were just about gone. I signed a couple for David Frith who collects that sort of thing though I've no idea what he does with them.

We spent the night at a plush restaurant on Park Lane at a slap-up dinner for all the players, their wives and people who've supported us which was paid for by John Cornell and Austin Robinson. They're great supporters of Australian cricket and would have been with us had they not been in Los Angeles working on another project.

We were even picked up from the Westbury in limousines and driven the full two kilometres to the restaurant. You can tell you're in a posh restaurant when there is more cutlery and glass on the table than you'll ever need and when there's one waiter to pour your drinks, another to serve the food, another to pull your chair out and another to fold your napkin. It must have cost 300 to 400 pounds a head, but it didn't take much thinking to convince ourselves that we deserved it.

Merv conducted interviews throughout the dinner so everyone got a chance to say something. Maysie was brilliant.

The other diners, separated by a thin partition, were probably shocked however when Boonie got up on a table and led us in one more 'Underneath the Southern Cross' complete with colourful language. Our wives joined in with enthusiasm.

From the restaurant we went to a nightclub where the drinks had already been paid for by the same supporters. A big night with several couples seeing in the dawn and then some.

**AUSTRALIA 468 AND 4-219 DECLARED, ENGLAND 285 AND 5-143.**

## WEDNESDAY, 30 AUGUST

Graeme Fowler (the media man — not the Lancashire and former England batsman), rang this morning to ask me to do something for his forthcoming BBC show, 'A Question of Sport'. That shortened the sleep-in as we had to do it today. He had me lie on a bed with several models so it should be an interesting sequence. I did an interview for Channel 7 at 10.30 am and then headed off to a luncheon at the Rooftop Gardens in Kensington given by XXXX. They showed a video of the series called 'Heroes' which brought out some emotion in the players, their wives and the Australian journos who've been with us from day one.

That night Julie and I went with the Boons, the Marshes and Tugga and Lynette to see 'Phantom of the Opera' thanks to John Kelly, a London friend and cricket lover who organised the tickets for us.

## THURSDAY, 31 AUGUST

Julie and I did some banking today then bought some clothes — presents for ourselves after all the hard work. We had a short team meeting to tidy things up and organise the trip to Holland and Denmark. There was also another swag of things for us to sign.

Almost the whole of the touring party dined together tonight. It was a great farewell-to-England dinner although disaster struck the Mays again when Catherine, Tim's wife, had her bag stolen. Naturally it had her passport in it and she is due to leave with us tomorrow for Holland.

## FRIDAY, 1 SEPTEMBER

All the trunks had to be in the lobby by 9 am. We posed for a picture for Emery Airfreight, the people who are flying all the gear home for us. We said goodbye to the Aldermans, Marshes, Cambo, Cracka and Merv. The Aldermans are off for a well deserved holiday in the Greek Islands; Swampy and Michelle and the kids are stopping over in Singapore before Swamp has to get back to the farm. No doubt he'll arrange to have a net during the stop-over. Cambo is hurrying home to Hobart to that fiancée we've heard so much about; Cracka is keen to get back to Brisbane and see his family for the first time in four months and Merv just wants to have a drink in his local at Werribee. It's a shame really. I'm sure he would have been a big hit in Holland.

The rest of us piled onto the bus to head for Heathrow and Holland. Austin was quite emotional when he dropped us at terminal 14. I think I saw a tear there somewhere. At 4.30 pm we took off for Holland and, would you believe it, more cricket.

# COMING HOME

OR TWELVE MEMBERS OF THE AUSTRALIAN
team, the tour did not quite end at Heathrow on
the afternoon of 1 September. Messrs Alderman,
Marsh Campbell, Hohns and Hughes left for
home or brief holidays, but the rest of us went to Holland
and Denmark for two games in each country. After four
months in England, we weren't overly keen on the idea,
especially as all six days were taken up with either playing or
travelling. We had to leave it to our wives to enjoy some
sightseeing. Still, it was a special occasion in Holland as we
were the first Australian cricket team to visit there.

Back in London before we headed off for holidays or
home, the news came through that Graham Gooch would
captain England, both in the Nehru Cup in October and on
the tour to the West Indies in early 1990. This came as no
surprise to us, nor it seemed to David Gower, who publicly
gave his full support to the new captain. However, it got
worse: when the touring teams were announced a day later,
Gower was not in any of them. We were stunned by this.
Gower might not have captained well in the Ashes series,
but he was still their second highest scoring batsman after
Robin Smith.

Ian Botham also missed selection for the West Indies
tour. And this after the selectors had spent weeks during the
summer convincing him to change his decision about never
touring overseas again. He finally agreed to make himself
available only to be passed over when the teams were
chosen. Thanks, but no thanks.

So, in one stroke England's selectors had felled two
exceptionally talented and experienced players. Whatever
problems English cricket is experiencing, I'm sure sure that
tried and tested men such as Gower and Botham are needed

for a recovery. The former may have been a disappointment as a captain, but he showed himself still to be a class above most English batsmen. The latter is not the player of 1981 or even 1985, but he showed in the two Tests he played that he can bring some fight and competitiveness to an otherwise dispirited England team. All those qualities will be needed in the Caribbean if England doesn't want to find itself with another group of battered and beaten cricketers.

For every backward step English cricket took this summer, Australia strode confidently in the opposite direction. For our skipper, Allan Border, it was a great personal

...............................................................

## Border breaks Australian record for most Test partnerships of 100 or more.

...............................................................

triumph. He might have been disappointed at not scoring a Test century, but he has always put team goals ahead of personal ones and would have found genuine satisfaction in seeing a number of players bloom into consistently successful Test cricketers.

Dean Jones played well in every Test innings bar one and confirmed himself as a world class Test batsman. When he arrived in England he must have harboured some self-doubts after such a poor Australian season, but he convincingly dispelled those and the doubts of his harshest critics.

Steve Waugh emerged from the shadowy category of the

...............................................................

## Waugh becomes only the 3rd Australian batsman to average more than 100 in an Ashes series.

.......................

'promising player' into the bright sunlight of the world class performer. That long-awaited maiden Test century at Leeds will be remembered as one of the game's classic innings. It proved he was capable of a long innings and brought him deep satisfaction.

Mark Taylor, given the job of opening for his country under the pressure of being the man for whom a great partnership had been split, took to it as if he was playing his tenth full Test series not his first. Just as Terry Alderman consistently destroyed England's batting to allow Australia to be victorious, Taylor was the player who set it up with his consistent and heavy run-scoring at the top of the order. His record on the this tour speaks for itself.

...................................................................

## Taylor scores 839 runs — the most runs scored by an Australian opener in a Test series.

...........

David Boon, like his captain, did not make a Test century, but that hardly mattered to the team. He averaged over 50 for the series and his success at his new position of number three brought the depth and stability the batting needed to allow it to post so many high totals. His fielding at short-leg was always high class.

The motivation to 'prove something', whether to yourself, your supporters, your critics or your opponents, should not be underestimated. It not only drove the batsmen to perform well, but was the main factor that pushed Terry Alderman and myself to ensure that our last Ashes tour to England would be successful. We were not satisfied until the last ball was bowled at the Oval and the series ended the way it began — with Australia on top. Terry's bowling in this series was of the highest quality and he thoroughly deserved his man of the series award. His knowledge of English conditions and players was invaluable. Like Clem, I was determined to make up for the disappointments of previous tours. This was the most rewarding series of my career even though the statistics weren't as healthy as they were in 1982–83 when we beat England in Australia. This will certainly be my last tour to England with an Australian team and to come home with the Ashes gave me the greatest satisfaction of my career.

It would have been much more difficult to take the wickets we did without the support of Merv Hughes, Trevor Hohns and Greg Campbell. Merv's continual encouragement, shouted from all corners of the field for all of the four months, was a great help to all of us.

I said at the start of this book that the achievements of this team were the result of the work of everyone, from the manager down to the players who did not take part in any Tests. We won because we wanted to 'do it' for each other and for our country. In the context of contemporary professional sport, that may sound trite, but it was true of us and would be of any team that really wants to succeed. Some of the opposition seemed more concerned with their counties or their insurance schemes than with a wholehearted effort for their team and their country.

A thrill to equal Boonie's winning hit at Old Trafford that won us the Ashes series awaited us when we arrived home. It was great to hear that the ACB with the Government and numerous others wanted to fete us on our homecoming. A couple of dinners, some ego-boosting words and a few pats on the back would have been enough, but the New South Wales Government and Allan Davidson's committee decided that a ticker-tape parade through Sydney was in order. The feeling among the players was one of apprehension. What if no one turned up? It could be more than a little embarrassing.

The subsequent response from the people in Sydney was overwhelming. One official told me he thought there were about 400,000 people at the parade that day, lining the streets of Sydney from the Regent Hotel down by Circular Quay all the way to the Darling Harbour complex. They were ten and twenty deep along the roadways with many more throwing paper on us from high above in the office blocks. I saw several friends along the way. At one stage a woman rang out of the crowd to get an autograph. It was my sister Carole. The whole day was a highly emotional experience for all of us. Our wives were on the footpaths waving furiously and taking photographs. At the Barrack Street corner, people were chanting 'Henry, Henry'. It was hard to hold back the tears. The car Tim May and I were in was so full of paper we had to throw it back out at the crowd. At the luncheon for 1,500 people that followed the parade, a man came up to me and said he'd come all the way from the Northern Territory just for the day. What can you say to that?

After a wonderful dinner in Melbourne earlier in the week, we went back there on the Saturday to receive a standing ovation from 95,000 people at the VFL Grand Final. It was a perfect end to a week we could never have envisaged. We had no idea we had brought so much pleasure to so many people.

As AB said at the end of the fifth Test when we had equalled the 1948 side's four-nil victory margin: 'I suppose in twenty years time we'll look back and think we were pretty good'.

*An unexpected bonus: some of the thousands of Sydneysiders who gave us such a stunning welcome home.*

# ASHES TOUR RECORDS

## Played 20 (Won 12, Lost 1, Drawn 7)

| Date | Opponent | Venue |
|------|----------|-------|
| 13–15 May | Worcestershire | Worcester |
| 17–19 May | Somerset | Taunton |
| 20–22 May | Middlesex | Lord's |
| 31 May–2 Jun | Warwickshire | Birmingham |
| 3–5 Jun | Derbyshire | Derby |
| 8–13 Jun | England (1st Test) | Leeds |
| 14–16 Jun | Lancashire | Manchester |
| 17–19 Jun | Northamptonshire | Northampton |
| 22–27 Jun | England (2nd Test) | Lord's |
| 1–3 Jul | Glamorgan | Neath |
| 6–11 Jul | England (3rd Test) | Birmingham |
| 19–21 Jul | Hampshire | Southampton |
| 22–24 Jul | Gloucestershire | Bristol |
| 27 Jul–1 Aug | England (4th Test) | Manchester |
| 2–4 Aug | Nottinghamshire | Nottingham |
| 5–7 Aug | Leicestershire | Leicester |
| 10–15 Aug | England (5th Test) | Nottingham |
| 16–18 Aug | Kent | Canterbury |
| 19–21 Aug | Essex | Chelmsford |
| 24–29 Aug | England (6th Test) | The Oval |

| Australia | | | Opponent | Result for Australia |
|---:|---:|---:|---:|---|
| 103* | 205 | 146 | 7–163 | Lost by 3 wkts |
| 8d–339* | 3d–144 | 140 | 3–235 | Drawn |
| 2d–233 | 7–243 | 245* | 227 | Won by 3 wkts |
| 3d–444* | 4d–195 | 235 | 3–105 | Drawn |
| 200* | 180 | 228 | 141 | Won by 11 runs |
| 7d–601* | 3d–230 | 430 | 191 | Won by 210 runs |
| 288 | 1–84 | 184* | 185 | Won by 9 wkts |
| 329* | 5d–229 | 180 | 106 | Won by 272 runs |
| 528 | 4–119 | 286* | 359 | Won by 6 wkts |
| 4d–373* | 5d–216 | 5d–301 | 5–135 | Drawn |
| 424* | 2–158 | 242 | – | Drawn |
| 6d–343* | 246 | 6d–275 | 0–81 | Drawn |
| 438 | – | 200 | 92 | Won by an innings & 146 runs |
| 447 | 1–81 | 260* | 264 | Won by 9 wkts |
| 284* | 4d–255 | 195 | 148 | Won by 196 runs |
| 305 | 1–99 | 157* | 243 | Won by 9 wkts |
| 6d–602* | – | 255 | 167 | Won by an innings & 180 runs |
| 8d–356* | – | 191 | 9–237 | Drawn |
| 7d–387* | 2d–258 | 6d–290 | 205 | Won by 150 runs |
| 468* | 4d–219 | 285 | 5–143 | Drawn |

* Denotes batted 1st

# First Test
## Headingley, Leeds, 8-13 June

**Umpires**: J.W. Holder and D.R. Shepherd
**Toss:** England
**Man of the Match:** T. Alderman
**Australia won by 210 runs.**

## 1ST INNINGS

### AUSTRALIA

| | Runs | Balls | Mins | 4s |
|---|---|---|---|---|
| **G. Marsh** lbw b DeFreitas | 16 | 63 | 78 | 1 |
| **M. Taylor** lbw b Foster | 136 | 315 | 394 | 16 |
| **D. Boon** c Russell b Foster | 9 | 24 | 31 | 1 |
| **A. Border** c Foster b DeFreitas | 66 | 118 | 141 | 9* |
| **D. Jones** c Russell b Newport | 79 | 172 | 267 | 7 |
| **S. Waugh** not out | 177 | 242 | 309 | 24 |
| **I. Healy** c & b Newport | 16 | 31 | 38 | 2 |
| **M. Hughes** c Russell b Foster | 71 | 105 | 131 | 6* |
| **G. Lawson** not out | 10 | 13 | 13 | 1 |
| **G. Campbell** did not bat | | | | |
| **T. Alderman** did not bat | | | | |
| Sundries (13LB, 7NB, 1W) | 21 | | | |
| **Seven wickets (dec) for** | **601** | | | |

FALL: 44, 57, 174, 273, 411, 441, 588.

| BOWLING | Overs | Mdn | Runs | Wkts |
|---|---|---|---|---|
| **P. DeFreitas** | 45.3 | 8 | 140 | 2 |
| **N. Foster** | 46 | 14 | 109 | 3 |
| **D. Pringle** | 33 | 5 | 123 | 0 |
| **P. Newport** | 39 | 5 | 153 | 2 |
| **G. Gooch** | 9 | 1 | 31 | 0 |
| **K. Barnett** | 6 | 0 | 32 | 0 |

**Innings time:** 704 min. **Overs:** 178.3.
\* Denotes six. (Border 1, Hughes 2.)

| | Runs | Balls | Mins | 4s |
|---|---|---|---|---|
| **G. Gooch** lbw b Alderman | 13 | 46 | 58 | 2 |
| **C. Broad** b Hughes | 37 | 74 | 107 | 5 |
| **K. Barnett** lbw b Alderman | 80 | 118 | 165 | 10 |
| **A. Lamb** c Boon b Alderman | 125 | 205 | 281 | 24 |
| **D. Gower** c Healy b Lawson | 26 | 38 | 60 | 5 |
| **R. Smith** lbw b Alderman | 66 | 132 | 192 | 8 |
| **D. Pringle** lbw b Campbell | 6 | 15 | 16 | 1 |
| **P. Newport** c Boon b Lawson | 36 | 73 | 107 | 3 |
| **R. Russell** c Marsh b Lawson | 15 | 33 | 53 | 3 |
| **P. DeFreitas** lbw b Alderman | 1 | 6 | 11 | 0 |
| **N. Foster** not out | 2 | 5 | 5 | 0 |
| Sundries (7LB, 5B, 1W, 10 NB) | 23 | | | |
| **TOTAL** | **430** | | | |

**FALL:** 35, 81, 195, 243, 323, 338, 392, 421, 424, 430.

| BOWLING | Overs | Mdn | Runs | Wkts |
|---|---|---|---|---|
| **T. Alderman** | 37 | 7 | 107 | 5 |
| **G. Lawson** | 34.5 | 6 | 105 | 3 |
| **G. Campbell** | 14 | 0 | 82 | 1 |
| **M. Hughes** | 28 | 7 | 92 | 1 |
| **S. Waugh** | 6 | 2 | 27 | 0 |
| **A. Border** | 2 | 1 | 5 | 0 |

**Innings time:** 533 min. **Overs:** 121.5.

# 2ND INNINGS

| | Runs | Balls | Mins | 4s |
|---|---|---|---|---|
| **G. Marsh** c Russell b Foster | 6 | 22 | 22 | 0 |
| **M. Taylor** c Broad b Pringle | 60 | 112 | 121 | 8 |
| **D. Boon** lbw b DeFreitas | 43 | 95 | 138 | 6 |
| **A. Border** not out | 60 | 76 | 97 | 8 |

| | Runs | Balls | Mins | 4s |
|---|---|---|---|---|
| D. Jones not out .......................... | 40 | 33 | 56 | 3 |
| Sundries (5LB, 2B, 9W, 5NB) ................... | 21 | | | |
| **Three wickets (dec) for** ...................... | **230** | | | |

FALL: 14, 97, 129.

| BOWLING | Overs | Mdn | Runs | Wkts |
|---|---|---|---|---|
| N. Foster .................... | 19 | 4 | 65 | 1 |
| P. DeFreitas ................... | 18 | 2 | 76 | 1 |
| D. Pringle .................... | 12.5 | 1 | 60 | 1 |
| P. Newport ................... | 5 | 2 | 22 | 0 |

**Innings time:** 220 min. **Overs:** 54.5.

## ENGLAND

| | Runs | Balls | Mins | 4s |
|---|---|---|---|---|
| G. Gooch lbw b Hughes ..................... | 68 | 118 | 175 | 10 |
| C. Broad lbw b Alderman .................... | 7 | 12 | 19 | 1 |
| K. Barnett c Taylor b Alderman .............. | 34 | 46 | 50 | 7 |
| A. Lamb c Boon b Alderman .................. | 4 | 6 | 9 | 1 |
| D. Gower c Healy b Lawson .................. | 34 | 44 | 53 | 6 |
| R. Smith c Border b Lawson ................. | 0 | 3 | 4 | 0 |
| D. Pringle c Border b Alderman .............. | 0 | 27 | 39 | 0 |
| P. Newport c Marsh b Alderman .............. | 8 | 27 | 41 | 1 |
| R. Russell c Healy b Hughes ................. | 2 | 22 | 27 | 0 |
| N. Foster not out ......................... | 1 | 16 | 19 | 0 |
| P. DeFreitas b Hughes ...................... | 21 | 18 | 26 | 0 |
| Sundries (4B, 3LB, 5NB) ..................... | 12 | | | |
| **TOTAL** ............................ | **191** | | | |

FALL: 17, 67, 77, 134, 134, 153, 153, 166, 170, 191.

| BOWLING | Overs | Mdn | Runs | Wkts |
|---|---|---|---|---|
| T. Alderman ................. | 20 | 7 | 44 | 5 |
| G. Lawson ................... | 11 | 2 | 58 | 2 |
| G. Campbell .................. | 10 | 0 | 42 | 0 |
| M. Hughes ................... | 9.2 | 2 | 36 | 3 |
| A. Border ................... | 5 | 3 | 4 | 0 |

**Innings time:** 238 min. **Overs:** 55.2.

# Second Test
## Lord's, London, 22–27 June

**Umpires**: H.D. Bird and N.T. Plews
**Toss:** England
**Man of the Match:** S. Waugh
**Australia won by six wickets.**

## 1ST INNINGS

### ENGLAND

|  | Runs | Balls | Mins | 4s |
|---|---|---|---|---|
| **G. Gooch** c Healy b Waugh | 60 | 123 | 167 | 9 |
| **C. Broad** lbw b Alderman | 18 | 44 | 54 | 3 |
| **K. Barnett** c Boon b Hughes | 14 | 24 | 29 | 2 |
| **M. Gatting** c Boon b Hughes | 0 | 1 | 6 | 0 |
| **D. Gower** b Lawson | 57 | 62 | 104 | 8 |
| **R. Smith** c Hohns b Lawson | 32 | 36 | 52 | 6 |
| **J. Emburey** b Alderman | 0 | 2 | 3 | 0 |
| **R. Russell** not out | 64 | 115 | 161 | 9 |
| **N. Foster** c Jones b Hughes | 16 | 51 | 57 | 3 |
| **P. Jarvis** c Marsh b Hughes | 6 | 14 | 15 | 1 |
| **G. Dilley** c Border b Alderman | 7 | 51 | 70 | 0 |
| Sundries (9LB, 3NB) | 12 | | | |
| **TOTAL** | **286** | | | |

**FALL:** 31, 52, 58, 131, 180, 185, 191, 237, 253, 286.

| BOWLING | Overs | Mdn | Runs | Wkts |
|---|---|---|---|---|
| **T. Alderman** | 20.5 | 4 | 60 | 3 |
| **G. Lawson** | 27 | 8 | 88 | 2 |
| **M. Hughes** | 23 | 6 | 71 | 4 |
| **S. Waugh** | 9 | 3 | 49 | 1 |
| **T. Hohns** | 7 | 3 | 9 | 0 |

**Innings time:** 371 min. **Overs:** 86.5.

## AUSTRALIA

| | Runs | Balls | Mins | 4s |
|---|---|---|---|---|
| **G. Marsh** c Russell b Dilley | 3 | 14 | 17 | 0 |
| **M. Taylor** lbw b Foster | 62 | 162 | 221 | 8 |
| **D. Boon** c Gooch b Dilley | 94 | 189 | 255 | 12 |
| **A. Border** c Smith b Emburey | 35 | 62 | 84 | 5 |
| **D. Jones** lbw b Foster | 27 | 31 | 45 | 1 |
| **S. Waugh** not out | 152 | 249 | 330 | 17 |
| **I. Healy** c Russell b Jarvis | 3 | 30 | 40 | 0 |
| **M. Hughes** c Gooch b Foster | 30 | 52 | 71 | 4 |
| **T. Hohns** b Emburey | 21 | 38 | 53 | 3 |
| **G. Lawson** c Broad b Emburey | 74 | 94 | 108 | 11 |
| **T. Alderman** lbw Emburey | 8 | 39 | 37 | 1 |
| Sundries (11LB, 8NB) | 19 | | | |
| **TOTAL** | **528** | | | |

**FALL:** 6, 151, 192, 221, 235, 265, 331, 381, 511, 528.

| BOWLING | Overs | Mdn | Runs | Wkts |
|---|---|---|---|---|
| **G. Dilley** | 34 | 3 | 141 | 2 |
| **N. Foster** | 45 | 7 | 129 | 3 |
| **P. Jarvis** | 31 | 3 | 150 | 1 |
| **J. Emburey** | 42 | 12 | 88 | 4 |
| **G. Gooch** | 6 | 2 | 9 | 0 |

**Innings time:** 636 min. **Overs:** 158.

## 2ND INNINGS

### ENGLAND

| | Runs | Balls | Mins | 4s |
|---|---|---|---|---|
| **G. Gooch** lbw b Alderman | 0 | 3 | 2 | 0 |
| **C. Broad** b Lawson | 20 | 30 | 43 | 4 |
| **K. Barnett** c Jones b Alderman | 3 | 21 | 27 | 0 |
| **M. Gatting** lbw b Alderman | 22 | 82 | 117 | 4 |
| **D. Gower** c Border b Hughes | 106 | 198 | 273 | 16 |
| **R. Smith** b Alderman | 96 | 206 | 272 | 16 |
| **R. Russell** c Boon b Lawson | 29 | 65 | 61 | 4 |

|                                    | Runs | Balls | Mins | 4s |
|------------------------------------|------|-------|------|----|
| **J. Emburey** not out             | 36   | 96    | 138  | 4  |
| **N. Foster** lbw b Alderman       | 4    | 2     | 2    | 1  |
| **P. Jarvis** lbw b Alderman       | 5    | 16    | 18   | 0  |
| **G. Dilley** c Boon b Hughes      | 24   | 64    | 83   | 3  |
| Sundries (6LB, 6B, 2NB)            | 14   |       |      |    |
| **TOTAL**                          | **359** |    |      |    |

**FALL:** 0, 18, 28, 84, 223, 274, 300, 304, 314, 359.

| BOWLING          | Overs | Mdn | Runs | Wkts |
|------------------|-------|-----|------|------|
| **T. Alderman**  | 38    | 6   | 128  | 6    |
| **G. Lawson**    | 39    | 10  | 99   | 2    |
| **M. Hughes**    | 24    | 8   | 44   | 2    |
| **A. Border**    | 9     | 3   | 23   | 0    |
| **T. Hohns**     | 13    | 6   | 33   | 0    |
| **S. Waugh**     | 7     | 2   | 20   | 0    |

**Innings time:** 531 min. **Overs:** 130.0.

## AUSTRALIA

|                                      | Runs | Balls | Mins | 4s |
|--------------------------------------|------|-------|------|----|
| **G. Marsh** b Dilley                | 1    | 12    | 16   | 0  |
| **M. Taylor** c Gooch b Foster       | 27   | 61    | 77   | 2  |
| **D. Boon** not out                  | 58   | 121   | 157  | 6  |
| **A. Border** c sub (Sims) b Foster  | 1    | 10    | 15   | 0  |
| **D. Jones** c Russell b Foster      | 0    | 4     | 8    | 0  |
| **S. Waugh** not out                 | 21   | 40    | 68   | 2  |
| Sundries (3B, 4LB, 4NB)              | 11   |       |      |    |
| **Four wickets for**                 | **119** |    |      |    |

**FALL:** 9, 51, 61, 67.

| BOWLING        | Overs | Mdn | Runs | Wkts |
|----------------|-------|-----|------|------|
| **G. Dilley**  | 10    | 2   | 27   | 1    |
| **N. Foster**  | 18    | 3   | 39   | 3    |
| **P. Jarvis**  | 9.2   | 0   | 38   | 0    |
| **J. Emburey** | 3     | 0   | 8    | 0    |

**Innings time:** 175 min. **Overs:** 40.2.

# Third Test
## Edgbaston, Birmingham, 6–11 July

**Umpires**: H. Bird and J.W. Holder
**Toss:** Australia
**Man of the Match:** D. Jones
**Match drawn.**

## 1ST INNINGS

### AUSTRALIA

|  | Runs | Balls | Mins | 4s |
|---|---|---|---|---|
| **G. Marsh** lbw b Botham | 42 | 133 | 147 | 2 |
| **M. Taylor** st Russell b Emburey | 43 | 100 | 137 | 5 |
| **D. Boon** run out (Jarvis) | 38 | 111 | 134 | 5 |
| **A. Border** b Emburey | 8 | 21 | 16 | 1 |
| **D. Jones** c sub (I. Folley) b Fraser | 157 | 293 | 396 | 17 |
| **S. Waugh** b Fraser | 43 | 54 | 78 | 6 |
| **I. Healy** b Fraser | 2 | 12 | 15 | — |
| **M. Hughes** c Botham b Dilley | 2 | 16 | 21 | — |
| **T. Hohns** c Gooch b Dilley | 40 | 99 | 121 | 4 |
| **G. Lawson** b Fraser | 12 | 28 | 34 | 2 |
| **T. Alderman** not out | 0 | 8 | 10 | — |
| Sundries (20LB, 17NB) | 37 | | | |
| **TOTAL** | **424** | | | |

**FALL:** 88, 94, 105, 201, 272, 289, 299, 391, 421, 424.

| BOWLING | Overs | Mdns | Runs | Wkts |
|---|---|---|---|---|
| **G. Dilley** | 31 | 3 | 123 | 2 |
| **P. Jarvis** | 23 | 4 | 82 | 0 |
| **A. Fraser** | 33 | 8 | 63 | 4 |
| **I. Botham** | 26 | 5 | 75 | 1 |
| **J. Emburey** | 29 | 5 | 61 | 2 |

**Innings time:** 563 min. **Overs:** 142.

## ENGLAND

|  | Runs | Balls | Mins | 4s |
|---|---|---|---|---|
| G. Gooch lbw b Lawson | 8 | 33 | 40 | 1 |
| T. Curtis lbw b Hughes | 41 | 81 | 121 | 7 |
| D. Gower lbw b Alderman | 8 | 26 | 39 | 1 |
| C. Tavare c Taylor b Alderman | 2 | 9 | 10 | — |
| K. Barnett c Healy b Waugh | 10 | 21 | 31 | 2 |
| I. Botham b Hughes | 46 | 110 | 154 | 6 |
| R. Russell c Taylor b Hohns | 42 | 131 | 156 | 3 |
| J. Emburey c Boon v Lawson | 26 | 58 | 77 | 5 |
| A. Fraser run out (Hughes/Healy) | 12 | 29 | 25 | 1 |
| G. Dilley not out | 11 | 63 | 86 | 1 |
| P. Jarvis lbw b Alderman | 22 | 31 | 39 | 2 |
| Sundries (1B, 2LB, 11NB) | 14 | | | |
| **TOTAL** | **242** | | | |

FALL: 17, 42, 47, 75, 75, 171, 171, 185, 215, 242.

| BOWLING | Overs | Mdns | Runs | Wkts |
|---|---|---|---|---|
| T. Alderman | 26.3 | 6 | 61 | 3 |
| G. Lawson | 21 | 4 | 54 | 2 |
| S. Waugh | 11 | 3 | 38 | 1 |
| M. Hughes | 22 | 4 | 68 | 2 |
| T. Hohns | 16 | 8 | 18 | 1 |

Innings time: 397 min. Overs: 96.3.

## 2ND INNINGS

### AUSTRALIA

|  | Runs | Balls | Mins | 4s |
|---|---|---|---|---|
| G. Marsh b Jarvis | 42 | 86 | 110 | 4 |
| M. Taylor c Botham b Gooch | 51 | 148 | 169 | 4 |
| D. Boon not out | 22 | 112 | 116 | 1 |
| I. Healy not out | 33 | 46 | 56 | 3 |
| Sundries (4B, 24LB, 2NB) | 10 | | | |
| **Two wickets for** | **158** | | | |

FALL: 81, 109.

| BOWLING | | Overs | Mdns | Runs | Wkts |
|---------|---|-------|------|------|------|
| G. Dilley | . . . . . . . . . . . . . . . . . . . . | 10 | 4 | 27 | 0 |
| P. Jarivs | . . . . . . . . . . . . . . . . . . | 6 | 1 | 20 | 1 |
| A. Fraser | . . . . . . . . . . . . . . . . . . . | 12 | 0 | 29 | 0 |
| J. Emburey | . . . . . . . . . . . . . . . . . . | 20 | 8 | 37 | 0 |
| G. Gooch | . . . . . . . . . . . . . . . . . . . . | 14 | 5 | 30 | 1 |
| T. Curtis | . . . . . . . . . . . . . . . . . . . | 3 | 0 | 7 | 0 |

**Innings time:** 227 min. **Overs:** 65.

# Fourth Test
## Old Trafford, Manchester, 27 July–1 August

**Umpires**: B. Meyer and J. Hampshire
**Toss:** England
**Man of the Match:** R.C. Russell
**Australia won by nine wickets.**

## 1ST INNINGS

### ENGLAND

| | Runs | Balls | Mins | 4s |
|---|------|-------|------|-----|
| G. Gooch b Lawson . . . . . . . . . . . . . . . . . . . . . . . | 11 | 32 | 50 | 1 |
| T. Curtis b Lawson . . . . . . . . . . . . . . . . . . . . . . | 22 | 103 | 134 | 4 |
| R. Robinson lbw b Lawson . . . . . . . . . . . . . . . . . . | 0 | 9 | 15 | — |
| R. Smith c Hohns b Hughes . . . . . . . . . . . . . . . . . . | 143 | 285 | 355 | 15 |
| D. Gower lbw b Hohns . . . . . . . . . . . . . . . . . . . | 35 | 51 | 87 | 6 |
| I. Botham b Hohns . . . . . . . . . . . . . . . . . . . . . | 0 | 6 | 6 | — |
| R. Russell lbw b Lawson . . . . . . . . . . . . . . . . . . . | 1 | 11 | 14 | — |
| J. Emburey lbw b Hohns . . . . . . . . . . . . . . . . . . . | 5 | 34 | 37 | 1 |
| N. Foster c Border b Lawson . . . . . . . . . . . . . . . . | 39 | 68 | 100 | 4* |
| A. Fraser lbw b Lawson . . . . . . . . . . . . . . . . . . . | 2 | 9 | 17 | — |
| N. Cook not out . . . . . . . . . . . . . . . . . . . . . . . | 0 | 10 | 15 | — |
| Sundries (2LB) . . . . . . . . . . . . . . . . . . . . . . . | 2 | | | |
| **TOTAL** . . . . . . . . . . . . . . . . . . . . . . . . . . | **260** | | | |

**FALL:** 23, 23, 57, 132, 140, 147, 158, 232, 252, 260.

\* Foster hit one 6.

| BOWLING | | Overs | Mdns | Runs | Wkts |
|---|---|---|---|---|---|
| T. Alderman | . . . . . . . . . . . . . . . . . | 25 | 13 | 49 | 0 |
| G. Lawson | . . . . . . . . . . . . . . . . . | 33 | 11 | 72 | 6 |
| M. Hughes | . . . . . . . . . . . . . . . . . | 17 | 6 | 55 | 1 |
| T. Hohns | . . . . . . . . . . . . . . . . . | 22 | 7 | 59 | 3 |
| S. Waugh | . . . . . . . . . . . . . . . . . | 6 | 1 | 23 | 0 |

**Innings time:** 424 min. **Overs:** 103.

## AUSTRALIA

| | Runs | Balls | Mins | 4s |
|---|---|---|---|---|
| **M. Taylor** st Russell b Emburey . . . . . . . . . . . . . . . | 85 | 180 | 179 | 10 |
| **G. Marsh** c Russell b Botham . . . . . . . . . . . . . . . . . | 47 | 100 | 157 | 5 |
| **D. Boon** b Fraser . . . . . . . . . . . . . . . . . . . . . . . | 12 | 40 | 40 | 2 |
| **A. Border** c Russell b Foster . . . . . . . . . . . . . . . . | 80 | 266 | 311 | 10 |
| **D. Jones** b Botham . . . . . . . . . . . . . . . . . . . . . . . | 69 | 141 | 172 | 7* |
| **S. Waugh** c Curtis b Fraser . . . . . . . . . . . . . . . . . | 92 | 174 | 202 | 7 |
| **I. Healy** lbw b Foster . . . . . . . . . . . . . . . . . . . . . | 0 | 1 | 1 | — |
| **T. Hohns** c Gower b Cook . . . . . . . . . . . . . . . . . . . | 17 | 64 | 63 | 2 |
| **M. Hughes** b Cook . . . . . . . . . . . . . . . . . . . . . . . | 3 | 6 | 9 | — |
| **G. Lawson** b Fraser . . . . . . . . . . . . . . . . . . . . . . | 17 | 31 | 30 | 3 |
| **T. Alderman** not out . . . . . . . . . . . . . . . . . . . . . | 6 | 12 | 23 | — |
| Sundries (5B, 7LB, 1W, 6NB) . . . . . . . . . . . . . . | 19 | | | |
| **TOTAL** . . . . . . . . . . . . . . . . . . . . . . . . . . . . . | **447** | | | |

**FALL:** 135, 143, 154, 274, 362, 362, 413, 423, 423, 447.

| BOWLING | | Overs | Mdns | Runs | Wkts |
|---|---|---|---|---|---|
| N. Foster | . . . . . . . . . . . . . . . . . | 34 | 12 | 74 | 2 |
| A. Fraser | . . . . . . . . . . . . . . . . . | 36.5 | 4 | 95 | 3 |
| J. Emburey | . . . . . . . . . . . . . . . . . | 45 | 9 | 118 | 1 |
| N. Cook | . . . . . . . . . . . . . . . . . . | 28 | 6 | 85 | 2 |
| I. Botham | . . . . . . . . . . . . . . . . . | 24 | 6 | 63 | 2 |

**Innings time:** 602 min. **Overs:** 167.5.

\* Jones hit one 6.

# 2ND INNINGS

## ENGLAND

| | Runs | Balls | Mins | 4s |
|---|---|---|---|---|
| G. Gooch c Alderman b Lawson | 13 | 23 | 50 | 2 |
| T. Curtis c Boon b Alderman | 0 | 2 | 6 | — |
| R. Robinson lbw b Lawson | 12 | 28 | 30 | 1 |
| R. Smith c Healy b Alderman | 1 | 8 | 5 | — |
| D. Gower c Marsh b Lawson | 15 | 40 | 68 | 1 |
| I. Botham lbw b Alderman | 4 | 23 | 25 | — |
| R. Russell not out | 128 | 293 | 351 | 14 |
| J. Emburey b Alderman | 64 | 183 | 220 | 10 |
| N. Foster b Alderman | 6 | 28 | 39 | — |
| A. Fraser c Marsh b Hohns | 3 | 32 | 38 | — |
| N. Cook c Healy b Hughes | 5 | 11 | 10 | 1 |
| Sundries (6LB, 2W, 5NB) | 13 | | | |
| **TOTAL** | **264** | | | |

FALL: 10, 25, 27, 28, 38, 59, 201, 223, 255, 264.

| BOWLING | Overs | Mdns | Runs | Wkts |
|---|---|---|---|---|
| T. Alderman | 27 | 7 | 66 | 5 |
| G. Lawson | 31 | 8 | 81 | 3 |
| M. Hughes | 14.4 | 2 | 45 | 1 |
| T. Hohns | 26 | 15 | 37 | 1 |
| S. Waugh | 4 | 0 | 17 | 0 |
| A. Border | 8 | 2 | 12 | 0 |

Innings time: 430 min. Overs: 110.4.

## AUSTRALIA

| | Runs | Balls | Mins | 4s |
|---|---|---|---|---|
| M. Taylor not out | 37 | 83 | 111 | 4 |
| G. Marsh c Robinson b Emburey | 31 | 94 | 94 | 1 |
| D. Boon not out | 10 | 23 | 15 | 2 |
| Sundries (3NB) | 3 | | | |
| **One wicket for** | **81** | | | |

FALL: 62.

214

| BOWLING | | Overs | Mdns | Runs | Wkts |
|---|---|---|---|---|---|
| N. Foster | ..................... | 5 | 2 | 5 | 0 |
| A. Fraser | ..................... | 10 | 0 | 28 | 0 |
| J. Emburey | .................. | 13 | 3 | 30 | 1 |
| N. Cook | ...................... | 4.5 | 0 | 18 | 0 |

**Innings time:** 111 min. **Overs:** 32.5.

# Fifth Test
## Trent Bridge, Nottingham, 10–15 August

**Umpires**: D. Shepherd and N.T. Plews
**Toss:** Australia
**Man of the Match:** M. Taylor
**Australia won by an innings and 180 runs.**

## 1ST INNINGS

### AUSTRALIA

| | Runs | Balls | Mins | 4s |
|---|---|---|---|---|
| **G. Marsh** c Botham b Cook ................... | 138 | 382 | 430 | 15 |
| **M. Taylor** st Russell b Cook ................ | 219 | 461 | 550 | 23 |
| **D. Boon** st Russell b Cook .................. | 73 | 183 | 207 | 9 |
| **A. Border** not out ......................... | 65 | 143 | 222 | 7 |
| **D. Jones** c Gower b Fraser ................. | 22 | 44 | 49 | 3 |
| **S. Waugh** c Gower b Malcolm ............... | 0 | 8 | 14 | — |
| **I. Healy** b Fraser ......................... | 5 | 7 | 11 | — |
| **T. Hohns** not out .......................... | 19 | 45 | 53 | 2 |
| **M. Hughes** did not bat ..................... | | | | |
| **G. Lawson** did not bat ..................... | | | | |
| **T. Alderman** did not bat ................... | | | | |
| Sundries (6B, 23LB, 3W, 29NB) .............. | 61 | | | |
| **Six wickets (dec) for** ...................... | **602** | | | |

**FALL:** 329, 430, 502, 543, 553, 560.

215

| BOWLING | Overs | Mdns | Runs | Wkts |
|---|---|---|---|---|
| A. Fraser | 52.3 | 18 | 108 | 2 |
| D. Malcolm | 44 | 2 | 166 | 1 |
| I. Botham | 30 | 4 | 103 | 0 |
| E. Hemmings | 33 | 9 | 81 | 0 |
| N. Cook | 40 | 10 | 91 | 3 |
| M. Atherton | 7 | 0 | 24 | 0 |

Innings time: 774 min. **Overs:** 206.3.

## ENGLAND

| | Runs | Balls | Mins | 4s |
|---|---|---|---|---|
| T. Curtis lbw b Alderman | 2 | 16 | 25 | — |
| M. Moxon c Waugh b Alderman | 0 | 3 | 2 | — |
| M. Atherton lbw b Alderman | 0 | 2 | 1 | — |
| R. Smith c Healy b Alderman | 101 | 150 | 206 | 16 |
| D. Gower c Healy b Lawson | 11 | 25 | 32 | — |
| R. Russell c Healy b Lawson | 20 | 63 | 91 | 1 |
| E. Hemmings b Alderman | 38 | 83 | 102 | 5 |
| A. Fraser b Hohns | 29 | 55 | 85 | 3 |
| I. Botham c Waugh b Hohns | 12 | 49 | 53 | 1 |
| N. Cook not out | 2 | 15 | 23 | — |
| D. Malcolm c Healy b Hughes | 9 | 15 | 12 | * |
| Sundries (18LB, 13NB) | 31 | | | |
| **TOTAL** | **255** | | | |

FALL: 1, 1, 14, 37, 119, 172, 214, 243, 244, 255

| BOWLING | Overs | Mdns | Runs | Wkts |
|---|---|---|---|---|
| T. Alderman | 19 | 2 | 69 | 5 |
| G. Lawson | 21 | 5 | 57 | 2 |
| T. Hohns | 18 | 8 | 48 | 2 |
| M. Hughes | 7.5 | 0 | 40 | 1 |
| S. Waugh | 11 | 4 | 23 | 0 |

Innings time: 325 min. **Overs:** 76.5.

* D. Malcolm hit one 6.

## 2ND INNINGS

### ENGLAND

| | Runs | Balls | Mins | 4s |
|---|---|---|---|---|
| **T. Curtis** lbw b Alderman | 6 | 10 | 21 | 1 |
| **M. Moxon** b Alderman | 18 | 48 | 71 | 3 |
| **M. Atherton** c & b Hohns | 47 | 127 | 172 | 3 |
| **R. Smith** b Hughes | 26 | 44 | 60 | 4 |
| **D. Gower** b Lawson | 5 | 5 | 7 | 1 |
| **R. Russell** b Lawson | 1 | 14 | 15 | — |
| **E. Hemmings** lbw b Hughes | 35 | 48 | 57 | 5 |
| **A. Fraser** b Hohns | 1 | 9 | 14 | — |
| **I. Botham** absent — hurt | — | — | — | — |
| **N. Cook** not out | 7 | 27 | 43 | 1 |
| **D. Malcolm** b Hughes | 5 | 9 | 6 | 1 |
| Sundries(3B, 6LB, 1W, 6NB) | 16 | | | |
| **TOTAL** | **167** | | | |

**FALL:** 5, 13, 67, 106, 114, 120, 134, 150, 167.

| BOWLING | Overs | Mdns | Runs | Wkts |
|---|---|---|---|---|
| **T. Alderman** | 16 | 6 | 32 | 2 |
| **G. Lawson** | 15 | 3 | 51 | 2 |
| **T. Hohns** | 12 | 3 | 29 | 2 |
| **M. Hughes** | 12.3 | 1 | 46 | 3 |

**Innings time:** 242 min. **Overs:** 55.3.

# Sixth Test
## The Oval, London, 24–29 August

**Umpires**: H.D. Bird and K.E. Palmer
**Toss:** Australia
**Man of the Match:** D. Jones
**Match drawn.**

## 1ST INNINGS

### AUSTRALIA

|  | Runs | Balls | Mins | 4s |
|---|---|---|---|---|
| **G. Marsh** c Igglesden b Small | 17 | 62 | 77 | 2 |
| **M. Taylor** c Russell b Igglesden | 71 | 126 | 160 | 4 |
| **D. Boon** c Atherton b Small | 46 | 90 | 123 | 6 |
| **A. Border** c Russell b Capel | 76 | 157 | 156 | 11 |
| **D. Jones** c Gower b Small | 122 | 180 | 214 | 17 |
| **S. Waugh** b Igglesden | 14 | 28 | 43 | 1 |
| **I. Healy** c Russell b Pringle | 44 | 44 | 58 | 6 |
| **T. Hohns** c Russell b Pringle | 30 | 62 | 95 | 4 |
| **M. Hughes** lbw Pringle | 21 | 42 | 46 | 3 |
| **G. Lawson** b Pringle | 2 | 8 | 8 | — |
| **T. Alderman** not out | 6 | 10 | 16 | 1 |
| Sundries (1B, 9LB, 9NB) | 19 | | | |
| **TOTAL** | **468** | | | |

**FALL:** 48, 130, 149, 345, 347, 388, 409, 447, 453, 468

| BOWLING | Overs | Mdns | Runs | Wkts |
|---|---|---|---|---|
| **G. Small** | 40 | 8 | 141 | 3 |
| **A. Igglesden** | 24 | 2 | 91 | 2 |
| **D. Pringle** | 24.3 | 6 | 70 | 4 |
| **D. Capel** | 16 | 2 | 66 | 1 |
| **N. Cook** | 25 | 5 | 78 | — |
| **M. Atherton** | 1 | — | 10 | — |
| **G. Gooch** | 2 | 1 | 2 | — |

**Innings time:** 651 min. **Overs:** 132.3.

## ENGLAND

| | Runs | Balls | Mins | 4s |
|---|---|---|---|---|
| **G. Gooch** lbw Alderman | 0 | 3 | 2 | — |
| **J. Stephenson** c Waugh b Alderman | 25 | 66 | 121 | 2 |
| **M. Atherton** c Healy b Hughes | 12 | 34 | 50 | 2 |
| **R. Smith** b Lawson | 11 | 19 | 18 | 2 |
| **D. Gower (c)** c Healy b Alderman | 79 | 120 | 165 | 11 |
| **D. Capel** lbw Alderman | 4 | 3 | 2 | 1 |
| **R. Russell (+)** c Healy b Alderman | 12 | 13 | 17 | 2 |
| **D. Pringle** c Taylor b Hohns | 27 | 90 | 150 | — |
| **G. Small** c Jones b Lawson | 59 | 97 | 138 | 8 |
| **N. Cook** c Jones b Lawson | 31 | 102 | 123 | 2 |
| **A. Igglesden** not out | 2 | 23 | 37 | — |
| Sundries (2B, 7LB, 1W, 13NB) | 23 | | | |
| **TOTAL** | **285** | | | |

**FALL:** 1, 28, 47, 80, 84, 98, 169, 201, 274, 285.

| BOWLING | Overs | Mdns | Runs | Wkts |
|---|---|---|---|---|
| **T. Alderman** | 27 | 7 | 66 | 5 |
| **G. Lawson** | 29.1 | 9 | 85 | 3 |
| **M. Hughes** | 23 | 3 | 84 | 1 |
| **T. Hohns** | 10 | 1 | 30 | 1 |
| **S. Waugh** | 3 | — | 11 | — |

**Innings time:** 417 min. **Overs:** 92.1.

## 2ND INNINGS

### AUSTRALIA

| | Runs | Balls | Mins | 4s |
|---|---|---|---|---|
| **G. Marsh** lbw Igglesden | 4 | 13 | 15 | — |
| **M. Taylor** c Russell b Small | 48 | 120 | 152 | 7 |
| **D. Boon** run out | 37 | 107 | 141 | 4 |
| **A. Border** not out | 51 | 74 | 108 | 5 |
| **D. Jones** b Capel | 50 | 79 | 68 | 4 |

|  | Runs | Balls | Mins | 4s |
|---|---|---|---|---|
| **S. Waugh** not out . . . . . . . . . . . . . . . . . . . . . . . . . | 7 | 12 | 23 | — |
| Sundries (2B, 7LB, 13NB) . . . . . . . . . . . . . . . . . . . | 22 | | | |
| **Four wickets (dec) for** . . . . . . . . . . . . . . . . . . . . . . | **219** | | | |

**FALL:** 7, 100, 101, 189.

| BOWLING | Overs | Mdns | Runs | Wkts |
|---|---|---|---|---|
| **G. Small** . . . . . . . . . . . . . . . . . . . . | 20 | 4 | 57 | 1 |
| **A. Igglesden** . . . . . . . . . . . . . . . . . | 13 | 1 | 55 | 1 |
| **D. Capel** . . . . . . . . . . . . . . . . . . . . | 8 | — | 35 | 1 |
| **D. Pringle** . . . . . . . . . . . . . . . . . . . | 16 | — | 53 | — |
| **N. Cook** . . . . . . . . . . . . . . . . . . . . . | 6 | 2 | 10 | — |

**Innings time:** 263 min. **Overs:** 63.

| ENGLAND | | | | |
|---|---|---|---|---|
|  | Runs | Balls | Mins | 4s |
| **G. Gooch** c and b Alderman . . . . . . . . . . . . . . . . . . | 10 | 34 | 51 | — |
| **J. Stephenson** lbw Alderman . . . . . . . . . . . . . . . . | 11 | 23 | 29 | 1 |
| **M. Atherton** b Lawson . . . . . . . . . . . . . . . . . . . . . | 14 | 47 | 63 | 2 |
| **R. Smith** not out . . . . . . . . . . . . . . . . . . . . . . . . | 77 | 99 | 144 | 11 |
| **D. Gower** c Waugh b Lawson . . . . . . . . . . . . . . . . . | 7 | 24 | 23 | — |
| **D. Capel** c Taylor b Hohns . . . . . . . . . . . . . . . . . | 17 | 60 | 56 | 2 |
| **R. Russell** not out . . . . . . . . . . . . . . . . . . . . . . . | 0 | 6 | 9 | — |
| Sundries (2LB, 5NB, 1W) . . . . . . . . . . . . . . . . . . . | 7 | | | |
| **Five wickets for** . . . . . . . . . . . . . . . . . . . . . . . . . | **143** | | | |

**FALL:** 20, 27, 51, 67, 138.

| BOWLING | Overs | Mdns | Runs | Wkts |
|---|---|---|---|---|
| **T. Alderman** . . . . . . . . . . . . . . . . . . | 13 | 3 | 30 | 2 |
| **G. Lawson** . . . . . . . . . . . . . . . . . . . | 15.1 | 2 | 41 | 2 |
| **M. Hughes** . . . . . . . . . . . . . . . . . . . | 8 | 2 | 34 | — |
| **T. Hohns** . . . . . . . . . . . . . . . . . . . . | 10 | 2 | 37 | 1 |

**Innings time:** 199 min. **Overs:** 46.1.

# TEST AVERAGES

## BATTING

### AUSTRALIA

|  | Tests | Innings | Not Out | Total | Highest Score | Average |
|---|---|---|---|---|---|---|
| Steve Waugh | 6 | 8 | 4 | 506 | 177* | 126.50 |
| Mark Taylor | 6 | 11 | 1 | 839 | 219 | 83.90 |
| Allan Border | 6 | 9 | 3 | 442 | 80 | 73.66 |
| Dean Jones | 6 | 9 | 1 | 566 | 157 | 70.75 |
| David Boon | 6 | 11 | 3 | 442 | 94 | 55.25 |
| Trevor Hohns | 5 | 5 | 1 | 127 | 40 | 31.75 |
| Geoff Marsh | 6 | 11 | 0 | 347 | 138 | 31.54 |
| Geoff Lawson | 6 | 5 | 1 | 115 | 74 | 28.75 |
| Merv Hughes | 6 | 5 | 0 | 127 | 71 | 25.40 |
| Terry Alderman | 6 | 4 | 3 | 20 | 8 | 20.00 |
| Ian Healy | 6 | 7 | 1 | 103 | 44 | 17.16 |

Greg Campbell – played one match – did not bat

* Denotes not out.

### ENGLAND

|  | Tests | Innings | Not Out | Total | Highest Score | Average |
|---|---|---|---|---|---|---|
| Allan Lamb | 1 | 2 | 0 | 129 | 125 | 64.50 |
| Robin Smith | 5 | 10 | 1 | 553 | 143 | 61.44 |
| Gladstone Small | 1 | 1 | 0 | 59 | 59 | 59.00 |
| Robert Russell | 6 | 11 | 3 | 314 | 128* | 39.25 |
| Eddie Hemmings | 1 | 2 | 0 | 73 | 38 | 36.50 |
| David Gower | 6 | 11 | 0 | 383 | 106 | 34.81 |
| John Emburey | 3 | 5 | 1 | 131 | 64 | 32.75 |
| Kim Barnett | 3 | 5 | 0 | 141 | 80 | 28.20 |
| Nick Cook | 3 | 5 | 3 | 45 | 31 | 22.50 |
| Phil Newport | 1 | 2 | 0 | 44 | 36 | 22.00 |
| Graham Dilley | 2 | 3 | 1 | 42 | 24 | 21.00 |

* Denotes not out.

| | Tests | Innings | Not Out | Total | Highest Score | Average |
|---|---|---|---|---|---|---|
| Chris Broad . . . . . . . . . . . | 2 | 4 | 0 | 82 | 37 | 20.50 |
| Graham Gooch . . . . . . . . . | 5 | 9 | 0 | 183 | 68 | 20.33 |
| Mike Atherton . . . . . . . . . | 2 | 4 | 0 | 73 | 47 | 18.25 |
| John Stephenson . . . . . . . . | 1 | 2 | 0 | 36 | 25 | 18.00 |
| Neil Foster . . . . . . . . . . . | 3 | 6 | 2 | 68 | 39 | 17.00 |
| Ian Botham . . . . . . . . . . . | 3 | 4 | 0 | 62 | 46 | 15.50 |
| Tim Curtis . . . . . . . . . . . . | 3 | 5 | 0 | 71 | 41 | 14.20 |
| Philip DeFreitas . . . . . . . . | 1 | 2 | 0 | 22 | 21 | 11.00 |
| Mike Gatting . . . . . . . . . . | 1 | 2 | 0 | 22 | 22 | 11.00 |
| Paul Jarvis . . . . . . . . . . . | 2 | 3 | 0 | 33 | 22 | 11.00 |
| Derek Pringle . . . . . . . . . . | 2 | 3 | 0 | 33 | 27 | 11.00 |
| David Capel . . . . . . . . . . . | 1 | 2 | 0 | 21 | 17 | 10.50 |
| Angus Fraser . . . . . . . . . . | 3 | 5 | 0 | 47 | 29 | 9.40 |
| Martyn Moxon . . . . . . . . . | 1 | 2 | 0 | 18 | 18 | 9.00 |
| Devon Malcolm . . . . . . . . . | 1 | 2 | 0 | 14 | 9 | 7.00 |
| Tim Robinson . . . . . . . . . . | 1 | 2 | 0 | 12 | 12 | 6.00 |
| Chris Tavare . . . . . . . . . . | 1 | 1 | 0 | 2 | 2 | 2.00 |
| Alan Igglesden . . . . . . . . . | 1 | 1 | 1 | 2 | 2 | – |

# BOWLING

## AUSTRALIA

| | Overs | Mdn | Runs | Wks | Average | 5 WI | 10 WM | Best |
|---|---|---|---|---|---|---|---|---|
| Terry Alderman . . . . . . . . | 269.2 | 68 | 712 | 41 | 17.36 | 6 | 1 | 6–128 |
| Trevor Hohns . . . . . . . . . | 134.0 | 53 | 300 | 11 | 27.27 | 0 | 0 | 3–59 |
| Geoff Lawson . . . . . . . . . | 277.1 | 68 | 791 | 29 | 27.27 | 1 | 0 | 6–72 |
| Merv Hughes . . . . . . . . . | 189.2 | 48 | 615 | 19 | 32.36 | 0 | 0 | 4–71 |
| Steve Waugh . . . . . . . . . | 57.0 | 15 | 208 | 2 | 104.00 | 0 | 0 | 1–38 |
| Greg Campbell . . . . . . . . | 24.0 | 0 | 124 | 1 | 124.00 | 0 | 0 | 1–82 |
| Allan Border . . . . . . . . . | 24.0 | 9 | 44 | 0 | – | 0 | 0 | – |

## ENGLAND

|  | Overs | Mdn | Runs | Wks | Average | WI | WM | Best |
|---|---|---|---|---|---|---|---|---|
| Neil Foster . . . . . . . . . | 167.0 | 42 | 421 | 12 | 35.08 | 0 | 0 | 3–39 |
| Angus Fraser . . . . . . . . | 144.2 | 30 | 323 | 9 | 35.88 | 0 | 0 | 4–63 |
| John Emburey . . . . . . . . | 152.0 | 37 | 342 | 8 | 42.75 | 0 | 0 | 4–88 |
| Alan Igglesden . . . . . . . | 37.0 | 3 | 146 | 3 | 48.66 | 0 | 0 | 2–91 |
| Gladstone Small . . . . . . . | 60.0 | 12 | 198 | 4 | 49.50 | 0 | 0 | 3–141 |
| David Capel . . . . . . . . . | 24.0 | 2 | 101 | 2 | 50.50 | 0 | 0 | 1–35 |
| Nick Cook . . . . . . . . . . | 103.5 | 23 | 282 | 5 | 56.40 | 0 | 0 | 3–91 |
| Derek Pringle . . . . . . . . | 86.2 | 12 | 306 | 5 | 61.20 | 0 | 0 | 4–70 |
| Graham Dilley . . . . . . . . | 84.0 | 12 | 318 | 5 | 63.60 | 0 | 0 | 2–123 |
| Graham Gooch . . . . . . . . | 31.0 | 9 | 72 | 1 | 72.00 | 0 | 0 | 1–30 |
| Philip DeFreitas . . . . . . . | 63.3 | 10 | 216 | 3 | 72.00 | 0 | 0 | 2–140 |
| Ian Botham . . . . . . . . . | 80.0 | 15 | 241 | 3 | 80.33 | 0 | 0 | 2–63 |
| Phil Newport . . . . . . . . | 44.0 | 7 | 175 | 2 | 87.50 | 0 | 0 | 2–153 |
| Paul Jarvis . . . . . . . . . | 69.2 | 8 | 290 | 2 | 145.00 | 0 | 0 | 1–20 |
| Devon Malcolm . . . . . . . | 44.0 | 2 | 166 | 1 | 166.00 | 0 | 0 | 1–166 |
| Eddie Hemmings . . . . . . . | 33.0 | 9 | 81 | 0 | – | 0 | 0 | – |
| Kim Barnett . . . . . . . . . | 6.0 | 0 | 32 | 0 | – | 0 | 0 | – |
| Mike Atherton . . . . . . . . | 8.0 | 0 | 34 | 0 | – | 0 | 0 | – |
| Tim Curtis . . . . . . . . . . | 3.0 | 0 | 7 | 0 | – | 0 | 0 | – |

# FIRST CLASS AVERAGES — AUSTRALIA

## BATTING

|  | M | Innings | Not Out | Runs | Highest Score | 50 | 100 | Average | Ct/St |
|---|---|---|---|---|---|---|---|---|---|
| Jones . . . . . . . | 14 | 20 | 3 | 1510 | 248 | 8 | 5 | 88.82 | 8 |
| Waugh . . . . . . | 16 | 24 | 8 | 1030 | 177* | 3 | 4 | 64.38 | 6 |
| Taylor . . . . . . | 17 | 30 | 1 | 1669 | 219 | 10 | 3 | 57.55 | 24 |
| Boon . . . . . . . | 17 | 28 | 5 | 1306 | 151 | 8 | 3 | 56.78 | 22 |
| Border . . . . . . | 16 | 22 | 4 | 979 | 135 | 9 | 1 | 54.39 | 18 |
| Veletta . . . . . . | 5 | 8 | 1 | 294 | 134* | 1 | 1 | 42.00 | 6 |
| Moody . . . . . . | 12 | 20 | 4 | 564 | 144* | 3 | 1 | 35.25 | 8 |
| Marsh . . . . . . | 18 | 33 | 4 | 934 | 138 | 2 | 2 | 32.21 | 14 |
| Healy . . . . . . | 14 | 19 | 4 | 442 | 73* | 1 | — | 29.47 | 33/2 |

| | M | Innings | Not Out | Runs | Highest Score | 50 | 100 | Average | Ct/St |
|---|---|---|---|---|---|---|---|---|---|
| Zoehrer ..... | 7 | 9 | — | 259 | 93 | 1 | — | 28.78 | 16/- |
| Hohns ...... | 15 | 18 | 4 | 393 | 95 | 2 | — | 28.07 | 8 |
| Hughes ...... | 15 | 18 | 4 | 246 | 71 | 1 | — | 20.50 | 1 |
| Lawson ..... | 14 | 12 | 2 | 174 | 74 | 1 | — | 17.40 | 4 |
| May ....... | 10 | 8 | 3 | 59 | 24 | — | — | 11.80 | 1 |
| Campbell .... | 11 | 10 | 2 | 87 | 31 | — | — | 10.88 | 3 |
| Alderman .... | 11 | 10 | 6 | 38 | 8 | — | — | 9.50 | 5 |
| Rackemann ... | 8 | 5 | 1 | 22 | 11 | — | — | 4.40 | 2 |

## BOWLING

| | M | Overs | Mdn | Runs | Wkts | Average | 5 WI | 10 WM | Best |
|---|---|---|---|---|---|---|---|---|---|
| Zoehrer ..... | 7 | 5.0 | — | 9 | 1 | 9.00 | — | — | 1/9 |
| Alderman .... | 11 | 411.2 | 103 | 1095 | 70 | 15.64 | 6 | 1 | 6/128 |
| Lawson ..... | 14 | 522.3 | 140 | 1447 | 69 | 20.97 | 3 | — | 6/30 |
| Rackemann ... | 8 | 225.5 | 47 | 747 | 32 | 23.34 | 1 | — | 5/85 |
| Waugh ...... | 16 | 176.1 | 39 | 571 | 23 | 24.83 | — | — | 3/10 |
| Moody ...... | 12 | 63.0 | 19 | 151 | 6 | 25.17 | — | — | 4/30 |
| Hughes ...... | 15 | 399.0 | 102 | 1242 | 47 | 26.43 | 3 | — | 5/37 |
| May ....... | 10 | 287.5 | 86 | 740 | 28 | 26.43 | — | — | 4/43 |
| Campbell .... | 11 | 250.2 | 50 | 824 | 30 | 27.47 | 1 | — | 5/54 |
| Hohns ...... | 15 | 321.4 | 108 | 809 | 26 | 31.12 | — | — | 4/87 |
| Border ...... | 16 | 68.0 | 21 | 154 | 1 | 154.00 | — | — | 1/55 |
| Jones ....... | 14 | 1.0 | — | 13 | — | — | — | — | — |
| Boon ....... | 17 | 1.0 | 1 | 0 | — | — | — | — | — |

# REMI KAPO
# A SAVAGE
# CULTURE
# REVISITED

# REMI KAPO
# A SAVAGE CULTURE
## REVISITED

## A Black British View

ACACIA
TREE
BOOKS

Also by Remi Kapo
published by Acacia Tree Books

*Reap the Forgotten Harvest*

*Torrents of Fire*

# Foreword

*A Savage Culture* was first published in September 1981. After sending the manuscript to the publishers, I drew breath. I believed that within ten years, the UK's social order would have experienced substantial social and political change, and that my manuscript would be redundant. Those beliefs feel so hollow now. Forty years have passed and virtually nothing has changed.

Alas, Britain's next generation are still experiencing what mine had to endure, making the pain worse. I am galled by the prospects of more of the same for the oncoming decades. It seems a pertinent moment to republish *A Savage Culture.*

Before I sat down to write this preface, the world was beset by the Covid-19 pandemic and shaken by the largest global protests in history proclaiming Black Lives Matter. The latter was triggered by the infamous 8 minutes and 46 second slow lynching of George Floyd in Minneapolis[1]. Helplessly, the entire world

---

[1] Later revised to 9 minutes and 30 seconds.

looked on. During those homicidal minutes, power balances of race, gender and class shifted.

England's calamity began long ago when, having impoverished and degraded the rights of her working-class majority and deprived them of land, her ruling class minority struck out from this tiny island in a crazed aspiration to subjugate the black beings of Africa and the Caribbean.

After the demise of serfdom within these sceptred shores, there should have been no such thing as free labour. Unless, of course, your skin happened to be black. Over four centuries, Britain's aristocrats and ruling elite were perfectly happy to stand, whip in hand, over the black people they had enslaved, who shed blood, sweat and tears for no pay. Thus slavery financed a goodly share of England's stately houses, bankrolled her industrial revolution, and underwrote her rulers' classy lifestyles. The continuous corollary of this heartless enterprise is that anyone the colour of a slave has questionable human rights.

The Black Lives Matter protests also exposed that most contentious old saw — reparations for the Atlantic slave trade and for colonisation — arising from the enslavement of Africans and the appropriation of their lands. No matter how many years pass, the grievances remain unforgotten and unforgiven, confirming that the black peoples of Africa and the Caribbean have yet to be paid an astounding sum by the UK's ruling class minority and institutions.

Sadly, at the end of these forty years we are witnessing yet another young generation being punished for their blackness and being hunted by the police while walking the streets.

Given the abolition of slavery, former colonies regaining their freedoms, diminished status with the loss of empire, and the consequential tenacity behind Black Lives Matter, it would appear that the latent rage towards the slave-owner, and subsequently the imperialist, lies patently in the offing. Will *A Savage Culture* come to be seen as the tale of Britain's ruling classes and their loathing of change?

There are issues of seemingly naked contempt. Given the UK's constant nationality machinations, dubbed the Backstabbers' Charters by generations of victims, invitees who arrived on the SS *Windrush* and her sister ships, being just the latest victims getting short shrift. Consider this — would they have raised their families in the UK if they had known they would become refugees, to be thrown out of the UK 50 and 60 years hence? We should therefore be ready to receive back on Heathrow's brutal tarmac Africa's Anglo-Saxons, some of who are currently sunning themselves in Kenya's spectacular Highlands. Take care how you legislate. Be careful what you wish for.

In reissuing this volume, the original manuscript has been subjected to the deftest of editorial touches by Dr Jill Sudbury, both for clarity, and to reference past events that may not be familiar to contemporary readers. Many thanks to my son, Segun, for his counsel during the revision of this manuscript.

My gratitude to my dear friend Struan Dudman for his careful reading and advice on this edition. Thanks to Gareth and Melissa Hobbs of e-Digital Design, for their patience and diligence in the comprehensive redesign of this book.

As I prepare to send off this manuscript once more, I fervently hope that, in another four decades, there will be no need to reissue this book ever again. I do, however, have faith that my children and their generation will act differently, and take my words forward to do something demonstrably positive.

Remi Kapo
London, February 2022

*To the black and Asian peoples who died in the fires of New Cross and Southall.*

*To those whites who have also died for the same cause.*

*To Malcolm X whose death achieved his aims and ours. To Nelson Mandela whose very life and continued existence reinforces the flame of Human Rights into a permanent monument of resistance.*

*And finally, to those young Britons who have not yet made up their minds.*

# Contents

# Acknowledgements to the original edition

Many thanks to Jeannette de Haas, for her support and the innumerable late nights she spent reading and editing my manuscript; thanks also to the staff from the Humanities Department of the British Library who sought out and furnished much research material; and my everlasting gratitude to Roy Hiscock, who in Rock Road, Hackney, proved a friend.

The author and publishers would like to thank the following for permission to reproduce material quoted in this book:

Oxford University Press for lines from 'Epilogue' from *Rights of Passage* by Edward Kamau Brathwaite. Copyright Oxford University Press 1967

Monthly Review Press for *The Black Man's Burden* by E.D. Morel

Jan Morris for extracts from *Pax Britannica*, *Heaven's Command* and *Farewell the Trumpets*

Leicester University Press for *Colour, Class and the Victorians* by Douglas A. Lorimer

War on Want for *Now You Do Know* by John Downing and an extract from Bishop Colin O'Brien Winter's foreword; and for *From Massacres to Mining* by Janine Roberts.

*New Society* for 'It Couldn't Happen Here' and 'Dagenham's Way with Colour' by Remi Kapo. Copyright New Society 1977

*New Statesman* for 'Tolerated Guests' by Remi Kapo

George Allen and Unwin Publishers Limited for *Power* by Bertrand Russell

Penguin Books Limited for *Beyond the Limits of the Law* by Tom Bowden, published by Pelican Books 1978

Should you

Shatter the door
and walk
in the morning
fully aware

of the future
to come?
there is no
turning back

*Rights of Passage*,
Edward Kamau Brathwaite

# Preface

In 1980/81, street disturbances in Bristol, Brixton, Southall and Liverpool shocked the nation. Britain accidentally discovered that the customary gospel of cutting close to the edge without going down was impossible. Running out of luck, it was a psychic bring-down. For the sad, bittersweet suspicion of a possible racial struggle finally erupted. We were all straightened out by the stark, stretching reality that at the edge of any racial precipice is a very long drop. The Old Deal of righteously 'riding out a storm' had been hammered into perspective; sizzling in the bulletin is the fact that Britain is squatting on a permanent hornets' nest of colour/class reaction. But, the essence, the heart of the matter is: there is no Quality Time for some in the political and social justice of Britain.

Nevertheless, there have been gentle warnings chalked on the wall in a number of publications, which should have ripped down the mask of pretence that no other reality exists in present-day Britain. They were mostly presented by whites, some of whom were making a living 'taking care of business', but all had attempted to present the black or Asian reality. Additionally, if sincerity is a foundation, it is definitely impossible to write about *any* injustice with a muffled pen; for outrage demands the hot ink of belief for clarity. This book presents a black British view.

However, there are those, black, brown and white alike, who passionately care, and have spoken out against racial inequality only to be coldly dismissed by the silence of others. And silence is the acceptable lover of prejudice. Silence is the mouthpiece for injustice.

The *rigor mortis* reliance on the ability to control any racial confrontation through the possible use of naked power, or the rusty creed of 'repatriation' urged by reckless advocates, in my view, are giant miscalculations. In Britain, the biting use of naked power will most probably dominate any such racial protest. But at what cost? For humanity will weep. And why should anybody weep?

I was raised in Britain to believe in the moral reasoning of the democratic ideal. And growing through the passage of time, I learned the harsh reality that that ideal was, and is, immorally practised on the question of race. Therefore, black and Asian racial philosophy springs from the continual criticism of white race beliefs. But political timing is an art. Timing racial politics requires inspiration, and moral courage to carry out an equitable solution.

The principle forming the universal basis for belief in Human Rights is the single most important ideal for mankind. It is in this ideal I believe.

Remi Kapo
London, August 1981

# 1. An African Dream

Nineteen fifty-three was a decisive year for the Constitution of the United Kingdom: Queen Elizabeth II was crowned at Westminster Abbey. It was that same Constitution which held sway over the trial and conviction of Jomo Kenyatta and five other Kikuyu leaders for organising the Mau Mau rebellion in Kenya in 1952. It was also an important year for me, because on 30 August 1953, accompanied by my father, I arrived aboard the M/V *Apapa* at Tilbury Docks to begin an English education. I was seven.

The significance of Her new Majesty was completely lost on me, although it was something I was to question later. But the plight of Kenyatta was quite different. Despite my inability to comprehend the nature of his adversity, his black face on a newspaper page aroused a racial reflex in me.

Kenyatta was in trouble. This I gleaned from conversations I overheard between my father and other passengers on the long voyage out of Apapa, Lagos,

Nigeria. The added shipboard speculation that he might even be executed increased my sympathy.

I was born in a colonised Nigeria. I had heard pronouncements of 'death by hanging' of blacks by the white authorities many times before. This threat to Kenyatta's life was different. The attitude of my father and his friends was one of dismay, and the note of urgency in their voices added excitement. Their collective frame of mind, one of intensifying frustration and fear, was emphasised by many whispered conversations and continual checking at the cabin door. Outside on deck, fearing eavesdroppers, wary glances were thrown over the shoulder before anything was said.

From the little I could understand, I managed to grasp that a wind of change was blowing across Africa, that there were certain 'natives' who did not like the way the whites were running affairs in their countries, that those natives thought it was high time for whites to hand back to them the government of their respective countries; and that there were blacks who were quite prepared to force the whites to hand over everything. Kenyatta, they said, was one such man.

By this time, the ship-bound comrades were thinking of themselves as partners in a well-organised African guerrilla unit, permanently on call to any spot in Africa where whites were refusing to hand over power. They were not about to concede to the treasonous nature of their discussions, mainly because of the inspiration of Kenyatta, a black like themselves, who intended to free his people from the grasp of the British Empire. The fight for Independence was becoming a highly contagious colonial fever, and my father and his fellow-travellers, who obviously resented the theft of their land and the racist nature of British Administration, also wanted out. In a besieged garrison, every sentinel is a potential deserter. From what I understood, the British saw themselves as the garrison and the blacks as the deserters. Hence, what the authorities were bound to see as 'seditious conversations' were conducted mostly in our cabin at night, in low tones, and in our language, Yoruba.

Such was my introduction to the pernicious use of racial difference and the naked realities of African politics. I did not see it that clearly at the time, still less did I realise its meaning as I sailed into the United Kingdom.

Nigerian parents in the fifties were obsessed by educational ambitions for their children. The energies and hopes of a people reacting to the prospect of Independence were manifested in a ferocious competition to educate the next generation.

India, for so long a jewel in Britain's crown, became the Joan of Arc of colonised peoples. Her recently won self-emancipation fired the lust for freedom in other colonies. In the minds of most Nigerians who felt soured by their recent history, there was craving to make news. For them, the Empire was a confusing mixture of exploitation, inefficiency, brutality and greed. If it could not be exported for Britannic gain, then Britain was not interested, and many things were left under- and undeveloped. Education was one of them.

To have a son at King's College, Ibadan, twenty miles north of Lagos, was a family distinction. The rivalry for places at such fee-paying institutions was so fierce that family feuds shook neighbourhoods and parted lifelong friends. With such high stakes, some parents were even suspected of poisoning others' children. They dreamed of their offspring as cabinet ministers, captains of industry and commerce, lawyers, doctors and so on, as well as guarantors of their own future security. Failure meant that their thwarted ambitions were bestowed on the children, occasionally with horrifying effects. Beatings meted out by success-oriented parents sometimes resulted in hospitalisation, if they were lucky enough to live near one of the few infirmaries. At school, minor offences, such as lateness and incorrect uniform, invariably led to expulsion, the cause of which may have been the deliberate tactic of a 'friend', who had delayed a school-bound child, or persistently reported him for unruly behaviour. The 'friend's' child, it was hoped, would fill the vacancy.

Out of this crusade grew another mania: educating children at English boarding schools. Parents devoured the enticing advertisements. A child who had been educated in Britain fetched a higher premium on returning; he would not only possess an English qualification, but would also dress like an Englishman and, to crown it all, talk like one. Evening discussions would find many parents glowing with ambitious pride, dreaming of Reunion Day at Apapa Wharf where they would meet their now elongated babies with names on a degree certificate. Those port scenes were frantic and filled with frightening expectations. Yesterday's dreams, when realised, could lead the aspirants on the road to either becoming just another casualty of political ambition – especially when they discovered that their allegiance to nationalism was stronger than their allegiance to the Church – through a *coup d'état* and execution, or to success and eminence.

Someone had sold the idea to my father of a boarding school in St Leonards-on-Sea, Sussex, England. On this school his sights were set and his hopes founded. Ledsham Court School became my destination. After being told about my conscripted journey, passports, packing luggage, packing me – by this time my reluctance to leave my mother and everything I had ever known was becoming a problem – vaccinations and tickets were completed in a blur. And such were the methods of the savage Afro/British education market, that I found myself on the road to the docks on the way to obey my father's decree: to become a barrister. Time was anaesthetised. The farewells at Apapa Wharf were swiftly accomplished with the full expectation, in my head, that I would literally return in a few days, fully qualified.

Landing in England, the 'mother country', whose streets I had been reassured were paved with gold, produced in me an overwhelming emotion. I was stunned. I felt parts of me trembling; my body chemistry altered and I was revitalised. I goggled at the sea of faces and was frightened by its whiteness. I felt myself drowning in the intensity of its stare. Confused and dazzled by the fug of a thousand cars, the sights, sounds and smells of an alien country, we arrived at a hotel in Earls Court, London. The image of Ibadan, my home town in Nigeria, was already beginning to fade.

Next day, Ledsham Court School loomed into my present through the impending visit to my new headmistress. We travelled down to Sussex, the exchange was made with me as the currency, and my father returned to Nigeria, alone. Such was the pain, the shock, the surprise and the magic of my English 'homecoming'.

The school was a masterpiece; a beautiful mansion with a facade of woven ivy, set in acres of placid green fields and woodland. A boulevard-wide tarred oval drive, with a rhododendron bush dead-centre, completed the impressive frontage. My vision expanded as we entered a gargantuan assembly hall with a harlequin-tiled floor and a gallery half-way up the walls, leaving me gazing up through a glass roof to the sky above. From an African landscape to this, I was astonished. Pride died and I crumbled, as memories of Ibadan flooded back. Tears were wiped away, military fashion, as I was prepared for my first meal.

Salad was for lunch but a plateful of lettuce was not for me. I was dragged out of the dining room in front of the entire school, pulled along the corridor to the assembly hall and caned. I was filled with dread. It was only my first day. What would the rest be like? This ceremony completed, I was hauled back in. The stares, whispers and murmurs that heralded my initial entrance to the dining room increased in volume on my return, stiffening my resolve. I still refused to eat the lettuce and was promptly banished to the dormitory.

Later that afternoon I was again presented with the lettuce, to no avail. On closer inquiry by members of the staff, who finally decided that it might be time to ask me why I would not eat what they thought was good for me, I revealed that in my country only animals ate raw vegetables. They reluctantly relented. But the punishment of being smacked by hand was followed very quickly by exercise books across my face, the ruler's edge across my knuckles and, the ultimate sanction, the cane.

In these tortures, I was treated no differently from any other member of the co-educational school, except perhaps in that the frequency of these punishments was peculiar to me. The reaction of the school to my repetitive visits to the Headmistress's study for punishment set the racial trend. Golliwog in Enid Blyton's *Noddy* books came to life in the guise of 'that naughty black boy from Africa'. The jungle stereotype was complete.

Despite the shock of my entry into this school, I had my moments: summer nights that seemed to last forever; early evenings when a few of us would play endlessly down by The Rocks, without a care in the world; days with nature study, near a hide-out by the pond, where a single dragonfly with its long brilliant body and large wings would hold me spellbound and where waterboatmen careened across the mirrored surface, capturing my spirit, while the gentle seduction of the teacher's voice opened up a world seemingly uninterrupted by time. These were beautiful and memorable moments.

On the negative side of the school curriculum, however, were history, geography, mathematics and English. In history, I was taught how magnificent the British Empire was, how lucky I was to be part of it, and how the English had conquered half the world. Being the only black in the school, I was that half. In geography, I learned just how dark Africa was. Maths began as no problem, but it became one through a lack of encouragement and fulfilled the myth of my academic inability. But English was the *pièce de résistance*. It went something like this. English and Civilisation were considered synonymous. Africa was uncivilised and I was an African. So it was decided to begin the civilising process with me. I would speak perfect English and elocution was drafted in. My accent today stands as a tribute to their thoroughness.

Due to a family crisis, I had to leave this school.

The Headmistress and I said farewell with tears in our eyes. The goodbyes were sad and sudden. I was heartbroken, for it felt as if I was leaving home again. Someone accompanied me to my next boarding school in Kent, and somebody else to my next in Surrey, all in descending order of fees.

It was 1958, and the last step on my spiral staircase covering the British social and educational spectrum was Beechholme, and this one was free. On the list of other activities, of which there were many, was a necessary course of study familiarly termed street sense. Beechholme was an institution for orphans, deserted children and children of parents with 'difficulties'. It was the property of and administered by the old London County Council. At the age of twelve, after five years in Britain, my feet finally touched the ground.

Beechholme was a place of disgrace. The Public Eyes who comfortably inhabited the nearby villages of Nork, Banstead, Banstead Village and Belmont used Beechholme as a slur. To make the gulf absolute, we were from The Home. That meant we were either social lepers or a bunch of thieves. Outside its walls, to claim residence of a respectable neighbourhood was natural.

In Beechholme, the pollution of social disgrace penetrated our mentality. Scorn guarded its gates avidly like a limpet. The inmates, now devalued in social terms, struggled with hope as an idea, particularly if they were black. It was a place to steal away from and snuff from the memory as a bizarre, embarrassing dream. It never happened. The concrete aggression of the general public blew out any hope of contact. There was no let-up. I found this to be the crushing reality of English life, that it can so destabilise an individual, flattening his ego, that he soon knows his place. In Beechholme, this cut-rate resignation was refreshed by the monotony of discouragement and lack of interest from the staff, and leaden hours of boredom. Most insiders were crushed by their sentence. But some damaged beings climbed above their abasement with rebellion, or a craving for getting out of their own life in their hearts. I was placed in Acacia House with Gale Parsons. Little did I know I would soon lose my close friend. At nineteen, she was to die of a heroin overdose in a Lots Road squat. A BBC *Man Alive* documentary entitled *Gale is Dead* was made about her short tempestuous life. *Gale is Dead*. In this society, what does that mean?

In a very real sense, Beechholme and the London school I attended, Alvering Secondary in Wandsworth, were my Centres of Racial Studies. One reinforced the other in countless ways. In Beechholme, I was treated as separate and unequal; at Alvering, I found out why. I came to realise that inequality was the capital of black Britain. And Britain, from my experience, in every sense was always graded into and partitioned by class and colour, red and blue, black and white.

Frequently, I lay awake at night dreading the

thought of the next day's persecutions. I had reached a sensitive point, and other people's switch-offs carved up my soul. It hurt.

Contempt for my colour took many forms, from comparisons with apes to the white preoccupation with the size of the black male organ. The incredible sexual stamina blacks were supposed to possess produced the retort 'go and fuck your own kind' whenever I spoke to a white girl. Accordingly, all blacks were dirty, ignorant and stupid, they caused trouble, lived on Social Security benefits and ate smelly food. But, and this was real praise, blacks were great singers, superb athletes and good in bed. Whites, on the other hand, were scientifically-minded and tough, good-humoured and sportsmanlike. And they had an Empire to prove it.

The social brainwashing had its desired effect. If I wanted to be better, to be like them, I had to be white. So I tried. At Easter in 1960, when I was fourteen – Easter, because that was when Jesus was in the mood to forgive all sins and by now being black had become a sin – I went down on my knees and prayed, real hard. Every time I was alone I prayed, sometimes for hours. I prayed with tears in my eyes, imploring God to listen to my plea. I prayed to God to make me white. The myth of black inferiority, having been preached at me for so long, convinced me that the way out was to become a white man.

I closed my mind to Africa by not reading, thinking or talking about her. Whenever Africa or black people

29

were derided, I joined in the derision, albeit carefully just in case they turned on me. Moreover, whenever the topic of African or West Indian Independence hit the headlines, I slunk into the background. Britain's media traditionally commented negatively on these events with 'how will they manage to look after themselves without us?', thus exposing me to further ridicule. At those moments I kept quiet while seething inside. In keeping a low profile, I denied everything, myself as well.

A series of battles irritated my mind and aided my denials – it became a habit. One of these was triumphant in its execution. It happened on a train journey from school back to Beechholme. As the train pulled into Belmont Station (Banstead was the next stop) I peeked out of the window and waited until the porter drew level with my compartment. I then let out a terrible groan. The porter reacted, believed what he saw, and called for an ambulance. At the local hospital, constipation was diagnosed. Since I intended to stay there a while, I improved very slowly. On returning to Beechholme two weeks later, the pressure of racism was, for a while, much reduced.

I was still recovering eight weeks later when the unexpected happened. It was May 1960. My father, who I had not seen since August 1953, was coming to see me, along with my uncle, a member of the Royal College of Surgeons. I had mixed emotions, for what could I say when the situation I had long ceased to dream about was now with me? I saw the pain of failure written across my father's face as tears welled up in his eyes. His African dream and ambitions had ended up here in Beechholme, a children's home. I perceived the effort my father made to render harmless the abyss of time since we last met. We had a pleasant afternoon together, my father, my uncle and I.

For many years I had lived under the head-knocking hang-up that Britain was my permanent pawnbroker. I owed. As a debtor, I thought I should be grateful. But grateful for what? What did I owe? I was tormented. I had lost my culture, I had lost my longing to see others like me. I had seen through the empty smiles of those who derided me. I had so many feelings and ideas waiting to be freed. But it was impossible. As a black, white society had confined me in solitude in the middle of a crowd. Every crowd.

But something inside me stirred, and stirred again. I thought back to the time when there were no rules, no aggression, no fear in the gut, just me and my beach and the wind. And I shared them with my white friend, Jonathan.

But I was psychologically violated and I began to smoulder. My pain turned to energy, fuelling my resistance. I began to rebel. I refused all help because it had been proven shallow. I spent hours by myself eating thoughts. I took advantage of everything, every ounce of knowledge, about where I was from, who my people were and where I was, now.

Apart from my friend, there was no warmth

in this atmosphere. I started to read and eventually, looking up from my readings, I skipped anger and went straight to rage.

Before 1962, Britain's blacks existed insensibly in a cloud of tolerance. Because of the availability of white gospel worshippers, carefully sustained by subversive white liberals, we developed no political philosophy. Ideas of 'revolution' were just the preserve of lone individuals. Any Anglophobic bitter-mouths were coupled to blacks on the white side of the street. Cash, making no enemies, induced some whites to cut a path for the black sell-out, a 180-degree black. This shackled achiever broke out to all and sundry his confessions of 'Don't rock the boat'. Sadness melts. He came on real strong, with white handcuffs on and presented whites with the message 'I'm yours'. Due to his 'Marster', who saw him as a pile of bricks, Joe Sad lived a Christian path. It was a belly habit. He was a cupboard, a desk, a piano, a chair, in fact anything the white wanted him to be. Joe Sad walked straight into a flash pad, and stood beside the chair. Today, he is the filing cabinet, selling out verbal rip-offs. It has taken an explosion of world-wide categorical black imperatives, proclamations of black power and hosannahs of negritude to undermine this position. In time, the Uncle Tom will no longer be trusted in Britain, as in America.

1962 was the year that captured the essence of imperial miscalculations. It was an auspicious moment for Britain's whites who were about to reinforce their superiority. Their mood refuted those expedient colonial promises of 'entry and Britishness'. White affections were effectively reversed, spawning the Commonwealth Immigrants Act.

It was a splendidly unguarded hour for the ethnic newcomers who believed the hallucinatory promises of the 'mother country', thumping the idea into their heads that their position here, that they had romanticised, was very arbitrary indeed. The Act concurred, by rendering unthinkable the idea of peaceful black, brown and white coexistence in the near future.

That year left in its acrimonious wake a dismayed ethnic presence and a racially boastful white population. The Act was seen by many whites as having put the coloureds in their place and, as if to underline this, numerous clubs all over Britain were closed to blacks overnight. Two near Wolverhampton had their own methods: Smethwick's Labour Club boasted a colour bar; Sandwell Youth Club Committee openly issued their racial bias – 'no coloured person shall be admitted to membership of the club'.

The press went to town with headlines: 'Spittoons wanted', for spitting blacks; 'More immigrants from West Indies' and 'Concern at total of Immigrants' accelerated media scoops about black and Asian immigrants and their right to be in Britain; 'Coloured folk dominating house buying', exclaimed the Smethwick Telephone, a West Bromwich newspaper.

Conservative councillor, Norman Phillips, appealed for a 'home security trust fund', claiming that young couples were leaving Smethwick because of 'immigrant domination' in house-buying. Another Conservative councillor, Donald Finney, blamed Smethwick's traditional centre of vice, Spon Lane, on 'coloured men'. He said his own wife had been accosted and white girls were associating with coloured men.

Educationalists played their part. In 1962, Terence Casey, Headmaster of St Joseph's Catholic School, Maida Vale, went even further. With a gibe at black people, he denounced the Twist dance craze: 'While the people of Africa struggle to free themselves from the dark shadow of a primitive past ... our young folk are initiated into the barbaric contortions of the Twist.'

This racial extremism touched a nerve inside me; that the framework of British society was built on a wind of sudden changes. In Britain, a nation of versatile chaos, the negative motivation for suppressing blacks in her former colonies developed into a counter-attraction – nigger culling.

Deportation became the focal talking point of the Immigration Act. In April 1962, a frosty Daily Mail headline announced: 'Britain to begin deporting criminals next month', suggesting that it was an unprecedented step to kick out lawbreakers not born here. In the same month, some Midlands conservatives capped the Daily Mail. They asked the Home Secretary to 'deport immigrants who did no work within a reasonable time'. The action of racial discrimination was no longer confined to antiquated white expatriates, and yesterday's Governors-General and District Commissioners. Now, a government decree, hypnotic to negrophobic whites irrespective of class and rank, welcomed them to tread on the black and the Asian peoples. Complaints underlining black inferiority sprouted. Hatred was taken further and, in 1963, among many repulsive incidents, came an event which startled me: Janta Singh, an Indian in Birmingham, had his grocery store bombed. The bombers had carefully packed a fire-extinguisher with explosives and planted it in the doorway of his shop.

This, I thought, was the writing on the wall for ethnic peoples. I was hurt when I saw white friends I had known all my life ooze into the shadows and side-step the consensus when faced with the blemishing topic of race. From out front, white people I knew focussed and measured and occupied my consciousness. At this time, I viewed Britain through the polemics of my school history lessons, and began to review the attitudes of her whites. I saw people flipping out, directionless from the trickeries, triumphs and romantic legends of their history, still percolating from Empire with a racism created by myths, sustained by conquest, cemented by long-term domination and conducted with an aggressive technology. The Empire mentality was alive and well and thriving in Britain. It was not an overstatement to say that the heart of the matter is that many of Britain's whites don't like blacks and Asians, and are having a hard time keeping it a secret. More significantly, blacks and Asians were faced with a dilemma: to be here 'gratefully' or to retaliate against the blitzkrieging media and public racism. For Britain's whites hold a cutting finesse in their arguments; of black race-reducing views repeated endlessly, coupled with a monstrous condescension which screams, 'Accept what we say. We're right, we're white'. The garage-mechanics are here. The black man has long since been the earthbound muscle, but the white man holds the heavenly tools of supremacy.

The turbulence inside white Britain's black-panic resolved my decision. I set a new course. Iced by white hypocrisy, I met with a group in a house in Lavender Hill, Battersea. We listened and watched while they decided our lives and what we should do and what was going to happen to us. We listened to them cackling on about us having a place in Britain. As I walked the streets, I noticed the white answers looking at me. It was then I began to realise that the depth of condescension for my colour in Britain was deeper than I wanted to believe. I came to terms with the blatant fact that racism was (and still is) latent in Britain's adult white population.

I also came to terms with another fact. I was fed up with being manoeuvred into unimportance by whites. Their belief in black sub-humanity was so far gone that it was instinctive. They did not know how to change their own myths about us.

Decolonisation, which I had once thought would give them a new picture, merely focussed their attentions on how black nations would fail as independents. With the colonial departure, the meaningless title 'Third World' was added, rubbing in second-classness and conjuring up another physical but directionless globe like a naughty moon in the paranoid white imagination.

Immigration of blacks into Britain made no room for the white mental shock experienced when they realised that those so-called 'coloureds' intended to compete. They had been enticed to Britain to assume their traditional places labouring away at jobs whites didn't want. Hence any failing black pupil gave more credibility to the white myth of black intellectual inferiority. Any black who achieved unsettled them more, intelligence having been solidly identified with whiteness.

It was up to the black to prove their intellectual capability and equality to the white who permanently 'failed' to see black achievement and was constantly deaf when they heard any black ideas. But the race competition of equalising imperatives was on. Because of the racist attitudes of most of our teachers, who taught us with a look of 'failures' in their eyes, we helped them succeed, by failing. Realistically we knew it made little difference either way. The result, we thought by our collective experiences, was already decided. That blacks were basically factory-fodder in this nation of 'opportunities' did not encourage us to aim for stardom; we gave up. In other words we purposely failed. Anyone who succeeded was a sell-out.

I began making changes as the colour question distracted my attention from the lore of knowledge to the lore of the street. Street sense became a permanent picnic; I feasted with the intent of thoroughly understanding white behaviour. I got a Degree in Aggression. I also became ignorant and oversensitive about it; piling opprobrium on the head of any white who picked up on it. 'He has a chip on his shoulder.' I most certainly did. Do as you would be done by, but do it first, guided my ethics. I burned British history books and relegated their entire contents to mere lies and wishful thinking on the part of the whites. In geography, the Russian Steppes could have been halfway down the Bethnal Green Road for all I cared. 1066 and all that was fantasy, and the white version of the slave trade was hype and a hustle. In my destructive attitude to Britain, I hacked the whiteness out of my mind. I religiously hammered any white who tried to lay a pretentious superior intellect on my soul. This showcase nigger cased up the white show. It was quality time. When I was a negro I had many white friends, but now that I am black I have few.

I carried on running heavy black changes, and I was cold. And then in October 1963 a tragedy occurred that iced up my innards. It happened in South Africa, where the oppression of black people by whites was also a way of life.

Nelson Mandela, a former member of the African National Congress, was to be tried for sabotage and conspiracy to overthrow a regime. Not so long before that, on 21 March 1960, during a demonstration in Sharpeville, the police had opened fire on demonstrators killing 69 blacks and wounding 300, while continuing to brutalise the rest. The only difference I could see between Sharpeville and Mandela's crisis was that it was occasionally necessary for white South Africa to demonstrate to the world her nodding acquaintance with her own one-sided statute laws in relation to blacks. It struck me that in a land where whites devised the constitution, by sowing racism into it and thus into the law, all blacks stood a sure chance of being guilty of something. In a country where racial vindictiveness explodes the lives of black people with such immoral amorality, Mandela and others were convicted and sentenced long before they came to trial. However, our group, pained by that injustice, defended Mandela and anyone who used violence in similar situations.

I screamed with fury, not only at Mandela's prosecution, but also at the attitude adopted by Britain's whites towards his dilemma. Was he or was he not guilty seemed to be the basis of their questioning, never seriously challenging the life-blood of such a brutal regime. But at the same time, with shallow profundity, they carefully examined the ability of black Africans to govern themselves after Independence. Intuitively I felt that their demeanour could only be so because of the emotional similarities of the Afrikaners and Britain's whites. It dawned on me that their only dissimilarities lay in method and sophistication.

In comparison to South Africa and America, British race relations are apparently harmonious. But the truth of the matter is that these so-called relations are an edifice, a cardboard facade and rotten to the core. In reality, the British are more subtle than the South Africans, being older at the game, and do not need 'Whites Only' signs with which to do their discriminating. But the result is similar in its effect. South Africa's racism enforces the oppression of black people by Statute Law and legislates against all forms of demonstration by blacks fighting against the very laws forbidding them to demonstrate.

In fact, Britain's whites out-Herod Herod with Machiavellian determination, evaluating blacks and Asians with the stake they hold in the racism of the doctrine of white sovereignty. Not unlike the South Africans, but with their own highly refined version of apartheid, tried and tested with whole-hogging success on Britain's working classes and women, the whites now practise, with subtlety a sophisticated form of subjugation on Britain's ethnic minority.

But Britain's blithe spirit, grounded in racial condescension, is being demolished brick by brick. With black equality of every kind slapping him in the face, his new question is: 'If this savage is as talented as myself, then what have I been all along?' In Britain, the racial equality yardstick is under hypercritical invasion and is being scorched by a wind of searing black heat. It is not just the product of an ex-slave's memory.

In all my years here, I have always lived with some apprehension. I, like some others, function and act with an over-the-horizon radar covering both shoulders. The black man's thoughts of reactive aggression have always been decided by white prejudice. The relationship between black and white is a savage reality, the naked result of which can be seen in South Africa. For pain exists in every heart, irrespective of colour, that believes in what should be the first principles of humankind – humanity and human rights. If the black man living in Britain reacts, it will be akin to a razorblade slicing through white thoughts. The pain is great.

I have some white friends, principally being people who genuinely accept me as I am and consider my views as valid as their own. I have grown close to them, and skin colour is not a subject worth any consideration. Everything else is. Outside of this circle, fear is intuitive, teaching me that it is necessary to retain an opaque, indefinable distance from those whites I don't know.

But I still have hope, because I am a worshipper of optimism. I don't know any other way. I have hope in the youth of Britain, black and white. A youth who recognise their interdependence, unlike their parents. For this nation badly needs imaginations to be stimulated for its survival. There is hope, too, in its few but much-travelled wide-eyed citizens who cannot go along in its crazy flirtation with disaster. They refuse to believe in the governing ethic which has been using yesterday's ideas. Tradition stabilises Britain and holds her back at the same time. The Great Britannic Dilemma.

Nevertheless, many white youths cannot see how they can be schooled, often intimately, with black youth and then, on reaching adulthood, be asked to tread on the friendships of their past. They cannot believe in the directionless course of Britain's declining power; in preterit myths of superiority and contemporary political reactionaries, left or right.

I was shocked into colour reality at a time when labelling anyone 'coloured' denoted inferiority. A time when Britain's ethnic population accepted second best with little or no complaint. But as we enter a new epoch, black youth here will no longer accept the subordination meted out to their parents. They are saying, 'we have something to contribute' and 'gimme, it's our right'. The 'right' is theirs, and surely they will take it. Their struggle may have no organisation recognisable from outside, but it will make sense. If whites wish to know where to start with ethnic minorities, the answer is to stop. Stop patronising, stop harassing and stop treating them as educationally subnormal. Stop assuming that if a black is not acting like a slave, then he has a chip on his shoulder.

Stories discovered afterwards always have far more depth than the rumours circulated before. But before those stories can be related, the individual's curiosity is paramount. For understanding to be reached, that curiosity has to be satisfied. Curiosity is the essence. The essence I speak of here is black and Asian. Only now is there a story to relate. Tell on, tell all, tell everything.

# 2. Rule Britannia

Great Britain is a land of class, where the national perception is white. Numerous realities dictate the way each class makes the lives of black and Asian people *in general* more awkward. But the contemporary race quarrel of black versus white is making certain that British internal exploration, with determination, has begun.

When Britain abolished her part in the slave trade in 1833, black people regained their 'freedom', although they had been in Britain since the early part of the sixteenth century, when the white man's definition of freedom for blacks was created, which has changed only in degrees to this day. The guilt of morals is the space between fact and fiction. The fundamentals of British racism are hidden in the music of yesterday's Empire builders, in slavery. In 1562, the first British slave trader, John Hawkins, was backed by Queen Elizabeth I, who gave him a ship, ironically named the *Jesus of Lubeck*, with which he pursued a commission of slavery which became perpetually beneficial to the British nation. Hard on the heels of Hawkins's Honourable Company of Merchant Adventurers was a band of myth-makers – churchmen, traders and racial scientists – who were eager to evolve justifiable reasons for British greed.

Slave merchants returning with slaves and an avalanche of myths found a tonic in the theories of those skin-beating evolutionary scientists and clergy, who liberally sprinkled 'biology' with 'Christian morals' and 'God's will' as a guilt-relieving agent. Black peoples were therefore consigned into eternal slavery.

But the cry of the slave remains, so the clocks must be turned back and the act of slavery must be reviewed so that it can evoke a flashback in order to comprehend the magnitude of the black man's stake in white Britain.

The immoralities and inhumanities that froze the spirits of millions of slaves can only begin to assume their proper place in the British economic memory if it is recognised that this is the land where the profit motive mercilessly cuts down everything in its path. Which explains why John Hawkins was knighted by Queen Elizabeth I for his success 'to take the inhabitants with burning and spoiling their towns'. You may think this an understandable attitude towards other peoples in the context of the rampant violence of Elizabethan England. But what we shall perceive is that Britain's savage treatment of black slaves was malignant; that there exists a dynamic affinity between the treatment of black people as slaves, their treatment in Britain's colonies under the Pax Britannica, and the treatment black people are receiving in Britain today.

The history of oppression of black peoples by whites is two-fold. The first is the slave trade, which was followed by the second, a ruthless military fractionalisation which was covered up by a veneer of mendacity, called the Pax Britannica, to become the British Empire. It is to the first that we must turn our attention.

In the guise of the first slave, white men created their sum total of the black man. At the same time they affirmed that for their creation, the white fantasy of heaven would be the black's hell on earth. When the first African was kidnapped by Britain's whites and thrown by some bovine ruffian into the hold of a ship to become a slave, he confirmed white ideas of the black's earthbound hell. And the ease of the slaves to be taken, not in a trickle but a torrent of millions, gave even more foundation to the white myth of black sub-humanity. Failure to outwit their slave-masters was seen by those whites as justification for black enslavement.

Slavery was not only 'Made in Britain'; the hands of every European power are also smeared with black blood. Their gruesome 'family business' became a multinational enterprise when Columbus 'discovered' America.

When Spain struck gold in Hispaniola, now Haiti, white enslavement of black people became imperative, and the infamous Middle Passage to the New World was activated. Spain in the sixteenth century contracted with Portugal, who was to supply Spain with a steady supply of black slaves for her West Indian and American colonies. The Dutch won that right from Portugal in 1685, and kept it until 1702, when France grabbed it and kept it until 1713.

Under an arrangement of special contracts aptly named the 'Asiento de Negros', Spain conferred on any individual, company or nation the exclusive right to supply black slaves for its American colonies. Sir John Hawkins was one such individual, and Britain won this coveted glittering prize in 1713. Under the Treaty of Utrecht, she had obtained an 'absolute monopoly of the supply of slaves to the Spanish Colonies', making her the 'greatest slave trader in the world'. This was at that time considered to be a 'sound piece of mercantile policy'. The monopoly was in turn given to the South Sea Company by the British government.

The British take pride in their sophisticated accumulation of historical documents. Yet historical records pertaining to blacks have been loosely retained or filed away as unwanted memories – the only records of blacks kept faithfully by whites are their criminal records. How many slaves the British transported, for example, from Africa to make a profit for themselves in the West Indies and the Americas, has been quoted in British history books as ranging from one million to ten million landed alive. It is ironic that a country boastful of its business and accountancy methods can only approximate to within a few million the number of slaves it actually exported. The records of the Port of Liverpool, for instance, are remarkable explicit. Between 1783 and 1793, 921 ships from that port carried 303,737 slaves who landed alive, to the total value of £15,186,850. According to the Economics Division of the Bank of England, at 1981 prices this sum is now £350 million.[2]

In Britain, when everything else fails, they call out the record books of white fears about black numbers in Britain — black crime, black failure, black inability and white intellectual predominance. By this method, they can fetter a moment of turmoil which undermines the black and brown community. Other whites can, with underhand dealings, strategically manoeuvre black people along with their own devious interests. The result of the 1970 general election, an election laced with immigration as its main issue, is an example of this malignant technique.

It is no accident that I chose the election of 1970 to comment upon. In 1968, through Britain's Moses, Enoch Powell, race took on a new status, becoming a problem with true grit. 'Rivers of blood' was the subject chosen by a man with no political power other than his overwhelming ambition. As an indefatigable slithering adder, his immigration sums had great scare-power, swallowing up the Church-like pretence of many phoney liberal attitudes. And the fight against any black revolution was on.

---

[2] Worth approximately £1,207,700,000 in 2022.

Moreover, in the highly-structured class hierarchy which forms British society, black people lie at the bottom. People at the bottom of any society have little control over the transmitted information, or lack of information, put out, or not put out, by others about them. It follows, and is perfectly logical, that anything and everything can and is written about black people without any possibility of redress.

When Africans were first enslaved by the British in the racial dimwittedness of that era, it was thought that they should be slaves because the whites convinced themselves Africans possessed no souls. A rational argument. It was also a rational argument that Ian Smith's illegal Unilateral Declaration of Independence in 1965 in Rhodesia would find fertile ground among his kith and kin over here in Britain. The Achilles' heel of Britain's justifying arguments for not sending troops to end the oppression of Zimbabwean blacks by their mercenary white Rhodesian kinfolk was 'they fought beside us during the Second World War', showing us the quick-change artistry of British morality.

What Britons conveniently forgot was that Africans from their Empire fought beside them in a variety of places, including the march on Jerusalem and Damascus with General Allenby during the First World War. In addition, they fought at Gallipoli and Mesopotamia. The Indians went further, raising for Britain's beloved Empire the largest volunteer army in history. A mere one and a half million men. What my own Nigerian father, attached to the West African Frontier Force, was doing fighting the Japanese in Burma has never been clear, the Japanese having never perpetrated any act of violence against Africans.

British morality is clear cut and has always been. In the slave trade, they said 'toil for us', and millions of slaves did and died in huge numbers. In the colonies, during their white wars against each other, they said 'fight for us' and hundreds of thousands of Africans and Asians did and died for their trouble. Today the attitude still is, as it has always been, 'what ever good you do, we'll never recognise it and what's more we'll always forget it'.

According to Britain's two-tiered definition of morality in the nineteenth century, black people were menials and heathens. Therefore, ill-treatment of black people at the hands of whites was seen as their rightful lot. That was British custom and the popular feeling at that time. Time merely changed their methods and their morality towards black people, imprinting itself into the Briton's subconscious and preventing them from recognising that making profit through colonisation was an equally oppressive and subtle form of slavery.

In twentieth-century Britain, little has changed. Many black and Asian people have died and have been brutalised in outrageous circumstances, some in police stations, others on the streets. There are those who have been terrorised and discriminated against without any form of redress. In the eyes of the white media, all these acts merely warrant a cursory investigation, the result of which is always a foregone conclusion. But the death of a white school teacher, Blair Peach,[3] in 1979 sent a shockwave of revulsion throughout Britain, and one inquiry was not enough. The inference was obvious. White morality is clear-cut but Blair Peach, because he sided with the blacks, lost out. On hearing that an act of social or physical brutality has been committed against Britain's blacks or Asians, much of Britain's white media take a moral holiday.

Inside the racial arrogance of the British exists a crooked device known as *historical chauvinism*. In the most spectacular attempt in human history, through indifference, non-acknowledgement and conscienceless injustice, they have attempted to erase black history since the beginning of Britain's trade in slaves. Colonised black peoples, controlled by whites since that slave period, and having no control over the records of slavery and white colonial administrations, have phenomenal difficulty in preventing that attempted erasure. The *West Indian World*, a black community newspaper, recognising that black youths are not taught about their past, prints regular columns on black history.

If British black and Asian people want somewhere to attack, they should attack the archives of the British government and make them print whatever records are

---

[3] Blair Peach was a New Zealand teacher who was bludgeoned by Special Patrol Group officers during an anti-racism demonstration against the National Front in Southall, Middlesex, England. He died in hospital that night.

still in existence about their shameful trade in slaves, print everything about the valuable black and Asian contribution toward their two great wars in which they involved almost everyone else, and print their records of economic trickery and physical violence committed on the peoples in their ex-colonies. It is all history now, and history is something we should learn from, not live in.

But we will look again at the wartime contribution of black and Asian peoples in chapter three in order that an important part of a people's history be categorised into its proper place.


It is remarkable that the popular slave trade story of how the black people sold each other, a get-out clause, has persisted for so many years; and how the media of Britain has expediently remained in ignorance in their perceptions of black people, and their myths about black people. The recipe for how this fraud was perpetrated and how it was used necessitates inquiry at this state.

It is important to quote E.D. Morel, a British Reformist, who *The Times* credited as being 'the most important factor in awakening both public and official opinion to the monstrous iniquity ... perpetrated with ever-increasing cynicism and effrontery in the Congo Basin'. His book, *The Black Man's Burden*, published in 1920, contains a description of the vicious methods used by British slave-catchers:

The trade had grown so large that mere kidnapping raids conducted by white men in the immediate neighbourhood of the coast-line were quite insufficient to meet its requirements. Regions inaccessible to the European had to be tapped by the *organisation* of civil wars. The whole of the immense region from Senegal to the Congo, and even further south, became in the course of years convulsed by incessant internecine struggles. A vast tumult reigned from one extremity to the other of the most populous and fertile portions of the continent. Tribe was bribed to fight tribe, community to raid community. To every native chief, as to every one of his subjects, was held out the prospect of gain at the expense of his neighbour. Tribal feuds and individual hatreds were alike intensified, and while wide stretches of countryside were systematically ravaged by organised bands of raiders armed with muskets, 'hunting down victims for the English trader whose blasting influence, like some malignant providence extended over mighty regions where the face of a white man was never seen.'

... Queen Anne saw no objection, it is said, to increase her dowry, like her celebrated predecessor, from its operations. A statute of King William of pious memory affirms that 'the trade was highly beneficial to the kingdom'; another of George II declared it to be 'very advantageous to Great Britain,' and 'necessary to the plantations,' while the 'Society for propagating Christianity,' including half the episcopal bench, derived, as masters, from the labour of their slaves in the West Indies, an income which they spent in 'teaching the religion of peace and goodwill to men.' [My italics]

But the ever-victorious British were still not converted to the idea that it was unworkable to exist as dependants on the backs of their black victims. With an interest in guaranteeing white working-class approval for a political list of immoral doings, Britain's ruling and trading elite, with resourceful vision, fabricated yet another myth. The British Empire, it was said, only possessed immense tracts of land in Africa because those lands were wasting away. And the black inhabitants were wickedly lazy. In that continent, as in Britain, the heart of the matter lay in the land.

With the experience gained from depriving Britain's working classes of land, the ruling and trading classes went into action once more. The formula was to separate the blacks from their land, thus transforming them into titleless wage-earners, and their dependence on their new bosses would be assured.

The truth of the matter was that, in minority

white-ruled South Africa, a foreign body had dispossessed black people of their land, demolished their way of life and assaulted the bedrock of their freedom. On reflection, and in the searchlight of contemporary racial reality, the infliction of such bondage can only be preserved by the unwavering use of violence.

The difference between Britain's working classes and African peoples since colonisation is that Britain's have-nots' attentions are being diverted by sophisticated consumer items and public facilities that soften life.

Conversely, then as now, Africa's masses, without the distractions acquired by Britain's working classes, and without a profusion of choices, depend almost completely on the land and its uses. Britain had perceived in her slaves a way of developing, not Africa, but her interests in the Americas and the West Indies. In the racial myopia of the nineteenth century, she looked hungrily again at Africa, revised her original conception of her interest in that continent, and 'discovered' an enormous deposit of manpower and a gigantic store of untapped material resources fundamental to her new-fashioned industry. The temptation to impress that manpower force into her employ, this time in Africa itself, proved too powerful. Colonisation had finally arrived and with it the policy, first devised when trading in slaves, of setting 'tribe against tribe and community against community'. 'Divide and rule' was once again put into action.

An example of the methods used, gleaned from

Britain's experience of the slave trade, was the story of Rhodesia, now known as Zimbabwe. Albert Henry George Grey, who later became Earl Grey, Governor-General of Canada, wrote:

> Throughout this part of the British Dominions the coloured people are generally looked upon by the whites as an inferior race, whose interest ought to be systematically disregarded when they come into competition with their own, and who ought to be governed mainly with a view to the advantage of the superior race. And for this advantage two things are considered to be specially necessary: First, that facilities should be afforded to the White colonists for obtaining possession of land heretofore occupied by the native tribes; and secondly, that the Kaffir population should be made to furnish as large and as cheap a supply of labour as possible. [Quoted in E.D. Morel's *The Black Man's Burden*]

This razored summary of colonial attitudes reveals the stance taken by Britain's whites towards the peoples within their African, West Indian and Asian colonies. In October 1888, the following epic occurred:

Chief Lobengula, of the then ruling group, the Amandebele, was approached by Cecil Rhodes and his conspiring companion Charles Rudd. They were in pursuit of concessions 'for a place to dig for gold'. Their idea of 'a place' became encapsulated in a document signed between themselves and Chief Lobengula. It was the blueprint for Britain's acquisitive mentality abroad, euphemistically known as exploration. Under its terms, in exchange for a monthly payment of £100 and British products in the shape of 1,000 Martini-Henry rifles and 100,000 rounds of ball cartridges, Rhodes and Rudd were to receive 'the complete and exclusive charge over all the metals and minerals' in Zimbabwe, together with 'full power to do all things that they may deem necessary to win and procure the same, and to hold, collect and enjoy the profits and revenues, if any derivable from the said metals and minerals'.

This multi-purpose exploitative document, known as the Rhodes-Rudd Concession, eventually became the basis for the initial British occupation of Zimbabwe, and finally the foundation of the white Rhodesian self-styled Constitution.

At that time, few whites realised or cared how many Africans would have to die in order to regain what was rightfully theirs, and what had been deceitfully gotten by the exploring hands of white Rhodesians, Britain's sons. As far as they were concerned, a black-dominated Zimbabwe under a black Prime Minister, as Rhodesia's wonder man Ian Smith himself believed, was a 'thousand years away'.

While white Rhodesians turned the original

black landowners into subjects without security, they also began to do everything in their power to goad the Amandebele and the Mashonas into rebellion. This they did by setting up courts, and the British South Africa Company, which was not a sovereign power but had gained Britain's imperial assent, also carried out executions.

Under Leander Starr Jameson, BSAC's manager in Africa and incidentally the instigator of the Jameson raid into Transvaal, the Company's divisive plans came to fruition in July 1893. They began by stealing cattle from the Mashonas which they had hired from Lobengula, chief of the Amandebele. Jameson informed Lobengula that the cattle theft had been carried out by the Mashonas who had no intention of returning his cattle. Cattle being a sovereign symbol, the theft of which is an affront to the entire tribe, Lobengula punished the Mashonas in an avenging expedition in which several Mashonas were killed. Captain Lendy, under the direct orders of Jameson, completed the Company's plans by shooting thirty Amandebele warriors dead as they were retreating from their confrontation with the Mashonas. Jameson pleaded self-defence; no white lost his life.

The 'divide' completed, the climate was right for their 'rule' to be put into effect. The lands of the Amandebele was invaded by the British South Africa Company, with the British government mouthing protests but doing nothing, setting the precedent for its procrastinating attitude seventy-two years later, when Ian Smith declared Rhodesia's Unilateral Declaration of Independence (UDI) in 1965. The British South Africa Company's Loot Committee appropriated 6,000 square miles of land, and slavery, through forced labour, returned. Chief Lobengula died in January 1894.

In a letter to King George V, quoted in E.D. Morel's *The Black Man's Burden*, members of Lobengula's family wrote:

> The members of the late King's [Lobengula's] family, your petitioners, and several members of the tribe are now scattered about on farms so parcelled out to white settlers, and are practically created a nomadic people living in this scattered condition, under a veiled form of slavery, they being not allowed individually to cross from one farm to another, or from place to place except under a system of permit or pass and are practically forced to do labour on these private farms as a condition of their occupying land in Matabeleland.

Who created apartheid?

In his book, *The Heart of Africa*, published in 1954, Alexander Campbell quoted a friend who delivered a penetrating truism:

> The black man in a white dominated society,

said Hans Leuenberger, is equipped with X-ray eyes. He not only can study and understand the white man's techniques, but can see inside the white man's mind, penetrate his thoughts, and follow his motivations. But the white man only sees black bodies. He has never entered into the black man's thoughts, does not know what is going on in his heart, and seldom speaks his language.

That home truth fuses Britain's past with her present.

Brutality and injustice towards black and brown peoples as a British way of life did not end in Africa. Suppressive methods tried and tested during Britain's trade selling black human beings, crowned with success, promoted the use of the same racist formula in her colonies.

In Britain's international career of racial gangsterism and banditry, the peoples of the Caribbean, too, felt the long arm of her oppression. These black peoples were divided through the slave trade and ruled by sheer terror from the moment they landed on those faraway islands where a selection of Britain's landed gentry as plantation owners, busily building the financial base of their twentieth-century fortunes and estates, unleashed their pitiless inhumanities on defenceless blacks.

On 11 October 1856, in Jamaica, a crowd of blacks

went to Morant Bay courthouse to complain about the heavy-handed treatment meted out to blacks found squatting on uncultivated land. In reply to this protest, the white authorities murdered seven of the so-called rioters, who in turn killed two hated white overseers. In the words of Jan Morris, writing in *Pax Britannica*, the then Governor of Jamaica, Edward John Eyre, characteristically put down the demonstration 'with unusually ferocious zeal, killing or executing more than six hundred people, flogging six hundred more, and burning down a thousand homes...'

Quoting from *Colour, Class and the Victorians* by Professor Douglas A. Lorimer, the press reaction was:

> On 4 November *The Times* declared that this latest news from Jamaica proved that blacks were unsuited to freedom.
>
> On 11 November the *Standard* admitted that little news had been received of the insurrection, surveyed previous slave revolts in Jamaica, and concluded that black rebellions were far worse than white ones. The indolent black savages of Jamaica, the *Standard* claimed, had no grievances, but sought only to satisfy their greed, hatred, and lust for white property, white lives, and white women.

The voice of the *Standard* set the formula for the master plan on how black and brown protests and rebellions against white authority in the twentieth century should and would be treated by the British media and their readers, listeners and viewers. Do you remember the media reports concerning the unsuitability of the independencies of Britain's West Indian possessions, of India, Pakistan, Kenya, Nigeria, Tanzania, Ghana, Somalia, Zambia, and Zimbabwe, etc?

The Pax Britannica was a pretentious and self-glorious deception, maybe not in British eyes but certainly in the eyes of black people and Asians. The black and white definitions of their 'Peace' were always totally opposed. Britain's idea of peace was a violent nightmare, both for blacks whom they had brutalised and murdered over three centuries, and for Asians whom they ritually had 'blown from cannon'. In the words of Jan Morris in *Heaven's Command*, Indians were tied 'to the muzzles of guns and blown to pieces to the beat of drums'.

But the magnificent imperfection of the British Empire, which was also its latent strength, was distance; due to the far-flungness of its imperial territories, it was impossible for a counter-revolution to be mounted by its unenthusiastic, constricted black and brown peoples acting in concert.

Take India, the jewel in the British crown. After a century of persecution, in 1857, the Indians fought against the British Raj, which slid into British history as the Indian Mutiny. We are told that the misnamed Mutiny was the result of Indian resentment at Britain's issue of animal-fat greased cartridges, which were offensive to Hindu and Muslim soldiers. That was the advertised fantasy. In reality, the rebellion was due to enforced Christianisation and also the fact, expediently dismissed in Britain's history books, that India's masses hated the British presence in their country and had always done so.

In the sheer desperation of the British to remain on what was seen as priceless territory, they were unable to recognise in the determination of the so-called mutineers, in the act of their rebellion, a conqueror's maxim. 'In Imperialism', wrote William Inge in his *Outspoken Essays on Patriotism*, 'nothing fails like success'. What has gone down in Britain's books as a 'mutiny' must at the very least be re-recorded as India's First War of Independence.

However, while the British Raj jackbooted its mark into the heart of India, but not the Indians, it was never a secret to the majority of trigger-happy British individuals there that India's masses resented the colonial administration and were always psychologically in rebellion against them. They succeeded in subverting Indian resentment and agitation in 1857. But to ensure that the crown jewel remained in Britain's keeping, a tighter round-the-clock watch was kept. Through a system of paid Indian informers, India's powerful princes and the Indian Civil Service (ICS), the divide and rule was maintained with spasmodic bursts of military repression.

Furthermore, it was the princes, some of whom were rulers of states geographically larger than Britain, who were India's sell-outs. Thomas Macaulay, a member of the East India Company's Supreme Council, put British social engineering in the following context. If Britain was to succeed in India she had 'to form a class of interpreters between us and the natives we govern, a class of persons Indian in blood and colour but English in tastes, in opinions, in morals and in intellect'. The princes and darker-skinned individuals joining the Indian Civil Service aptly fitted this description: 'Moulded by nannies, tutors, advisers, the example of visiting officials and perhaps the schooling of Eton and Oxford, many of the princes became quasi-Englishmen themselves – English aristocrats buffed to an oriental polish.' (Jan Morris, *Pax Britannica*).

In other words, they were glorified houseboys and could be trusted to hold for Britain's whites what was not theirs in the first place. But in 1947, under the pressure of increasing violence, Britain pulled out of her 250-year Indian freehold in seventy-three days as 200,000 Indians died. The drama on the Indian sub-continent was over.

But we must look again at the slave trade in order to examine the role of the Abolitionists.

It is true that William Wilberforce, Thomas Clarkson, Granville Sharp and Secretaries of the British and Foreign Anti-Slavery Societies, John Tredgold and

John Scoble, campaigned to abolish the British slave trade. But the trade was becoming an increasingly unprofitable stumbling block. And in keeping with the liberating ideal of changing one thing by replacing it with something similar, Wilberforce proposed alleviating white guilt by turning that stumbling block into stepping stones, with the perceptive introduction of Colonisation, Commerce and Christianity.

Colonisation, being a veiled form of slavery, was acceptable to the Abolitionists, and more than acceptable to the liberal idea. The ideal of liberalism is the outcome of the basest instinct subscribed to by those who hold immense prejudices, but don't want to be seen obviously believing in malevolent practices, be they of a racial or class nature. But if those liberals also have something to lose in the way of status or property, that malevolence assumes another dimension.

As a result, it was necessary to manufacture for public consumption an illusion tinged with benevolent integrity, namely an Empire with Pax attached.

Ironically, those 'humane and determined men' (E.D. Morel) never had any intention of radically altering the very idea of slavery. Any change they intended was purely cosmetic. In fact, the Abolitionists had every intention of reinforcing Britain's hand in the trade by submerging out of international sight the unpleasant visual aspects of it which offended delicate liberal sensibilities.

The Abolitionists' heirs, the present-day liberals, wracked with guilt by the obscene deeds of their ancestors, advertise their moral concern under a facade in which they attempt to rationalise away Britain's historical contempt for black people by implying that Britain's slave trade was an inexplicable accident of long-gone generations, thus almost succeeding in turning the painful black reality of having been slaves into a legend.

Yesterday's abolitionists and today's liberals are one and the same. From the following accounts taken from Professor Lorimer's book, *Colour, Class and the Victorians*, can you recognise patterns and personalities?

When painting 'The Anti-Slavery Convention', in 1840, Benjamin Haydon devised a test of abolitionist attitudes. As each noted philanthropist sat to be sketched for the painting, Haydon asked him where Henry Beckford, an ex-slave from Jamaica, should be placed in the picture. First the painter tested John Scoble and John Tredgold, Secretaries of the British and Foreign Anti-Slavery Society. Both men objected to the Negro occupying a prominent place on the same level as the leading abolitionists.

An attitude reminiscent of those whites from Oxfam, War on Want, Christian Aid, the British Council, etc.? They persistently and religiously work 'helping' develop their 'Third World', but why are there not blacks and Asians in any significant capacity on their committees? Do they forget them at the planning stages of what can only be described as their guilt-alleviating projects? Back to Professor Lorimer:

> The abolitionists' concern for the slave did not necessarily lead to an acceptance of the free Negro as a brother and equal... A few regarded a black skin and slave origins as a sign of inferiority, but rarely did they openly display these feelings through hostile or insulting behaviour.

Zilpha Elaw, a black American preacher who toured England from 1841 to 1846, reported of her meeting with the Board of the British and Foreign Anti-Slavery Society:

> It was really an august assembly; their dignity appeared so redundant, that they scarcely knew what to do with it all. Had I attended there on a matter of life or death, I think I could scarcely have been more closely interrogated or more rigidly examined; from the reception I met with, my impression was, that they imagined I wanted some pecuniary or other help from them; for they treated me as the proud do the needy. [Quoted in Lorimer's *Colour, Class and the Victorians*]

The slave trade had been important and indispensable to the health and wealth of Britain. And the expansion of the cities of Liverpool and Bristol was due almost completely to the trade and, crucially, it kept vast numbers of those cities' labour pools employed, e.g. in shipyards, seamen and ships' chandlers, etc. Obviously, there was much to lose. As compensation to British slave merchants for the loss of their slave cargoes, the Abolitionists struck upon palm oil as a substitute. Palm oil was an ingredient necessary for the production of lubricants, candles and soap.

Hence, what Wilberforce and Co. failed, or rather avoided, to tell the British public, was that the same barbarities practised against black people in their slave trade, would again be employed in making those Africans toil for them, producing oil from the palm. And if colonisation were achieved, the Abolitionists' expectations of trade in a variety of resources and minerals would be realised. In other words, the slave trade was disguised as legitimate trade.

The Abolitionists, steeped in Britain's mythical tradition of fair play and justice for all, were well aware that that tradition depended comprehensively on how it was seen, and who saw it. Therefore, whatever diabolical deeds were vented on black and brown skulls by whites outside the white public gaze or knowledge did not happen. And cruelties committed by whites against blacks in their colonies, firstly during their palm oil trade, and thereafter in every other trade, according to whites, bore little substance or did not exist either. That opinionated attitude, never really questioned by Britannic whites, has lived on into the twentieth century.

Naturally, to consummate their soul-saving pilgrimage, the Abolitionists proposed reforming Africa's blacks by spreading the gospel of the Christian way of life, by a down-payment for Christianity through religious imperialism. William Wilberforce wrote:

> Let us endeavour to strike *our* roots into *their* soil by the gradual introduction and establishment of *our* own principles and opinions; of *our* laws, institutions and manners; above all, as the source of every other improvement, of *our* religion, and consequently of *our* morals. [Quoted from Jan Morris's *Heaven's Command*. My italics.]

Through this statement can be glimpsed accurately the intentions of Wilberforce and Co. And to accomplish what should now be called the *Wilberforce Doctrine*, the racial revolutionaries stampeded into the membership of the Kingdom of God: the Church Missionary Society, Baptist Missionary Society, London Missionary Society, and the British and Foreign Bible Society. This way they could, with evangelical determination, teach what they saw as Africa's stone-age relics the virtues of what those 'black children' would eventually classify as an intransigent white hypocrisy, conducted in the name of Christ.

Bishop Heber also lent his religious talents with his composition, 'From Greenland's Icy Mountains', with one notable verse ending in, 'The heathen in his blindness, bows down to wood and stone'. Sentiments of betterness, but understandable considering the racial indigestion rampant in that era. But what necessitated the singing of this intolerant religious lyric in the era of Queen Elizabeth II?

During the slave trade, the clergy of the Church of England along with their soul-siblings, the Roman Catholic Church, justified slavery and soothed their inward monitors by rewriting a certain Christian doctrine: that the righteous possessed a heavenly incentive and sinners were heading for hell (which, as we have seen, for some began on earth). Their new version of this doctrine was: since whites were morally superior to blacks, white maltreatment of blacks did not blot out any heavenly credits, and thus did not bar their way to the long-awaited appointment with the Right Hand of God. It should also be remembered that at this time, the clergy consisted of men who had long grown accustomed to seeing poor whites executed for petty theft and transported for minor offences. And while witnessing crimes against blacks and poor whites, their horror of injustice was tempered by the property-owning motives of the landed classes and their own.

The paramount issue on which the Churches have been consistently united is that of property and the property motive. Being slave and plantation owners themselves explains their belief in the upholding of the rules and regulations regarding the rights of property owners. Their vested property interests permitted no difference in their attitude to the commerce surrounding livestock and that of black human beings. But in accepting the concept of the abolition of slavery, the clergy implicitly accepted the concept of losing a vital and lucrative source of income. No capitalist does that.

The idea of colonisation through missionary work became more determined when its financial significance was realised. Through their new religious imperialism, many more territories could be conquered and their old slavery income, with the help of their respective governments, would at the very least be quadrupled. The religious advocates set forth to conquer yesterday's slaves by moral crucifixion, resurrecting them through conversion as newly loyal and ardent Jesus freaks, holding aloft the banner of Christ while, through a whitewashed slavery, they filled the bottomless coffers of the Protestant and Catholic Churches.

Meanwhile, having enthused their own flock with spiritual fervour, they reinforced in them a conviction that the lateness of the coming of the Messiah was due to the fact that there were so many black sinners at large. A big clean-up was needed and it must begin in Africa (what better place to begin than Africa?). The conversion-anthem rose to a crescendo, and the Church, along with the Abolitionists, announced a mission of good works led by the Salvationists with banner headlines declaring that the well-being of Africa's spirit-rappers was justification for their intended crusade. True to imperialistic type, it was not long before their initial aims of furthering God's work gave way to their meddling in African affairs.

It follows, with their African and Asian experience, that contemporary clergymen in Britain have transformed themselves into the 'Mouth and Ears of Black Grievances' and 'Apologists for Black Behaviour', the black and Asian people considered to be incapable of defending or speaking for themselves.

The moral lesson is that black and Asian people have white overseers, and conversely, those overseers have their blacks and Asians. But the basis of Britain's truths is determined by the overseers, and today it is no secret that those truths clash in practically every way with the life of each black and Asian individual.

The upshot being, in the everyday scenario of British life, that *truth* has come to be accepted as *customary*. Implicit in that fixed condition, it is for instance the custom to discriminate against women, and to ignore the poor and aged. It is also customary to oppress and degrade black and Asian people and blame them as the source of Britain's problems, e.g. Britain's economic decline, unemployment, housing shortages, declining services and overpopulation, requiring black and Asian immigration controls.

In a nutshell, there are those who, steeped in immorality, constantly strum trite racial remarks and speeches, and those who design Race Relations laws, head to tail with the others who congregate, either silently or visibly, under the National Front or British Movement banners.

# 3. A Savage Culture

The price of African and Asian independence in the twentieth century alone has been very high. In a very real sense, World War One was the beginning of the struggle for independence from Britain. In the words of A.J.P. Taylor in *English History 1914-1945*:

> The white populations of the Empire rallied eagerly to the mother country. Some 50 million Africans and 250 million Indians were involved, without consultation, in a war of which they understood nothing against an enemy who was also unknown to them.

With a vengeance, the Great War provided African and Asian people with the beginnings of their apprenticeship for freedom. And for some, almost immediately, poison gas proved to be that freedom's epitaph. At Ypres, Belgium, in 1915, Germany, who possessed the poison gas, was the enemy. In an account based on the first use of this terrible weapon, A.J.P. Taylor, as Editor-in-Chief of *The Illustrated History of the World Wars*, wrote about the German testing of this new weapon in actual battle conditions:

> The area selected was a quiet four-mile stretch of front at the northern corner of the Ypres salient. The line was held by French colonial troops whose erratic tactics and discipline had been a source of friction between the British and French commanders for some weeks. Ill-fitted to resist a determined conventional attack, they collapsed immediately under the impact of this new and frightening weapon ... Sir John French staged a series of ill-managed and extravagant counter-attacks against the new enemy positions (the British troops were told to protect themselves against gas by dipping their handkerchiefs in a solution of water and Boric acid and tying them across their mouths). These achieved little except the destruction of two brigades of the Indian Army and the dismissal of Sir Horace Smith-Dorrien, the first – and last – senior commander to protest against the cost in casualties of repetitive frontal attacks.

The 'destruction of two brigades of the Indian Army', referred to above actually meant a loss of

6,000 men who just happened to be Indian. It is also significant that the only losses suffered by Germany's enemies in that battle were African soldiers fighting for France and Indians dying for Britain.

Historically, with reference to black and Asian capability and the contribution to Britain, *accidental amnesia* is the guiding principle of the white British state of mind. Take Mary Seacole, a black woman born in Jamaica in 1805. She developed techniques that significantly reduced the loss of life in both the 1850 Kingston cholera epidemic and the 1853 yellow fever epidemic of Jamaica.[4]

But it was her activities in the Crimean War in 1854 that have been erased from the amnesia-prone British memory. Turned down by the Crimean Fund, who refused to send her to the Crimea along with the white nurses they did send, Mary Seacole, with the assistance of a relative, paid her own fare to make the 3,000 mile journey from London to the Crimea. With her own funds she established the 'British Hospital' in the war zone. And like Florence Nightingale, whose lamp was mostly spent burnishing Britain's newspapers, Mary Seacole dispensed aid to the sick and wounded. William Russell, war correspondent for *The Times*, with the future in mind wrote:

> She is always in attendance on the battlefields to aid the wounded ... I have seen her go down

---

[4] Mary Seacole saved her first cholera patient by using the following remedies: mustard emetics to make the patient vomit, warm cloths to combat chills, mustard plasters on the stomach and the back, and Calomel (mercury chloride) as a purgative and to kill bacteria.

under fire with her little store of creature comforts for our wounded men and a more skilful hand about a wound or a broken limb could not be found among our best surgeons ... I have witnessed her devotion and her courage; I have already borne testimony to her services to all who needed them ... and I trust that England *will not forget* the one who nursed her sick and who sought out her wounded to aid and succour them and who performed the last office for some of her illustrious dead. [My italics]

In 1855, when the war ended, Florence Nightingale returned to Britain to national honours and public adulation. Mary Seacole, on the other hand, returned to Britain bankrupt and forgotten, and died in Paddington in May 1881. She was buried in St Mary's Catholic Cemetery in Kensal Green. And white Britain suffered a traditionally convenient loss of memory.

It was no great leap in the dark when Asquith's government sent for what they considered to be *their* Africans and Asians. And to ensure that, among black people, slavery had not become just an idea, and to make black people and Asians admit, by their very presence on the battlefield, that they were still subject to white British control, they were included in Britain's Great War against Germany, to be used as guinea pigs on the battlefield of Ypres. Or had the black and Asian peoples expected Independence in return for their wartime contribution? According to G.M. Trevelyan, author of *A Shortened History of England*, writing about the contribution of the white populations of Empire who also fought for Britain the mother country:

> When the war was over, each Dominion insisted on a full recognition of its nationhood. They claimed individual representation in the League of Nations, and the right to retain those German colonies they had themselves taken in the war. And finally, in 1931, the Statute of Westminster has given legal force to the long-established custom that the Parliament of Great Britain should legislate for the Dominions only at their own request. Laws affecting the succession to the Crown can only be altered with the concurrence of each of the Dominions, and the King can take no advice about appointments or other action in the Dominions except from Dominion Statesmen.

A magnificent reward. Canada had raised 650,000 men, New Zealand and Australia about 300,000 men each, and the whites got their way. The West Indies and blacks contributed 135,000 men, and India raised a force of one and a half million men, and Africans and Indians got their traditional desserts. Nothing.

A reaction was not long in coming. India grew angry. A storm of nationalist hostilities and political agitation against the continued British presence on Indian territory swept the subcontinent. Independence from Britain was their ambition. And Mahatma Gandhi would be their Messiah.

In Amritsar, British tempers scaled the heights after riots ended with the deaths of four or five British nationals, although many more Indians than whites died as a result of those riots. It was April 1919, and rumours of insurrection abounded, conjuring up inherited memories of a former pseudo-Indian Mutiny. A significant reminder was needed, and Brigadier-General Reginald Dyer CB, Britain's agent by proxy and her revengeful instrument of suppression, was the man.

At Jallianwalla Bagh, in the centre of Amritsar, on 13 April 1919, hundreds of Indians attending a banned political rally were the target. Like a nightmare, the demonstrators were surrounded by General Dyer's men, and they weren't out sightseeing. To make sure that his intentions were carried out with complete success, an armoured car was also present.

The reality of their position struck home to the crowd when the soldiers fired point-blank into the brown mass of humanity for several minutes. The 'official' British figures for this act of supreme insanity were 379 dead with 1,500 wounded. Not surprisingly, the Indian figure was 800 dead with many more wounded. Amritsar would be an object lesson. And if Indians, indeed if any of Britain's colonised black and brown peoples, ever needed a salutary reminder of their position in Britain's eyes, Amritsar was it, with a vengeance. But what was important was that the end of the Great War signified Britain's confused and abrupt arrival into the twentieth century, and the era of any African and Asian doubts pertaining to true British intentions had ended.

Even though a rebellion against Britain's political and military control at that time seemed impossible, some Africans tried it. A Britain at war, they felt, was Britain off her guard. Nyasaland, now Malawi, was one such example. Reverend John Chilembwe was the black nationalist, and the misuse of his people by Britain spearheaded his case. He published an article in November 1914 criticising the forcing of Africans to fight for Britain in the Great War. On 23 January 1915, he wrote this to his men:

> This very night you are to go and strike the blow and then die ... This is the only way to show the white man that the treatment they are treating our men and women was most bad and we have decided to strike a first and a last blow, and then all die by the heavy storm of the white man's army. The white man will then think, after we are dead, that the treatment they are treating our people is almost bad, and they might change. [Quoted in Jan Morris's *Farewell the Trumpets*]

One fact is plainly obvious. Chilembwe knew that British firepower was superior to his own, but his resolve can be seen as an act of supreme frustration, to be equated with the reaction of Bristol's blacks in 1980 and Brixton's in 1981.

In those frustrating circumstances, the strength of the opposition is unimportant. Consequently, Chilembwe led an abortive revolt against British rule and white exploitation of blacks. The result was that Chilembwe was shot and his followers were hanged.

Dr Walter Rodney, author of *How Europe Underdeveloped Africa* (1972) wrote:

Sustenance given by colonies to the colonisers was most obvious and very decisive in the case of contributions by soldiers from among the colonised. Without colonial troops, there would have been no 'British forces' fighting on the Asian front in the 1939–45 war, because the ranks of the 'British forces' were filled with Indians and other colonials, including Africans and West Indians. It is a general characteristic of colonialism that the metropole utilised the manpower of the colonies. The Romans had used soldiers of one conquered nationality to conquer other nationalities, as well as to defend Rome against enemies. Britain applied this to Africa ever since the early 19<sup>th</sup> century, when the West Indian Regiment was sent across the Atlantic to protect British interests on the West African Coast. The West Indian Regiment had black men in the ranks, Irish (colonials) as NCO's, and Englishmen as officers. By the end of the 19<sup>th</sup> century, the West Indian Regiment included lots of Sierra Leoneans.

The most important force in the conquest of West African colonies by the British was the West African Frontier Force – the soldiers being Africans and the officers English. In 1894, it was joined by the West African Regiment, formed to help suppress the so-called 'Hut tax war' in Sierra Leone, which was the expression of widespread resistance against the imposition of colonial rule. In East and Central Africa, the King's African Rifles was the unit which tapped African fighting power on behalf of Britain. The African regiments supplemented military apparatus in several ways. Firstly, they were used as emergency forces to put down nationalist uprisings in the various colonies. Secondly, they were used to fight other Europeans inside Africa, notably during the first and second world wars. And thirdly, they were carried to European battlefields or to theatres of war outside Africa.

Furthermore, Indians under British orders fought against Africans. An example is given in the 1977 issue of *Africa Yearbook* published by *Africa Journal*, quoting the case of Nyasaland: 'In 1893, the name of the country was changed from Nyasaland Protectorate to the British Central African Protectorate. The country was finally "pacified" in 1897, with the help of Indian troops.'

With only 150 white land-grabbers in Nyasaland at the time, it is not surprising they used their colonised Indians to colonise the Africans. Furthermore, from *African Yearbook*:

> During the First World War, the country was invaded by German troops from Tanganyika. The Germans were repulsed and later Nyasaland became a base for British operations against German forces in East Africa. A total of 18,920 Nyasalanders were recruited for service with the King's African Rifles, and 191,200 rendered service as carriers and non-combatants.

Most significantly, Britain's military colonial practices had sown enmities among Asians, West Indians and Africans, by giving them a Roman holiday and U-turning them into exterminators of each other. A historic tool, as we shall see, to be used when those Asians, West Indians and Africans arrived to settle in Britain. It relied on completely ignoring their common denominators, while exploiting and accentuating any difference that could be found.

World War Two prophesied the severing of the lifeline between Britain and her colonies, and the potential cutting of the master/servant Gordian knot. But all was not over just yet. Britain's scheming intention for her African and Asian soldiers was for them to remain passive when it suited her, and aggressive whenever she so ordered.

Africans and Asians were conscripted into World War Two, encouraged by hints of Independence as a reward when Britain's problems were over. But, as will be seen, the moment Britain had solved her problems of war, forgetfulness was the order of the day, and the relationship between her and her subject peoples would again revert to master and slave. But in this her greatest moment of crisis, she failed to notice the supposed inferiority of her 'inferior peoples', and thus she sowed the seed for future rebellion. The slaves who had fought for Britain in wartime would continue their fight for freedom against her in peace.

Nineteen forty-six heralded impending change, and dictatorship and/or Marxist philosophy became the new method of government for some emerging nations. Great Britain was no longer able to hold the inevitable in abeyance. In the process of annihilating her wartime enemies, like Germany, Italy and Japan, Britannia exposed herself. West Indians, Indians and Africans alike had witnessed that most Roman of all institutions, the British Army, suffer significant reverses during World War Two. The myth of her might had been, in their eyes, laid low. Her grand illusion had crumbled when her subject peoples recognised the weak link in Britain's historically unbreakable chain.

Harold Macmillan once wrote that the British were 'masters of the world and heirs of the future'. But now the United States of America was very much in evidence, turning the Pax Britannica into the Pax Americana. And Britain became shackled by a myriad of homespun myths, legends and memories, and future heirs to trouble. The British Empire had reached its climax with Queen Victoria's Diamond Jubilee in 1897, and had been breaking apart ever since. The end was in sight. Great Britain had been the black man's burden, but the white man's burden was the stunning realisation that he was being given orders, marching orders, and the commanders were black. Decolonisation was the white man's Exodus.

Lord Curzon, Viceroy of India 1898–1905, had said:

As long as we rule India, we are the greatest power in the world. If we lose it we shall drop straight away to a third rate power ... Your ports and your coaling stations, your fortresses and your dockyards, your Crown colonies and protectorates will go too. For either they will be unnecessary, or the tollgates and barbicans of an Empire that has vanished.

And so it was.

From the moment Britain evacuated India, her Empire was in a perpetual state of breaking apart by instalments, leaving in its wake an obstinate 'Empire mentality'. When Britain lost her imperial possessions, the sense of superiority subscribed to by whites over Africans and Asians continued, based on a now defunct power. And the time of sham began. Today, Britain's politicians, in a cloud of bogus power, continue to formulate foreign policies assuming that they still hold, internationally, yesterday's influence sponsored by yesterday's source of power.

Inside the British Empire mentality lies the idea that she has a meaningful say in today's world events, but in fact she does not; that at times of international crisis she commands an equal vote with the USA, Russia and China at the negotiating tables of power. That too is far from the truth. In fact, it would be overestimating the case to believe that the prospects of any human being outside Britain depended on the state of affairs in Britain today. Because that was not always the case, it is therefore a painful reality for many of Britain's ruling and middle classes who feel frustrated and uneasy when confronted by the staggering realisation that world power is in the hands of the Americans, Russians and Chinese. And the decision as to whether Britain, on the world platform, moves this way or that will be made in Washington, not London. From King and Queen, to pawn.

The NATO Secretary General Dr Josef Luns warned in April 1981: 'I would take issue with the assumption that the less powerful members of the Alliance will be understanding if they are habitually excluded from deliberations bearing on their interests'. A statement based more on optimism than honesty. Dr Luns is well aware of the fact that within the history of the SALT[5] negotiations, within the reality of international politics, policy on such issues has always been and will continue to be decided by America on behalf of the West, and the Soviet Union on behalf of the East. He would do well to remember that if America was not effectively the West's decider, he would not need to make such an unrealistic statement. Moreover, if the United States of America is determined to force European and British acceptance of the Cruise missile, or any other type of missile, on their territories, America will succeed, and the British Empire mentality will have been dealt another wounding body blow.

Consequently, through the loss of her Empire, Great Britain has suffered continuous stinging reminders of the loss of her former global authority. But it was not until 1979 that the unfamiliar phrase 'negotiate not dictate' finally entered the British political vocabulary. It was Mrs Thatcher, the new Prime Minister, thinking of her new charge as an imperial power, who made the mistake. Her statement, made in Canberra, Australia, helped change a few ideas about using bully-boy tactics on Africans. Labelled the Iron Lady by the Russians,

[5] Strategic Arms Limitation Treaty.

Mrs Thatcher, while lecturing a press conference said that she was ready to grant recognition to the lurching regime of Bishop Muzorewa, the great white hope, and Ian Smith, the promised-land leader. And to lift – unilaterally – the mandatory UN sanctions.

According to *The Guardian* columnist, Patrick Keatley, in March 1981, the African reaction to her Canberra statement was totally unexpected. He wrote:

Total British exports to Nigeria had topped the £1,000 million mark by 1977 and reached £1,133 million the next year. Then came a setback, in which the largest factor was political. Hasty statements by the incoming Thatcher administration brought the overnight decision to nationalise the assets of BP in Nigeria. It was a warning shot to show that Nigeria would not idly tolerate a handover to white minority rule in Rhodesia.

The result was that Mrs Thatcher backed down, recognising economic reality, and in doing so, the British Lion was defanged and declawed. Nigeria, over this issue, represented the international black spirit, the jagged piece of glass stuck in the intestinal tract of white Britain.

It is a fact that Ian Smith declared UDI[6] on 11 November 1965. It is also a fact that successive British governments did nothing about that illegal declaration.

---

[6] Unilateral Declaration of Independence.

Furthermore, African people with their white allies fought against both the illegal white administration in Salisbury and against the racist inactiveness of Britain's governments. But the reality is that Zimbabwe's black people were and still are the majority. Therefore, power by political definition is rightly theirs. In recognition of that white-frightening fundament, Robert Mugabe, the so-called terrorist, became Prime Minister of Zimbabwe, *persona grata* for the black majority and their white allies.

The grand sham continues. One would have thought the moment of decolonisation was a glorious moment for the United Kingdom to seek new directions and fresh beginnings. But that was not so. It took several years, with a little help from vociferous African and Asian leaders, for Britain's politicians to recognise that *their* British Commonwealth was not in fact British, but international. Or was the British Commonwealth a cut-price variety of Empire?

Ultimately, the British Commonwealth gave way to The Commonwealth. And the ruling Britons finally settled for an imperial illusion through the continuance of imperial titles. The OBE (Order of the British Empire) and the MBE (Member of the British Empire), conferred while the Empire was still alive, continue to be bestowed. Or are the OBE and the MBE and other such imperial memorabilia still in existence in order to remind the nostalgic British that there had been an Empire?

Europe, too, became aware of the loss of British

power and colonial trading market through the public death of her Empire. It took ten years and many attempts before Britain was finally accepted into the European Economic Community. General de Gaulle's veto may have reflected that loss, as well as a reluctance to accept France's traditional competitor into an organisation in which France was pre-eminent. That there was anyone bold enough to humiliate Britannia without retribution was unthinkable. But there was, and de Gaulle was such a man.

There were conditions attached to her entry into the EEC. Conditions dictated by some members of the Community, principally France and Germany. It was because of those unacceptable conditions that she found it necessary to renegotiate the Treaty of Rome after her entry into the EEC, twice.

For Britons, this was a case of chickens coming home to roost. There had been a time when it would have been Britain who decided whether to create an EEC, or not. Britain also would have decided which European countries could become members. Most significantly, she would have dictated policy for such an august body, if necessary through her customary methods of gunboat diplomacy. But those days were over. Now here was Britain being dictated to by her rival, France.

Britannia's distress was that her power belonged to another era, and here in 1973 it was a new one, where no amount of bygone power could strengthen her obvious powerlessness. Britain could not dictate, but had to negotiate from a position of economic weakness. Neither the status nor the energy could be found to counter the confidence of some Common Market countries that were negotiating from a position of economic strength. In Place of Strife[7] was more strife to come.

Observed from a black or Asian position, it is an Empire mentality which compels Britain's ethnic peoples to exist in a white world of intolerance, injustice, unemployment, and continuous ill-treatment. They are not welcome but merely tolerated on British soil. But white intolerance continuously sharpens the ideas of the ethnic community. And brains honed to determination through necessity, heavily aided by racial injustice, are trembling potentials for spontaneous or purposeful rebellion at any moment. British television as a devil's disciple plays its part by constantly reminding black and Asian people what they will never be, i.e. equal, and what they will never have, i.e. status. So pressures continue to build, for to be reasonable in the alienated reserves of the Brixtons of Britain is tough. If conditions do not change, and soon, for black and Asian people, and if white rulers continue to rule through imperial attitudes, with illusions of racial pre-eminence, blacks and Asians living in Britain will prove to be the most costly of Britannia's imperial acquisitions.

Bishop Colin O'Brien Winter captured the essence of white treatment of black and Asian people living in

---

[7] In Place of Strife (1969) was a Government White Paper written by Barbara Castle, Secretary of State for Employment and Productivity.

Britain in his foreword to John Downing's publication *Now You Do Know*, published in 1980. He wrote:

Aneurin Bevan, ex-miner and M.P., once warned Winston Churchill in a memorable speech in the House of Commons, 'not to wince before the lash falls'. John Downing's report falls like a lash on the smug, the silent, the unconvinced and the uncaring people of Britain who either pretend that there is no racial prejudice in this country, or ignore the massive injustice, the daily violence and the sufferings that black people undergo. The author, in his preface, feels no hope that the mass of people here will face up to, let alone act on, the appalling reality of the racism that exists here and, because of this, he aims his report at the wider international readership. One is immediately reminded of the situation that pertained in Germany after the war with Hitler, when the overwhelming mass of the German people, having failed to challenge Hitler's murderous policies, tried to excuse their silence by pleading ignorance to what was going on in the county. The rest of the world judged them guilty of being accomplices to Hitler's atrocities against the Jews, adding that silence in such situations was tantamount to complicity. After reading this report, I am even more convinced that we in Britain are, for the most part, accomplices in the injustices suffered by black people here and that outside world opinion will condemn us for our appalling silence and our cold-hearted indifference to the racism that we harbour uncritically in our personal as well as national life...

Drawing on researched statistics, the writer shows that racism repeatedly goes unchecked and unchallenged as far as attitudes to the overwhelming majority of black people are concerned. When racism is exposed, as it is from time to time, white society prefers evasions, cover ups and excuses.

The 'cover ups' mentioned by Bishop Winter are the sweeping of nasty actualities, like colour discrimination, under a carpet of innocence. For instance, under the guise of 'doing their duty', some members of the British police force practise barefaced racism through a device known as the 'Sus charge'. Alternatively known as Section 4 of the 1824 Vagrancy Act, it was conceived to deal with the thousands of demobilised soldiers and sailors home from the Napoleonic wars. The end result was that huge numbers of able-bodied men roamed the country looking for work, often while starving. For Lord Liverpool's government this was a situation that called for drastic measures. Hence the Vagrancy Act, making it a criminal offence to be without a visible means of support. It also gave a police constable the power to arrest a person who the constable suspected of being *about to commit* a crime; along with the power to arrest a tramp, a reputed thief, an idle or disorderly person (known in law as rogues and vagabonds respectively), an incorrigible rogue and fortune tellers. In reality, it amounted to the arrest of anyone the constable did not like the look of. Which really meant that anybody who did not have a clearly defined position in British society, or no fixed address and no acceptable means of earning a living, was fair game. But the Vagrancy Act of 1824 was scarcely enforced because at that time there were literally no policemen. As a result, the fortune tellers and now unemployed ex-soldiers were not gravely harassed. For example, in the town of Oldham, Lancashire, with an 1820 population of 60,000, there was no resident magistrate and no effective force of law and order. Had there been people guilty of contravening the Vagrancy Act, they would have escaped detection and detention. There was nobody capable of effecting an arrest. In London, also, there were no police, but there were Bow Street Runners. They were nothing more than a bunch of thieves licensed by magistrates to carry on their trades, providing the magistrates received a percentage of their ill-gotten gains.

Two developments lessened the problem. Firstly, Britain's economic improvement at the end of the

1840s began reducing the number of unemployed and, secondly, Sir Robert Peel's creation of a police force, a disciplined body of uniformed constables who patrolled the streets. Prevention by presence had arrived.

But Britain's black community in the 1960s and 70s, with its increasing number of able-bodied unemployed, had fallen victim to the incredibly loosely defined power vested in the Vagrancy Act. An Act that is being used by many whites in police uniform as a stick to beat those who the white population has shown its dislike and fear of.

The prime minority white legal objection to the Vagrancy Act is that the evidence consists solely of the uncorroborated word of police officers who themselves must justify the arrests they have made. To grant an acquittal, the magistrate must say that they do not believe police evidence. Ignoring any bias that may exist on the part of the magistrate against the type of defendants concerned, disbelief of police evidence under this law rarely happens in practice. Thus, effectively the police can lay a charge on a person with near certainty of its success, relying solely on their own unsubstantiated evidence. No victim and no material evidence need be produced. In practice, no evidence is ever produced, apart from notebooks.

The prime objection of the black community to the Vagrancy Act comes in two stages. Firstly, the black community agrees with the minority legal objection. And secondly, in Britain's two-tiered society of black and white, where the interpretation of the law is two-faced, a law which gives *carte blanche* to white policemen who use white paranoia as a yardstick, invites itself to be misused in order to obtain an easy conviction. Politically, in the wake of the white racial insurgency against blacks, the Vagrancy Act, by its obvious misuse, is nothing other than an instrument of repression. Of all the youths charged under the Vagrancy Act in 1977, forty-two per cent were black. As all blacks in Britain (minus Asians) numbered under one million, out of a fifty-six million white population, forty-two percent is a high proportion of guaranteed success. So white dismissal of the cries of unfair treatment is another racial cover up.

But the largest white betrayal of all, being the most subtle, is openly practised in the run-up to a general election.

Election time, a time when issues are the currency of the language of politics. A time when the electorate is licensed to kill the government, and the issue is the provoking agent on which the government either retains power, or falls. The polling station, custodian of the nation's ability and right for peaceful change, is filled with voters on polling day, each carrying a holdall of national colics: inflation, unemployment, law and order, reduction of income tax, housing, education, health services, etc. And the prospective candidate, as a constituent instrument of the people's will, while promising change itself, will become the reason why an issue, locally or nationally, arises at the election.

Ever since the Commonwealth Immigrants Act was helped onto the statute books in 1962 by a phalanx of Aryan evangelists, The Issue for the ethnic minority at every general election since then has been immigration. Whole communities look on in horror as this issue is opportunistically manipulated by candidates seeking a white majority vote. At those elections, the polling booth holdalls carried by many white voters hold all that is uppermost in their minds; the fresh crop of racial resentment they carry as a guilty secret and, clinging to deep-rooted fears of racial impurity manipulated out at the dawn before *the* day by negrophobic sermonisers on the street and in the media, they dangerously intertwine their racial animosities with the privilege of the vote, and their guilty secret can finally be freed inside the covered-up secrecy of the polling booth where honesty, however dishonest, will prove their choice right or wrong for anything up to five years.

Nevertheless, it is a powerfully horrific feast for the eyes to witness so many of the so-called 'ethnic minorities' being bad mouthed and stamped upon, accompanied by the animosities of some of Britain's whites, for having come to Britain in search of anything. Those whites must sneer in the run-up period to a general election: after the black and Asian experience of centuries of white oppression in yesteryear's colonies, what did you black and Asian people expect to receive in the heart of racism itself? Or did you really believe that the cancer of injustice was only practised in your own countries by a white British minority? Did you believe that the long-drawn anguish of watching your people being crucified, physically and spiritually, would be ended on Britannia's soil?

After 1950, Britain's black and Asian white-house contract with convertible terms was given an extension clause. Traditionally, their life function had been to help Britain's whites achieve their obsessive deep-rooted ambitions in the West Indies, Africa and Asia. And that in-house duty had been to create a comfortable downy life in the sun for the colonial whites. It is true that Britain's colonial whites drew up the plans for technological advances – mostly to suit white purposes – but it is just as true that the physical and economically profitable side of Britannia's colonial enterprises was only achieved through the blood, sweat and tears of African and Asian labourers, who received a tenth of the rewards Britain's whites awarded themselves.

However, because of white Britain's post-war labour necessity, black people and Asians were still required to fulfil their traditional white-house duty, but now it was extended to help create a comfortable downy life for Britain's whites in Britain itself.

British attitudes have scarcely progressed since the following article appeared in volume 34 of *The Gentleman's Magazine* in 1764. At that time there existed

20,000 black servants out of a total London population of 676,250. And true to some white belief in the sub-humanity of black people, the inoculation of cattle was discussed in the same article. The article read:

> The practice of importing Negro servants into these Kingdoms is said to be already a grievance that requires a remedy, and yet it is everyday encouraged, insomuch that the number in this metropolis only, is supposed to be near 20,000; the main objection to their importation is, that they cease to consider themselves as slaves in this free country, nor will they put up with an inequality of treatment, nor more willingly perform the laborious offices of servitude than our own people, and if put to do it, are generally sullen, spiteful, treacherous, and revengeful. It is therefore highly impolitic to introduce them as servants here, where that rigour and severity is impracticable which is absolutely necessary to make them useful.
>
> The mortality among the horned cattle rages in *Saxony* to a terrible degree. Inoculation has been practised in other countries with success, and is recommended to the sufferers there as the most effectual means to prevent the loss of their herds.

The white 1764 opinion of how black people will not 'put up with an inequality of treatment, nor more willingly perform the laborious offices of servitude than our own people' is an opinion which, in 1981, as nearly every black and Asian woman, man and child knows, is subscribed to by the majority of Britain's whites. Furthermore, 'that they cease to consider themselves as slaves in this free country', is a fundamental Britannic Race Law. But few, if any, of Britain's black and Asian immigrants in the 1950s would have heard or read about the 1760s white opinion of black people. But they would soon know what that old opinion felt like in modern-day Britain.

The great white father needed BPE (black people's effort). And out went an ulcerated 'come and help' Pied Piper-type invitation. A sasine invitation *comme il faut*. Britain had discovered that her black peoples and Asians, having also helped her to win her wars, were multipurpose, and at this moment she considered that they could be very useful. In much the same way as the people of Hamelin town, when they cried for help to rid their town of an infestation of multicoloured rats, the Pied Piper answered. But what Britain's invited minorities had not taken into account, in a glorious moment of impetuosity, was that when they had achieved their Britannic mission they, like the Pied Piper, would have outlived their usefulness. Interestingly, the Pied Piper, with encouragement from Hamelin town council, left Hamelin town empty-handed. And the treacherous citizens of that town, much to their surprise, lost out as well.

Britain was advertised as a promised land through the circulations of postcards, brochures and posters of her more pleasant scenes. She had a plethora of schools and bustled with trade and commerce; there were scenes of London and its busy happy markets, its Mall, St James's Park and Trafalgar Square, crowded with a host of quaint two-storey buses called double-deckers; streets in a figurative sense were paved with gold. This all reinforced the ethnic's belief that living conditions, employment and educational opportunities in Britain were literally fantastic. Through all this visual feasting, many Britain-bound black and Asian travellers began to develop a mother-country world of fantasy, with the hope they saw in their much-trumpeted El Dorado, come-to-Britain invitations.

And together with the rest of the white Empire, they had sung the imperial anthem: Land of hope and glory, mother of the free. How shall we extol thee who art born of thee? The traditional white answer to that question for black people was: work, work and more work. But little did the hopeful blacks and Asians realise that their invitations carried with them a time-bomb, tick, tick, tick, slowly and inexorably ticking towards a racial crescendo, and more so towards the truth, which was: 'We don't want you to breed your children here, we really don't want you to settle here, but we won't say so at this moment because then you may not come

– Your Country Needs You'.

Necessity being the mother of invention, white necessity invented the *accidental blindness*, which prevented many of Britain's whites from seeing the racial, social and cultural threat they would suddenly see some years later. Superficially, the United Kingdom excreted a mirage of welcome. But in truth, she was a regurgitating Venus fly-trap, energised by underlying racial currents.

So into Britain came her new settlers, an assortment of people with their different magical hues, ignorant of the secret that they were really 'guest workers'. They came to feed her production lines, the ultimate hippodrome of inferiority in the testing ground of British class division; to feed her factories, fill her filthiest occupations and ultimately to be shot at like marbles from all sides of the ring. They had arrived to take their place on the arctic side of Britain's streets without complaint, to work as postmen, counter clerks, sorters, cleaners, messengers, porters, sweepers, on the buses as conductors and drivers, and on the railways. They worked for anyone who would employ them, and for wages so low that even those whites who considered themselves from the wrong side of the tracks refused to win the indignity of accepting wages accepted by blacks and Asians. By their very presence in Britain they had unknowingly elevated people whom the white upper and middle classes had always considered, by birth and by treatment, along with their perpetual acceptance of that negative treatment, to be the white niggers of Britain. They accepted treatment which had hitherto been reserved for the 'lowest' whites, and the workplace, the schools, the streets, working-men's and other clubs and their houses were turned into an arena, a racial testing ground. This drives one to ask, does the moral life of Britain incorporate any truth? Or is Britain's truth the following passage, gleaned from the inviting pages of *Going to Britain?*, published by the British Broadcasting Corporation for West Indians en route to the United Kingdom in the 1950s:

### Making Friends

Going to church is not likely to help you find a better room to live or a job. The people may have much the same problems as yourself and in any case they do not attend church to find someone they can help. Their presence in church, like yours, is no evidence of sainthood. If they smile with you in church and look away from your direction in the bus, it is just one of those things and you are free to do the same.

However, the friend you make at church will tend to be more sincere than those made – say at the pub, for instance, or dance hall. People will grow to respect you a little more if they see you often in the church. Sometimes they decide to give you credit for being truly converted, and then they expect big things from you simply because they may have it in their heads that coloured people are heathens who break the hearts of saintly missionaries who try to convert them.

But whatever people think, the church remains a good place to go. You may find friends there – you almost certainly will – but, if you don't, you can get there a truer picture of what you are really up against.

But there is another aspect of British truth which can be seen in the following passages from the same booklet, which encourage the then immigrant settlers to accept white antagonism:

**You are the Stranger**
However, your greater problem will be getting on with your white neighbours. One thing you must always keep in mind, is that their knowledge of your country is much less than your knowledge of theirs. Whenever you are inclined to get angry or fly off the handle at some remark – or because that person stares at you for a long time – remember that English people are ignorant of your ways and habits, and they may be just displaying a natural curiosity. There are some parts of England where the sight of a coloured

man is still an uncommon thing, and there are people who may never have seen a person like you before...

## No Offence Meant

Don't take offence at things like these. If, in the house you live, you see one or two of them whispering and pointing to you, it may well be that they are wondering why you wear your hat with the brim turned up all around, for instance, it doesn't have to mean that they are making fun of you. And where you find a healthy curiosity, it will pay you to go out of your way to explain things to them. You may be surprised at some of the questions they may ask you, and you might feel they are insulting you on the sly, but it is only their ignorance of you and your country.

## Politeness the Key

... They don't stand on the doorstep gossiping, or form a crowd on the pavement to talk about the latest ballad. I notice some West Indians still have that habit and I can tell you it isn't one that English people like. What they like is politeness.

In those passages from the BBC's introduction to Britain lies an obvious – to whites only – respect for the intelligence of Britain's black settlers. That *is* the truth, along with that other forgotten truth which was proven during Britain's slave trade, and again inside her colonies, and which was, with the influx of Britain's black and Asian settlers, about to be proved again. That is the internationally recognised assertion that everyone has rights which include responsibilities. But what blacks and Asians, side by side with their white allies, have long held to be universally axiomatic, is that in a world dominated by white power structures, it is the whites who have the rights, while everyone else bears the responsibilities for white actions. It is clear from the quoted passages from *Going to Britain?* that black people *were again asked* to bear the responsibility for white behaviour.

Consequently, it was not long before the Chapeltowns, the Bradfords, the Handsworths, the Smethwicks, the Southalls, the Notting Hills and the Brixtons[8] of Britain became synonymous with black or Asian. It took even less time for many white *tourists* to see into those places and pronounce them to be third-rate, places where failures lived. And it took only a glance to see that everywhere else sported 'Coloureds Need Not Apply' signs. A few did apply without success, but most gave up. You could see the 'No Coloureds' notices everywhere, for jobs, flats, bedsits and many hotels. There were many places which avoided advertising their racial hang-ups, and thus had no notices. They allowed a black person to enter,

---

[8] Areas of significant non-white populations.

but the glacial temperature of the atmosphere warned them to go elsewhere. Black people kept to themselves as did the Asians. Consequently, Britain's inner-city police forces, encouraged and strengthened by white race-conscious fellow travellers, did not immediately discover that it is virtually impossible to effectively police an antagonised and therefore antagonistic black society made secret by white racism. Where should they start? Obviously somewhere easy. On the streets? Is that why there has been a plethora of young black 'Sus' arrests under the Vagrancy Act of 1824?

In the 1950s, there were few whites who knew or could even hazard a guess as to what the ethnic minority did after leaving work. Of course, out of sight was out of mind. What whites did not see, if it happened to blacks, did not happen at all. Moreover, what all blacks and all Asians had in common, as per their lot, was to live inside white men's generalisations; simply because according to those generalisations, they were a stagnant people, brainless and changeless. Anything could and did happen to those types of people.

You could see black and brown men and women, some of whom were highly qualified, with university degrees, working on the underground and buses, cleaning faeces off hospital beds and floors, and, as I did, feeding J. Lyons kitchens with their labour. Sure, white people did those jobs as well, but at that time that is all black and Asian people ever did.

Amid the moral pollution that insufficiency

sponsors, you could perceive these settlers constantly seeking ways out of their overcrowded, damp and often dank and lightless abodes. Occasionally somewhere was found, usually a mirage where there were no NO COLOUREDS notices in evidence, but the price for these scarce 'glad pads' for black and Asian peoples was a doubled rent.

The moral crucifixion of black and Asian people began the day they landed on British soil. Those were the days when white men behaved (though many still do) as if they, individually, had had a hand in admitting them into Britain. The new settlers, in return, were supposed to behave gratefully to each and every white man. Therefore, each new settler started life in Britain three steps behind a white. One, he was not white. Two, he had to be grateful for being here. And three, he had to be grateful to each white individual for having allowed him in, so he must say wonderful things about Britain to justify his entry and his presence in Britain. The gospel of hundreds of thousands of great white fathers was refurbished. Advice usually given to their English-rose-complexioned, slender and sensitive daughters when travelling abroad was changed from 'Beware of Men in the Tropics' to 'Beware of Tropical Men'.

A generation grew up watching the humiliation and degradation heaped onto the heads of their parents, which they accepted with little complaint to white authority. Who could they complain to, and who would listen? It was also a time when other blacks turned away in shame if another black fell into an argument with a white. It was an era when to become involved in that argument might result in those whites who had a grudge against life, pointing accusingly with what became their standard black put-down, 'You have a chip on your shoulder', even though they seemed to be the only ones who could see it. It was a moment when the best way to avoid that accusation, even though it was meaningless, was to admit white right with black silence. Therefore, any black who defended him or herself was automatically labelled a trouble-maker.

So a generation grew up knowing full well that what was happening to them was morally, spiritually, politically and humanly wrong. Their parents' apparent crime was that they did not *en masse* protest hard enough. But maybe they had other things on their minds, like being grateful, making a living for their families and creating opportunities for their children, plus *knowing* that they would never rise above the street.

For a moment, black and Asian people lived in Britain inside their white stereotype in order to lessen the racist pressure on their skulls. For a moment, their silence, through continuous white dismissals of their many grievances, was deafening. For another moment, Britain's whites, in a racial sense, had never had it so good through having it all their own way. They had, temporarily, succeeded in relegating blacks and Asians to Meanwhile Alley.

Meanwhile, Mayfair and the more salubrious areas of London and other cities and all the places where the ethnics were never seen, were (and still are) the white man's gilded paradise. Whereas the Southalls and Brixtons of Britain were the blacks' and browns' exotically depressing shanty towns. Seen through white eyes, they were (and still are) human zoos on a grand scale, filled with prehistoric relics and, being out on a limb, they became the stamping grounds of otherwise unemployable white sociologists; along with racially-opportunistic bored middle-class whites who drove down to these zoos for their 'good times' while playing with and observing the ways of the relics. There were Oxbridge 'Leakeys' brushing up on their zoological studies being towed along by snappily-dressed musical burglars who plundered black rhythm by ear; accompanied by an advance guard of rebelling Hooray Henrys tearing down the beaten track just to try it black or brown; closely followed up by God's servants relieving their guilt by trying to clear up the Britannic mess. They were all prancing across the foreign but British L.S. Lowry tenement-scape, mouthing anachronisms: 'You people are such good dancers, and we bet you're good in bed. We bet you're good at running, but you don't have much in your heads.' It was, I suppose, the black and brown inauguration into the cultivated life of Britain.

None the less, these 'zoos' were seen by whites as the lands of darkness. As far as blacks were concerned, they were places where whites' conjured-up-and-conditioned ideas of black people happened. Where they spent all day sleeping and eating smelly food, all night partying, revelling, and leaping on loose white women while making their living trafficking in drugs. According to that charitable mentality, the Asians were just as guilty by keeping themselves to themselves: 'Goodness knows what they get up to without us'. A reflection of the white state of mind?

These things, somewhere at some time, may have happened, as surely as they could also happen, and probably did, inside white society. What is much more likely to be closer to the truth is that other things happened as well. Like work, like ignoring white racist attacks, like aspiring, like creating for themselves a stable community where their children could use the few opportunities their parents were giving them, like disregarding KBW (Keep Britain White), Wogs Out, Niggers Go Home and other racist graffiti. Like chasing illusive jobs by residing at the Labour Exchange; like trying to find better accommodation, or just finding accommodation; like contributing to Britain's economy and hence its society. It was that kind of activity black and Asian people were involved in and which white society did its best to disregard. For those whites, black effort did not exist. But with the obvious and often blatant animosity toward the black and Asian newcomers, the burning question was: had white Britain finally lost her innocence of racism?

She had lost it, brutally, several centuries ago, but with the presence of black and brown aliens on her much-coveted sceptred shores and pleasant pastures, she was *now* beginning to notice. And it hurt.

Britain hurt too. Walking through the crumbling ghettos where despair and dejection hung about in groups on lonely sidewalks, you could see them treading water in the shadows on the beat each night. These streets were full of hunters and the haunted. And the hot jazz of high-powered discrimination blew loud and clear into a growing mountain of determination, emitting the soul chorus, 'Keep the faith, baby'. Some would, some wouldn't. While the in-betweens just mouthed disbelief at the audaciousness and blatancy of white Britain's racial nepotism. I am making the scene. This is the main drag of many tears. This is Brixton. This is Southall. This is Chapeltown. This is Handsworth. This is Powis Square. This is Babylon. This is anywhere. And the ruling whites are somewhere else. Lost in Britannic pride.

Hope in white Britain for blacks and Asians was, and still is, a frail and delicious ordeal. Whereas hope, the black and brown sense in the 1950s and 1960s, was summed up on the lips of nearly every black and Asian human being with the words, 'When I Go Back Home'. They had yet to realise that their British-born children (a parent's hope) might one day ask the shock questions, 'Where is home?' and 'Where is *our* hope?' and 'What is hope?'. But those same children soon realised that life in Britain for them would be a long disenchantment, through the heavy news that being black or brown (or old, mentally handicapped or poor, or...) in Britain, is a crime.

Racism is moral in a racist country. At the very least, Britain's new settlers refused to accept that Britannic truth. For if you cannot refuse, you cannot control your past, present or future. Making us cognisant of the fact that blacks and Asians living in Britain have always lived, and continue to live, inside a white fabrication of reality; even though the spaces in between their facts is the reality of their senses. An intrinsic truth few white men will ever know or understand.

The facts on each of us are the details which other people might read about us, usually from the files or media reports. But reality is You, and the world will never really know or understand how you experience experience. Human experience is the pain, love, lust and happiness of human existence. And only You will ever really know what it smells like, looks like, tastes like, sounds like and feels like. My reality is politically, morally, spiritually, humanly and realistically black. And so are the others, who grasped that in being considered Britain's social liabilities by her whites, their colour-talk blew out the afterglow of previous optimism in Britain with, 'Look here sisters and brothers, we have a white problem over here'.

It is almost impossible to be an individual in any country. But when the victimising civilisation of

Britain is determined, in almost every way, to stop you from being somebody, that kind of mistake can be measured in terms of human misery. What happens then? Things get shattered into another plane, and so do people.

By 1958, black people had grown tired of being kicked in the face for being black. They reacted by fighting back and a minor race battle, known here as the Notting Hill *riots* [*sic*], blew the white breeze of racial resentment into a black storm of anger.

*Daily Mirror* columnist Keith Waterhouse, on 8 September 1958, had *the* answer and wrote:

> **Who – or what – is behind the race riots?**
> IGNORANCE is the real villain. Ignorance of how people live. Ignorance of their aims and their ambitions. Ignorance of what they are actually doing. Ignorance breeds fear. Fear breeds violence. The enemy of fear is FACT...
> ... Today – meet the West Africans ...
> WHO ARE THEY? GHANA – known until recently as the Gold Coast – is an independent country, equal in the Commonwealth with Australia, Canada and New Zealand. It has its own Prime Minister and its own Parliament.

That then is a white definition of being civilised. What makes those blacks *not* savages, in this case, is the possession of a form of government recognisable, by virtue of its Westminster similarity, to whites. It is that simple. Or is it? What happens when the facts do not tally (they never do) with the white-preferred traditional fiction of black and Asian people? The history of the oppression of blacks and Asians by whites continues.

It is tantalising to say that the 1958 Notting Hill *fracas* was straightforwardly due to white ignorance of black people. That the black Kelso Cochrane was slain because the white who dusted his life away did so because he was ignorant of how Kelso lived, ignorant of his ambitions and ignorant of the fact that he was a human being. Or did his black colour disguise his humanity to his white assailant, who accidentally thought that he was butchering a subhuman species? Had he not, somewhere at sometime, read or heard of how many other British whites had also decided centuries ago that wasting away black and Asian lives without retribution was acceptable to the white-erected system in Britain's colonial territories? Had he not watched his fellow whites' lack of interest that greeted the news of any slaying of a black by a white, even on Britain's streets?

What Keith Waterhouse – along with those other cliché-riding media men who perpetually use public ignorance as an excuse for unpalatable and unexplainable (by them) situations – forgot to mention, was that white ignorance of black and Asian facts is a white way of life and has always been so. The facts, even when *known* to whites generally, are not merely dismissed, but are genetically forgotten. They *really* forget.

Consequently, there exists in Britain no real majority white interest in knowing the facts about black and Asian people. Thus the basis of Keith Waterhouse's identification of ignorance as the cause of the 1958 Notting Hill *riots* is ignorance. His own, along with the others. Equality for the ethnic minority was a long time coming, but the reaction of Britain's whites to blacks who stood up for themselves against racism was not.

The answer to the ethnic presence in Britain, to the white fear of that presence, the answer to blacks who complained when they had no right to, the answer to the black refusal to accept their negative white definition, the answer to black questions as to why they should accept second-best, in everything, why they should be overjoyed to see 'Coloureds Need Not Apply' notices, why they should be grateful, why they must accept the blame for Britain's economic, housing and unemployment problems, the answer to Notting Hill 1958, the answer to white ignorance through fear was the answer to racism. The answer was to *legitimise racism*.

The field was still in play, the referee blew his whistle and the rules were changed. The 1962 Commonwealth Immigrants Act was spawned and qualifications were required of black and Asian people to enter the Britannic Kingdom of Heaven. Up on Lavender Hill, the day the Act was passed, a white man of octogenarian years with kindly eyes looked at me while I was reading a 'NO COLOUREDS' advert, noticed the anger splattered across my face and said: 'If you are shooting at us in twenty years' time, it will be because we put the gun in your hand today.'

# 4. On the Brink

Yes, God does move in a mysterious way, and He has left many people confused. For what is freedom's price in this ugly experience?

Britannia has a rigid caste system, where the *right-birth* people, by virtue of their birthright, stay at the top through fair means or foul. And the working-class masses, the leftovers, have been, over the centuries, buffeted and pummelled into dough to await orders from above, the star commandment being, 'promise you won't do anything rash, like demanding your rights'. *Ad infinitum*. Into this social conspiracy, with Establishment backing and crawling with clues, the middle-class mass-market media evaporates the best verbal gun-bearers through a system of reward or punishment, leaving the working classes without the incentive to rebel and leaderless. In Britain, moral standards fell ages ago, when there was a greater need – the profit motive – a greater competition; and the pulverised masses became the cheated debris of industrialised society. But truth, in its plain wrappings, became a delicate suffering, a modern-day luxury the ruling class could never afford; in dread, now, of granting anything for fear of losing everything, for fear of losing control. *Carpe diem*. They had practised a different form of democracy, alien to the theories of its Greek creators. Yes, the workers travelled on complacently, sabotaged by their own docility; enviously frustrated by the cakes-of-opportunity for the upper classes; highlighted in the present-day working-class conversational anathema and Britain's social separator: the public school for the privileged, private schools for the pretentious, standing an experience away from the comprehensive, comprehensively undereducating. Until a collection of black and brown Freedom Riders arrived. The working classes ascended a step closer to the middle classes. They were 'allowed' to, as a reward for continuing to 'see' *reason*, as a body politic, in their unreasonable lowly position. These Freedom Riders cultured in at the now vacant position, the bottom. The Britannic multiracial body politic was complete, with its ethnic, and potentially energetic, political scapegoats. Immediately, the counterfeit rumour, with *bona fides* attached, was sent abroad by upper and middle classes announcing that, 'the class system has broken down; there is no such thing, no such animal called class, alive in Britain today'. Some believed it, some didn't. Some, through apathetic insularity, did not care. *The* grand Britannic fantasy; for in naked class terms, due to the titanium-like rigidity of the British class structure, the past is the same as the present and presently will be the future.

A variety of exotic Freedom Riders perceived a Britannic factory-class triumvirate over them, each layer supportive of and dependent on the other. And those foreign bodies could see the differences, the lines of social division between the haves, the have-nots and the never-will-haves, who *now* have a grudge against life, a grudge against everything, a grudge against foreign bodies, who *all* whites tagged with one negative label after another, ending with, care of Scotland Yard's Labelling Department, 'Muggers'. There were lies and counter-lies and a geometric progression of exaggerations. The black and Asian peoples were given 'walking papers' in the form of forced and then voluntary repatriation, with much love from the management and staff of a depreciating Great Britain. Hey fellas, we've arrived. Or have we? Or are the foreign bodies half a stretch away from a new and more venomous insurgency?

White people said, 'you have no grievances'. Bristol 1980 said, 'we have'. White people said, 'Bristol was an isolated incident'. Brixton 1981 said, 'it wasn't'. White people said, 'you have no just causes'. Petrol bombs that burned alive entire Asian families, Asian youths stabbed to death in British streets and the New Cross Fire

Massacre 1981,[9] proved they did. White people said, '*you* have nothing to worry about'. Southall 1981 said, '*we* do'. The Great British Establishment (GBE) said, 'it's all the fault of the blacks'. Liverpool 1981 proved that class was involved. The GBE said, 'extremists have damaged race relations in Britain'. What relations? Or is what we have in Britain today what most people consider relationships should be like? I ask again. What *is* freedom's price in this ugly experience? It's the well-being of our children, the well-being of our sanity, the well-being of our next generation, the well-being of ourselves. Or is it?

In June 1977, I wrote an article for *New Society* about the well-being of our society and ourselves. Under the section 'Society at Work', *New Society* headlined it, 'It couldn't happen here'. It stated:

Since this time last year, when massive police presence elevated the Notting Hill street festival/brawl into the status of a riot, tensions in London and the United Kingdom seem to have relaxed. The black *revolution*, on the surface, has relapsed into its traditional, characteristic inactivity. The over-enthusiastic tribes have been put down. Jolly good show. What threatened to become a disruption, appears once again to be manageable as a problem. Praise be de Lawd.

---

[9] During a party in New Cross, a blaze occurred in the early hours of 18 January 1981, killing 13 young black people aged between 14 and 22 years.

Of course, the dark mutterings of discontent go on: racism, oppression, lack of opportunity, bad housing and so on and so on. These institutionalised grumblings have become a necessary part of normal life. And that other part of normal life, the painful and bloody saga of Northern Ireland, continues.

A logical development of the increasing violence and bitterness of the Anglo/Irish fracas is the emergence and daily reinforcement of no go areas. This is not confined to Ireland. It happens here (and has been happening for some time) in areas of black/white aggression, Brixton and Southall for instance.

It is often said that the racial problems of America could never happen here. A statement based more on English optimism than political honesty. For example, Brixton, Harlesden, Willesden, Southall, Brick Lane E1, Kensal Rise and so on are London's Harlems. What could not happen is already here. Considering the many difficulties of the black and Asian minorities, it should be no surprise if the same attitudes emerge as are already apparent in the Irish militants.

Events show that there are two types of no go areas, with a third 'hospitably' advocated by the CRC. The first is where the whites cannot go, such as clubs and illegal shebeens. In the second, entry is not restricted – but nor is hostility. The third, which could be a potential no go, is the recommendation by the CRC that local authorities should 'encourage the growth' of all-black communities on council estates. But how are council bureaucrats, many of whom are distrusted by minorities, supposed to encourage? A Brixton shopkeeper from Guyana, John Mansfield, compared it with the Bantustans or homelands scheme of South Africa. 'Blacks,' he feels, could be 'placed on the worst estates' and most significantly 'we would be surrounded'. This apparent fear is a real one amongst many blacks.

There are incidents which those professing to be racially alert must recognise as undeniable forecasts. For example, Alan Fenton, a social worker, walked into a dimly lit black hang-out, off the Westbourne Park Road in West London. Instantly, about 30 pairs of eyes followed him – Britain's lone white pioneer. 'Waddyah want?' shouted someone aggressively. 'To have a drink.' Three blacks moved up to him. 'Sorry boy,' said one, 'members only.' They had his arms, steering him towards the door.

'How do I get membership?' Fenton asked hurriedly. 'When you join.' The door flicked open. They let him go. He turned slowly (here, that's how a white has to move) to a blockade of hate. 'Who do I apply to?' Expectations in the room were high. 'You can't.' And not realising he was addressing an audience very touchy about put-downs, 'Well, how can I join when I can't apply?' He thought he had them. 'That's your problem, man.' He was forced out.

Amazingly, seconds later, he reappeared with two friends. 'Look,' he began, 'let's be reasonable...' He was cut off. Liberal reason is a commodity in short supply. Immediately, four other blacks joined the original three. Two with knives, one armed with a possession now common amongst some black militants – a small pistol. 'The talk is over.' With that, Fenton was kneed in the balls, falling out ... It was over in seconds. His friends hadn't moved since they entered. They left, backing out. This is, without a doubt, a no go area for whites. Here, if your colour's not in – you're out.

Among young blacks and Asians there is a growing number whose attitude towards the whites is not hardening, but has already hardened. After the recent slaying of a youth in Southall, Asians, often considered to be passive, changed. Today, vigilante groups operate in a well-organised grapevine in many Asian communities. Now they retaliate if provoked. For instance, six weeks ago, a defence force was created in Brick Lane E1 because of persistent aggro from the National Front.

In Brixton, the artery of the black community, pioneer streets have fallen into even more squalor. As unemployment increases, slums spread. And grievances fester. Here, below the slowly cohering top layer of blacks (traders in Brixton market), poor blacks wait, sporadically employed and disgruntled. They pass the time on street corners, talking, drinking, smoking and listening to countless funky records. Day in, day out. Their discontent growing in the sunshine and storm of racial politics. Their attitude to whites not hardening – but hardened. In parts, certainly along Railton Road SE24, the atmosphere is permeated with simmering tensions.

Anything can, and does, happen. Some of this tension expressed itself in a fight I saw between blacks when a scuffle broke out over a spilled drink. Two protagonists emerged, one with an iron pipe, the other with an empty Coke bottle. The jagged neck remained. It happened fast, against a background of shouting and jeering. They are pulled apart.

An old Jamaican at my table said these youths have 'studied different'. 'They're as disunited as we are, but more definitely against whites...' continuing, 'very few of them would go up to a white' and, significantly, '...that counts for their unity...' A unity against whites.

The quarter mile between Desmond's Hip City record shop and Mecca Bookmakers has seen and continues to see, bitter conflicts between police and blacks. It is not surprising that this section is known locally as 'the front line'. The activity denoted by that name speaks for itself. Now that firearms are obtainable by some black militants (who are admittedly a minority at present), the ingredients of big trouble are here. I've seen it. I'm black. If I'd been white, I might not have done so.

But white Britain has consistently persuaded itself that black and Asian people will permanently put up with oppression. In a society subscribing to the Utopian ideal of freedom of speech (which suggests freedom of thought), black criticism is tolerated as long as there is no action. And what of black and Asian warnings of dire consequences, like, 'it could happen here'? 'Poppycock, that coon was probably writing with his foot', or 'I do think you're being a little oversensitive'. The dismissive tactics come into play: people see it, they rationalise it, they walk away from it and then refute it. Was it ever written or said at all?

In March 1980, in St Paul's, Bristol, the unrealistic statement 'it couldn't happen here' was shattered. The disturbances were due to an oppressive white society which had decided that its short-term vision of life was truth, for everybody. But through a white-accepted participation of racism in the British practice of a warped democracy, a sophisticated form of *apartheid* has developed, promoting the leading question, what is life like for black and Asian people living in Britain today? In October 1976, in the *New Statesman* I wrote an article under the title, 'Dagenham's Way with Colour'. The article stated:

> Henry Ford, founder of the Ford empire and innovator of mass production, has always been considered a man ahead of his time. Certainly his dictum about the original Model T – 'You can have any colour you want, so long as it's black' – seems to apply equally well today at Ford's Dagenham Estate. Except an onlooker there might easily think he had meant, in fact, people and not cars.
>
> Of Dagenham's 23,000 workers, 60 per cent are black or Asian. In the body plant, 70 per cent of 6,000 workers are black or Asian, and in the PTA (Paint, Trim and Assembly) section the figure is 60 per cent of 5,000. However, of 1,200 foremen, only six

are black and the figures for shop stewards are barely more impressive: ten out of 300. These numbers speak for themselves; blacks form the majority of the workforce, but they are thinly represented when it comes to trade union or staff appointments. According to Sid Harraway, boss of the shop stewards' committee: 'You'd be right in thinking that the ratio is all wrong.' Ford-worker Herman Pinnock commented: 'We have very few of everything black, except for non-skilled production workers.'

With varying degrees of justification, black and Asian workers believe management to be racially prejudiced. It has been assumed that trade unions were not. Yet, most remarkably, Dagenham has never seen the promotion of a black man from shop steward to convener or district level official. Is it lace-curtain discrimination that inhibits blacks from attempting to climb the ladder? If so, is the discrimination at management level, or is it within the unions themselves? Or a combination of both? According to one black worker: 'Some of us have applied many times, but without success. Now many have developed a segregation mentality.'

The existence of veiled discrimination might go some way towards explaining why Bill Morris is the only black full-time official of the TGWU. And possibly it could explain, too, why Britain's largest union, with 1.7 million members (of whom 287,000 are women), has only one female official at the national level. She is Marie Patterson, and despite her token-female loneliness, Ron Todd, secretary of TGWU's Region 1, maintains: 'It is not a male preserve. Other than Ms Patterson, a woman has not yet emerged as the best person.' His stand on the other question is as adamant. He maintains that no racism exists in his organisation, and if he discovered a racist shop steward he would dump him 'because I don't think it's compatible with being a union representative'.

But there is still a curious lack of black stewards and officials, and Mr Todd could not deny that the few there hardly make for a racially integrated union movement. According, however, to a Ford official 'they don't have what it takes'. What does 'it' take? After a week at Dagenham you really begin to understand the cynicism of automobile workers, but the magical 'it' never becomes apparent. New workers are given a talk by a shop steward, and also by safety and personnel officers. Then, training: 'A *great* training programme,' as one of them said, 'two days, I think. You don't have to be full of "O" levels to work here.' Once trained, it's on the line. 'Hello,' says Bill. 'You put this here, so. And put that there, got it?' Then, mysteriously, as if it were all in the nature of a favour: 'I'm not paid for this, y'know.' A new worker either picks up the routine, or picks up his cards.

Real arguments or racial resentments are not aired on the factory floor. 'Those fights,' one worker says, 'happen outside the gates or in the pubs. But the tension is there most of the time.' 'The whole history of endeavouring to prove discrimination,' says Sid Harraway, 'is very difficult.' One Ford worker who might agree with this is Olatunji Taylor who, in 1971, applied for the post of trainee foreman. 'At the present time there are no vacancies,' he was told by the personnel officer, Mr Rossiter. But 'your application will receive consideration'.

Between 1971 and 1973 Taylor applied several more times with no tangible results, except that he was advised to re-apply in 1976. Feeling he was being discriminated against, Mr Taylor took his case to the Race Relations Board. Thirteen months, 16 letters, and four changes of Board Officials later he was told that 'no unlawful discrimination had taken place'. (My own enquiries at the Race

Relations Board produced the reply: 'We are not allowed to discuss any case which has not already received publicity.' A nice little catch-22 phrase, but small comfort to Mr Taylor.)

Doggedly, Taylor applied yet again in May 1976. In an interview with Mr Rossiter he was told that he was an unsuitable candidate because he hadn't the personality required, nor the ability to lead. Curiously, though, Rossiter suggested he apply again in 12 months. He was, in the meantime, to 'reassess yourself and your attitudes'. When asked to enlarge on this somewhat arcane advice Mr Rossiter told me over the phone that he did not wish to make any comment at this stage. Nonetheless, he did so. Taylor, he said, 'fell down in various respects' and 'does not meet the requirements'. It was stressed that Taylor could always apply again. This is all very well, but 45 is the age limit for foreman training, and as Taylor is now 41 he does not have many chances left.

What has Mr Taylor's union done about his case? Shop steward Alex French, who had initially helped Mr Taylor, was told by Ford that 'the union was not allowed to be party to any discussions on the appointment of foreman; it is a management function only'. This is apparently true, and it may be here that the union has surrendered some of its power to protect its members' rights. There is, of course, a recognised grievance procedure which can be invoked in cases of racial discrimination within a union. However, the process for registering and following through a complaint is very complex and would require a high degree of patience, courage and persistence for any grievance to be remedied. Among black and Asian workers, already handicapped by language and sophistication barriers, there exists, too, a fear of losing their jobs if they become known as trouble-makers. For these reasons, complaints such as Mr Taylor's tend not to filter up to union leaders, who, therefore, continue blithely to assume there is little trouble of a racial nature among their members.

According to a PEP survey, racial problems in the trade unions fall into two groups. In the first, the local union tolerates discrimination rather than acting to counter it. In the second, the union is not directly involved in discriminatory practices but such practices have, nonetheless, been allowed to develop. It is possible that Olatunji Taylor's case falls within this second group. Either way black workers are the casualties.

David Buckle, district officer of the TGWU based at British Leyland's Cowley plant, feels the most dangerous is for those in the trades union movement to 'kid ourselves that there is *not* discrimination in our unions'. Most significantly he says: 'What is going on in our society is going on in the trade union movement. It simply reflects the kind of society we've got.' The reflection is unfortunately, an unflattering one. If Olatunji Taylor's case is representative of black workers there is a very real risk that, discouraged by the failure of their attempts to gain promotion, they will become another unleavened lump of discontent in British industry.

How long before Britain sees and has to suffer a black workers' reaction to their second-rate position? It is on the cards, for the longest road has an end.

Today, in white immigrant-minded Britain, racism is impregnated powerfully into the white struggle against ethnic human rights and into the mind of the ethnic body politic through a successive series of undermining immigration controls, thus keeping the black and Asian whipping-boys 'mobile-minded': 'We don't want you coons to settle, you might think it's permanent – this is *not* your country'. A Britannic Reversal. Maybe the sun never really set on the British Empire, because God does not trust the Brits in the dark. Who does?

In Britain, racism is a highly inflammable issue, and

is the foundation of her system of justice, her criminal law, and the current white prejudices and negative attitudes towards black and Asian people. Immigration, quickly followed by other related issues, was the first fundamental white assault on the ethnic community. Immigration also prevented political unification of the so-called immigrants by diverting their attentions; and the immigrating statutory instruments surrounding the ethnic community, designed specifically for *them* by government of both political colours, completed the white immigration gang warfare.

In *Now You Do Know*, author John Downing, writing about immigration, stated:

When the 1971 Act cancelled the previous right of black Commonwealth members to citizenship after five years' residence in Britain, it created a situation where any black person walking the streets might be a post-1971 Act entrant. White immigrants did not stand out as much; black people wore no tag or lapel-button to indicate the date of their entry to Britain. Since the Act also gave the police the right to stop and search people in the street, or break into private premises without a warrant, if they had 'reasonable grounds' to suspect the presence of illegal immigrants, the police had carte blanche to harass black people on this pretext...

At airports as well, black people are regularly subjected to vaginal or anal examinations by immigration officials under pretext of a search for drugs, or checking for diseases, or at one time – until protests cancelled this excuse – to satisfy the officer that the woman was a virgin. It must be stressed that this loathsome behaviour, though congruent with the National Front and Powellite sympathies of many immigration officials, is perfectly legal under the 1971 Act.

Other practices include abusive questioning, separating parents and children and grilling them separately on details of their application form for entry; and a readiness to interpret the slightest such deviation, or the most marginal indication of a willingness to work during a holiday trip, as evidence of duplicity, and therefore a reason to refuse admission. In their time, British immigration officials have preferred to shuttle destitute British citizens of Asian descent around the world's airlines for weeks at a time rather than let them in.

Those who have been refused entry but who succeed in registering a rapid appeal against refusal, are kept in special detention centres, Harmondsworth near Heathrow airport being the best known. Conditions in these centres are pointlessly harsh, with inmates not allowed to rest on their beds during the day, with great difficulty of access for relatives, with inappropriate food, one telephone, and an extremely unpleasant attitude on the part of the Securicor guards. (The use of private police for public purposes is a dimension of contemporary policing not covered in II.d; that it should begin with black people is typical of the process.) The objective is clear: to grind in the message that black people are not wanted in Britain (Moore and Wallace 1975). The message is intended to spread out from those treated in this way, to as wide an audience as possible, nationally and internationally. State policy and immigration officials' attitudes are at one with each other. This hostile treatment arises because those who apply for immigration control work are given the necessary scope by the immigration rules to act out their prejudices.

In times like these, of social crisis springing from the racial hailstorm beating down on ethnic skulls, it is easy to be hoodwinked by the strength and depth of white racist attacks, and by the white mania for tribal security. It is easy to mistake eventual time-bound occurrences for never-ending reality. But the potency and unchangeability of the white kick-back is deceptive. Although this offensive engagement appears to have unflagging power, the necessary political ideas, however, are very much in the hands of those whites who have unfettered themselves from the myopia of Empire mentality, and those whites, blacks and Asians who have unshackled themselves from the lord/serf mentality.

However, there are other unhealthy stirrings on the national front. 'A great philosophy,' says Charles Péguy, 'is not one that passes final judgements and establishes ultimate truth. It is one that causes uneasiness and starts commotion.' Péguy has a point, and the 'uneasiness' and 'commotion' he speaks of, in this instance, is the British Nationality Bill 1981. It is a bill which suggests that Britain entered the race conflict by accident and now intends to exit by design. This political instrument, supposedly intended to streamline the rules and regulations about what constitutes a British citizen, is seen by its proponents as the white man's oasis in a racial desert of despair. In February 1981, *The Sunday Times* wrote:

> The new law will introduce three tiers of citizenship – British citizenship, British overseas citizenship, and citizenship of the British dependent territories. Only the first of these confers the normal full citizenship rights. Being born in Britain will no longer be enough to claim full citizenship on. Babies born abroad to parents themselves

born abroad, even if they are British will not automatically be deemed fully British.

The final decision rests on the Home Office 'discretion' and this could apply to millions of cases. Passport offices will demand evidence about parents' birth as well as the applicants. The new law will also tangle inextricably with the various Immigration Acts (1962, 1968 and 1971).

Both the Labour and Liberal parties have declared the Bill to be racist and it is expected to take a long time going through the committee stage.

A briefing published by the Action Group on Immigration and Nationality in October 1980 stated:

It is never easy for a country to re-define its nationality, but it has often been done. Problems little different from, or harder than, ours have been dealt with by nations which used to have larger overseas empires, such as France, Portugal and the Netherlands. France, for example, has a single nationality which carries the same rights for all holders and is held by people in the Overseas Departments (Martinique, Guadeloupe, Réunion) equally with people in metropolitan France. French citizens in all these territories can move freely in and out of them all: a black French citizen from Martinique can enter France freely and work there; a white French citizen can enter and work in Martinique; both can vote for the French Assembly and both have freedom-of-movement rights in the EEC. But former French possessions which have become independent countries have completely separate nationalities of their own, with no citizens' rights in France (e.g. Algeria, Chad).

The other colonial powers used to have different classes of citizenship, with different rights from each other, but since 1945 they have moved towards defining a single, clear nationality. The United Kingdom is going in exactly the opposite direction: it used to have one category for the whole Empire, but is now moving towards a ranking of superior and inferior classes, as though legislating for an empire that is now only a ghost.

It's that Empire mentality again. The international uproar over the white immigrants in South Africa and their system of 'separate development' known as apartheid, stems from the fact that racism is written into their constitution, along with their capitalist need for black enslavement. In Britain, racism has not needed to be written into British law. Subtlety has hitherto been used as the racists' weapon. A racist Nationality Act implies that that subtlety has failed, blacks, Asians and some whites having seen through it, and a majority of whites now demand open hostility to blacks and Asians.

Considering that the white Establishment minority fears a white working-class mass rejection of their conditioned docility, a Declaration of Human Rights must be avoided at all costs for the sake of keeping alive the status quo. Therefore, it should come as no surprise that the United Kingdom now wishes to declare what blacks, Asians and a white minority have known all along, that she intends to 'come out' by openly clasping to her superior bosom the doctrine of separate development by separately developing a first-class nationality for whites and a second-class one for blacks and Asians. So where to? Soweto? So, finally, we have the truth. Her Majesty's Government intends to stitch racism onto Britain's Constitutional blanket. The world, my friends, is definitely changing, for Doctor Footswitch is here. But, will Britain's vociferous anti-apartheid movement have the courage and the commonsense to demonstrate against British as it has continued to do against Britain's disaster-prone cousins in South Africa?

In a *Guardian* article of July 1980, Mrs Anne Dummett of the Joint Council for the Welfare of Immigrants was quoted as stating:

People should realise that the new category of British citizen with its rights of entry and abode in Britain, would be largely white, and the category of British overseas citizen, with no rights to anything, would be largely black.

So, let us make no mistake, the British Nationality Act today will be the gun in the hands of its victims, tomorrow. 'Some people are moulded by their admirations, others by their hostilities' (Elizabeth Bowen, *The Death of the Heart*).

To a swelling *guilt-fermenting* catalogue of expressions which intensifies the British educational Establishment's class-conscious sufferings, tack on the terms 'racist' and 'racism'. In the *Times Educational Supplement* of June 1981, journalist Diane Spencer wrote:

> Mr Donald Firth, general secretary of the Secondary Heads Association thought it 'scandalous to use the word "racist" as if it had a precise meaning, I find its use bitterly unhelpful – it is a term of abuse.'

There is in this statement the institutionalised 'deny-it-first' British habit, which comes into play whenever the uncomfortable cries of 'racism' (or sexism) rear their heads. Through this statement, we can detect the paramount need to flatly deny black accusational opinion without consideration. And seen against the backdrop of current racial tensions in all areas of Britain's social life, this revocation of the existence of racial antagonism in British schools is tantamount to implying: 'I cannot come to terms with unpleasant realities, so let us sweep it under the carpet by repudiating its existence; that way it might miraculously vanish'. The Head-in-the-Sand syndrome. The glaring facts are that, inside Britain's Houses of Knowledge, white teachers have given little quality time to those pupils who are, by white custom, not to be mentioned together with anything positive. Those pupils I refer to are The Unmentionables - the black and the Asian. It is true that racism and education should be completely unfamiliar to one another. But in Britain, if you are black or Asian, racism *is* education; in fact, through the constant teaching of negatives about black and Asian people found in Britain's history books; and in fiction, e.g. the perpetuation, by white teachers, of the fallacies and myths about black people being good at sport and music. Therefore, black pupils are encouraged at sport and not at academic subjects. There is a profound inability within the school system to promote and encourage black pupils to stay on and achieve academically. At this point the fundamental question must be: inside a racist atmosphere do people lose their prejudiced feelings on becoming teachers? Especially after their own conditioned schoolings about black and Asian people when they were pupils themselves. In the Inner London Education Authorities' house newspaper, *Contact*, the issue of June 1981, observing the Interim Report of the Committee of Inquiry into the Education of Children from Minority Ethnic Groups (Rampton Committee), stated:

Although the Committee believes that only a small number of teachers could be said to be racist in the commonly accepted sense, it believes that other teachers display signs of '*unintentional*' racism which may influence their attitudes towards ethnic minority pupils. [My italics]

Bernard Coard, author of *How the West Indian Child is Made Educationally Sub-Normal in the British School System*, published by New Beacon Books, pointed out a virulent aspect of the Rampton Committee's definition of 'unintentional'. He stated:

An Inner London Education Authority report entitled *The Education of Immigrant Pupils in Special Schools for Educationally Subnormal Children* (ILEA 657) reveals that five of their secondary ESN schools had more than 30 per cent immigrant pupils at the time of their survey in 1967. By January 1968, one of the schools had 60 per cent immigrant children!

In the ILEA's ESN (Special) Day Schools, over 28 per cent of all the pupils are immigrant, *compared with only 15 per cent immigrants in the ordinary schools* of the ILEA. This situation is particularly bad for the West Indians, whereas *West Indians are only half of the immigrant population in the ordinary schools.* The 1970 figures are even more alarming, for even though immigrants comprise nearly 17 percent of the normal school population nearly 34 per cent of the ESN school population is immigrant. And four out of every five immigrant children in these ESN schools are West Indian!

The ILEA report quoted by Bernard Coard also gave the numbers of black children attending ESN schools who the headmasters of those schools thought were wrongly placed: one school calculated that between 70 and 79 per cent of its black children were wrongly placed; two schools calculated that between 40 and 49 percent of black children were wrongly placed; another considered that between 30 and 39 percent were wrongly placed; and three schools calculated that between 20 and 29 per cent of their black children were wrongly placed.

Bernard Coard added:

... nine out of nineteen schools thought that 20 per cent or more of their immigrant pupils had been wrongly placed. This is from Table 9, page 9, of the report. The report states (page 5) that: 'Where children are suspected as being wrongly placed in the ESN school, this is *four times as likely* in the case of immigrant pupils.' [Author's italics]

Due to the unexpected gutbuckets of wrath poured out by black parents against the excessive loading of black children into those schools, the educational Establishment, which by now saw them as lands of darkness by virtue of how many black children they had exiled to them, mugged by their undisguised disinterest in black education, suffered withdrawal symptoms. And 'procrastination being the art of keeping up with yesterday' (Don Marquis), the educational Establishment certainly has done so. Keep on keeping on, with the art of sham. This ESN black-loading sham has re-emerged as the Disruptive Pupils Programme (ILEA 1979), which in secondary schools has resulted in Sanctuaries and Off-Site Peripatetic Groups, Nurture Groups and Withdrawal Groups. Very magniloquent titles, but what do they mean? They, successors of ESN schools, revamped in name only, *are* ESN schools. The possibility of any of their black pupils being readmitted to normal schooling is practically non-existent; and white children are prominent in their absence from these units.

Peter Wilby, *The Sunday Times* Education Correspondent, wrote in May 1980 that the existence of these 'sinbins' is a cause for concern. He stated:

A new survey by the Advisory Centre for Education shows that local education authorities have set up at least 450 sinbins – double the number in operation three years ago.

ACE calls them 'a threat to the rights of parents and schoolchildren' and, with the National Association for Multiracial Education, is holding a conference next week to highlight the problem. It will be told that:
- Sin-bin children are rarely returned to normal schooling;
- there is a disproportionate number of black children involved;
- the children often end up with a second-class education in sub-standard conditions.

... ACE says the procedures for sending children to them are too varied and too vague. In at least one area, the children may be attending the unit because they are 'peevish, dreamy, unpersevering, depressed and untidy' as well as because they are 'bullying and destructive'.

If a child is expelled, or sent to a school for the sub-normal or maladjusted, the authorities must go through formalities and give parents rights of appeal. Sin-bins, by contrast, have no legal status and a child can be sent to one – without the parents having any say.

But the parents of those children had dreams. And they toiled. What black parents endured so that they might give their children the opportunity of education cannot be quantified; nor can the humiliations those parents had to suffer when their children returned home from ESN schools more uneducated than before they left. I can see the pain, the sweat and the tears. I can also hear the white man's denials.

The Rampton Committee, with its now famed Rampton Report, comforted those parents with a new set of figures. Their report showed that three per cent of West Indian school leavers gain five O-levels. Ironically, the Rampton Committee had unknowingly provided a yardstick which can be used to measure the level of racism crushing the young black pupils attending English schools; a level which now, using 1981 Rampton figures, suggests that black children have to withstand a high level of racism while attending English schools. Well done, Britannia.

Or is their failure rate due to the perpetuated white myth that black people possess a lower IQ than whites? If that is true, metaphorically speaking, then Britain's multiracial society will never see a black man or woman rise to any level higher than the ground floor. Which also might suggest that, due to black repugnance at the positively-motivating-to-fail white IQ test, and visualising the possibility (through the black genetic instincts of slavery-avoidance) that they may never ascend, or afford that luxury known as 'aspiring', they may choose to take up other methods to attain their just education rights.

The Rampton Committee also provided another set of figures, regarding Asians. Eighteen per cent of Asian school leavers gained five O-levels. Could this be due to the fact that white Britain never fractionalised Asian communities like they did the West Indian community? The Asian family unit is still linguistically distinct and culturally intact, thus affording some Asian school children a steadier home life in which to study. Whereas the whites uprooted black people from their cultural roots through the slave trade, and in the Caribbean maintained the separation of African blacks from Africa so that the enforced emigrants could never regain their rightful hereditary links. Those blacks were murdered physically, spiritually and morally through the destruction of the black family unit in the West Indies. That there is still today a black family unit in the West Indies at all only goes to demonstrate the strength and determination of the Africans who were forced to reside there.

Of course black parents have a responsibility to help education authorities with the educating of their children. Furthermore, the rebuilt black family unit in Britain has recovered sufficiently from white repression to be strong enough to help and care for the education of their children. But do whites want to recognise that fact? Are teachers aware enough?

Which leads us on to the next divisive white tactic.

A tactic perfected in Britain's ex-colonies in Africa and the West Indies. The Asian Buffer Syndrome. In those colonies, Indians were transported by Britain's whites to act as buffers between the black majority and a white-ruling minority. By placing Asians over African heads to act as foremen and junior managers, rewarding them by enabling them to set up as small businessmen, they, now a British class above the blacks, made black-armed insurrection more difficult. They acted as informers in order to keep the position they had attained, even though the mass of Asians in the then British Asia were just as oppressed as the black people living in British Africa. A false enmity grew, not just between the black people of Africa and those few Asians in Africa, but between the black and Asian nations in general. The African result can be seen in this white-created problem which has left a very sad and difficult racial situation in Africa today, i.e. the Ugandan and Kenyan Asians. A tactic used successfully once, is one to be used again. Divide and rule.

The Rampton figures created the image that Asians are more intelligent than black people, and therefore a class above them. The British media used it, and the white population had grown used to hearing it, while subconsciously believing it. But because black and Asian peoples have seen through that white divisive device, it has lost its potency and it will not work again.

Sadly, what the Rampton Committee's Report really underlines is that there is an overall failure in the education of Britain's white, brown and black schoolchildren which is what this nation should be very concerned about, instead of making opportunistic political use of black and brown people as scapegoats for national educational failure, and continuing to ignore the real and obvious implications of the Rampton Report.

Philosopher Bertrand Russell, in his book entitled *Power* published in 1938, honing his grey matter with moral reasoning, pointed to reality with 'this is where it's at':

As the beliefs and habits which have upheld traditional power decay, it gradually gives way either to power based upon some new belief, or to 'naked' power, i.e. to the kind that involves no acquiescence on the part of the subject. Such is the power of the butcher over sheep, of an invading army over a vanquished nation, and of the police over detected conspirators. The power of the Catholic Church over Catholics is tradition, but its power over heretics who are persecuted is naked. The power of the State over loyal citizens is traditional, but its *power over rebels is naked*. Organisations that have a long career of power pass, as a rule, through three phases: first, that of fanatical but not traditional belief, leading to conquest; then, that of general acquiescence in the new power, which rapidly becomes traditional; and finally that in which power, being now used against those who reject tradition, has again become naked. [My italics]

Consequently, it is through those who do not conform that we can truly witness the naked power of the state and its institutions. The British education system is about conformity. Rightly or wrongly, therein lies Britain's stability. The majority, being a reliable army of conformists, have, by Bertrand Russell's definition, acquiesced.

Schools, therefore, severely curb the natural tendency of a child for individuality. They temper that instinct just sufficiently to conform that child to the will of the state; which twists its direction so that he or she becomes the factory-fodder of Britain's concrete jungles, or the heir to its controls.

However, there exists in Britain a selection of nonconformists. Some through their beliefs, i.e. campaigners against injustices; some through their political beliefs, i.e. Marxists; some by accident, i.e. the unemployed; some by misfortune, i.e. the handicapped; some through their sex, i.e. women; and others are seen as nonconformists through the nature of their nonconformity, which is their black or brown pigmentation. A fact that obviously permeated through to the classroom, by being an inherent part of a racist society.

More solidly, do the racial leanings of Britain's white teaching majority guide the practices of their teachings, by teaching white?

White is right, and black gets the sack. ESN forever. So, what is *contemporary* education for? And what are Britain's schools today educating toward? Divide and rule, as ever?

Most nightmares end at daybreak; Britain's, in education, is just beginning.

# 5. The Order Architects

The British police force is the wince of the nerve of the capitalist's frown and the organ of coercion for the State. This national all-weather bag-of-tricks is a social knuckleduster in the battleground of rebel deterrence; thus enabling the rule of law, through the shrapnel of the Blue Eminence, to prevail. That *is* the Standing Order. Created by the state to guarantee public obedience on behalf of the ruling propertied minority, which is seen to be in the so-called interests of the majority, these order-architects are paid legal informers. And On Her Majesty's Service, the policeman is your statutory friend. He can also be your Judas, so as to curb the natural tendencies of the nonconforming who, in his eyes, are permanently a hair's breadth removed from criminality. Thus he is ordained by the state to use his own discretion, when the rule of law has been infringed, in the amount of naked power needed as a remedy.

Power is a magnet for the self-revering and it demands a degree of megalomania from those who *seek* it. Bertrand Russell, in his book entitled *Power*, wrote:

> Thus love of power, as a motive, is limited by timidity, which also limits the desire for self-direction. Since power enables us to realise more of our desires than would otherwise be possible, and since it secures deference from others, it is natural to desire power except in so far as timidity interferes. This sort of timidity is lessened by the habit of responsibility, and accordingly responsibilities tend to increase the desire for power. Experience of cruelty and unfriendliness may operate in either direction: with those who are easily frightened it produces the wish to escape observation, while bolder spirits are stimulated to seek positions in which they can inflict cruelties rather than suffer them.

Consequently, it is inherent in the act of joining a police force than an individual, consciously or subconsciously, seeks a larger slice of the local power-cake. And it is in the position of being a police officer, that an individual in civil life comes closest to the smell of individual power of the naked kind. But, as guardians of the law they are morally assumed to be above misusing it. Obviously, effective policing through a willing public co-operation ensures that the use of his naked power is rarely needed. Conformity, being the secret police of the majority's senses, aids the policeman in the everyday execution of his duties. Therefore, nonconformers are seen, by the police, to be in direct need of external and visible policing.

But it will be a defunct nation which possesses no police force, and conversely, a nation with a police force allowed to misuse its invested power can hold that nation or an element of that nation in sheer terror; such is the power a nation invests in its police force.

Policemen are an integral part of this class-ridden society. They uphold the law through the ambitious white Darwinian maxim: 'survival of the fittest'. The fittest in the public eye are the propertied, and the rule of law is all about protecting property. In the Higher Mathematics of the police 'the fittest' are the best, the upper and middle classes. But, it is 'tough luck' for the masses who, through their greater numbers and lack of influence, co-operate easily with the promotional prospects of that officer. Being fair game, the chances of the white working classes depend upon the nature of the individual lonely God of the street in blue, and the mood he is in on that particular day. Have you ever witnessed the sycophantic crawlings of a policeman in the presence of a peer of the realm or an industrialist?

Additionally, a police officer who recognises that a citizen is without power, through lack of influence of social status, has it made. That citizen, by virtue of his negative-power situation, normally submits, especially if the officer is of the tyrannical kind. But in doing so, he might have to admit guilt so as to soften the action of this tyrant. In raw reality, and with everything else being pretence, a citizen with no social standing or connections in the hands of this policing state functionary is already in a hopeless position, being unrecognised for his social value. Anything is allowed, and does happen, to citizens like himself.[10]

Such are the benefits of an enterprising class system, and such are the benefits of enterprise. Tom Bowden, author of *Beyond the Limits of the Law*, states:

> For the poor, the dispossessed and the underprivileged, for those without property and hence with no stake in the system, the police appear more often as aloof and brutal authoritarians...
>
> ... We have said that the evidence supports the view that the policeman is a conventional personality; that he is politically and morally conservative and operates in such an environment that all his values and beliefs are based on the fact that he is *for* order and *against* change. In normal times, but particularly in crises, the policeman works to uphold or restore the *status quo*.

---

[10] Black people are statistically considered more likely to be arrested than any other group.

Therefore, through its worship of the god of property, and especially of those to whom it belongs, the British police force is itself the personalised property of those who have it, the British ruling class.

The reality of this was reported in *The Sunday Times* of July 1981:

An inquiry has been ordered by Scotland Yard into last week's death of a mentally disturbed man who lost consciousness in a struggle with police summoned to take him to hospital.

The investigation will try to find out how nine policemen came to overpower 27-year-old Winston Rose, a West Indian from Leyton, East London, who had a history of mental illness but who, according to his wife, had never been violent. It will also examine certain allegations that Rose was thrown face-down into a police van after losing consciousness...

... 'Two policemen tried to hold him. Then there were about eight policemen on top of him. I couldn't see him for policemen. One of them said: "Use your radio." What he meant I don't know. One of them said, "He's pretending to go unconscious." I saw a hand on a truncheon, I don't know if he was getting it out or putting it away.' ...

... 'The police carried him out and threw

him into the van. One of them said, "Face downwards," and they turned him over. They just threw him in like a piece of meat.'

The blue-rinse pretence of the flexibility of Britain's police forces has always been, and is still, a useful psychological image-softening weapon by presuming the gullibility of the British public into believing that advertised police image. But since there is latent mania for power lying in the cold storage inside every police individual, the Toytown Noddy image of the smiling 'unarmed bobby' you could talk to, ask the advice of and more unrealistically, trust, is fake. There is a massive difference between this advertised image and the cosh on the head of Blair Peach.

However, *the police are tragically powerless if they are not supported by public sentiment and that public sentiment is powerful when supported by the police.* Therefore police will react to any national crisis, psychologically and then physically. The police, being part of the white national-mind, are themselves subject to any mass paranoia sweeping the country at any given moment. In their position of being the guardians of the law, they are selective when using their naked power in reaction to mass fear and mass ignorance. Like it or not, contemporary police behaviour is a reflection of the type of society we live in; a society ruled by the mass white subscription to the ethic of white superiority. The difference between the police and the public is that the white public individual possesses an indirect power (i.e. the vote) which he cannot *legally* use directly on those who he dislikes or fears. But the policeman vested with naked power for use against those who the state views as nonconformist, (e.g. rebels or, as we have seen, the mentally handicapped, or those who intend to disrupt the workings of the state) can also secretly, in Britain's case not so secretly, oppress those he *knows* will produce very little outcry from the majority of the public who are white. Black and Asian people just happen to fit very neatly into this category. The problem here is that since there is white mass hysteria about the presence of black and Asian people in Britain, in the eyes of the police those ethnic individuals are fair game, since injustice only really exists in the eyes of the white power structure, where one of their own race had his or her rights denied. But there are exceptions to the rulers' rule. Once there is a *majority* dislike of a person or community, that individual or community, from that moment on, loses all their human rights, for example, the public and media crucifixion of the Liberal Party's Jeremy Thorpe. But the white working classes, too busy with conforming or rebelling (thus defending themselves), have little interest in defending the rights of those they themselves are frightened of. Black and Asian people are therefore abandoned to the tender mercies of the blue hot-shots in their houses of pain if they happen to suffer the misfortune of stumbling across the statutory muscles of the law. Tough luck for the restless natives.

I wonder if the British system's racial ethics, of denying rights to black and Asian citizens, coincides with Articles 1 and 2 of the Universal Declaration of Human Rights (1948), which states:

**Article 1**
All human beings are born free and equal in dignity and rights.

**Article 2**
Everyone is entitled to all the rights and freedoms set forth in this Declaration, without distinction of any kind, such as race, colour, sex, language, religion, political or other opinion, national or social origin, property, birth or other status.

Or does Britain's system only pay lip-service to those articles, considering itself above them? In that case do you recognise *anything* British about the following statement published in 1967 by UNESCO in a book entitled *Apartheid*, about black people in another white-dominated society (albeit a white minority), in South Africa? It states:

Thus, unless teachers are aware that nearly all textbooks perpetuate errors which historians have corrected by diligent research ... children in many schools still regard the

Xhosa as thieves and possibly murderers, and the European farmers as blameless, since many of the books employ ... emotive words calculated to arouse feelings of hostility against the Xhosa. The children are therefore likely to identify themselves virtuously with the blameless farmers, and some, if not all, present-day Africans with the Xhosa thieves.

Ironically, hitherto in Britain, major problems have decisively evolved an answer, or an individual to 'answer the call', e.g. Winston Churchill for World War Two. All, that is, except this one, of *race*. Britain has never been so faced with what some of her whites obviously consider to be the 'enemy within'. Therefore, because of the urgent requirement for a solution to this white-created crisis, the question that begs itself is: 'Is there a giant conspiracy by Britain's whites against her black and Asian peoples?' No. It is a conditioned way of life for many, but not all, of Britain's whites. But, sadly, it is also an attitude which exists deeply embedded in large quantities in much of this nation's police forces, who now find themselves in the 'inquisitor's dilemma', kissed-to-life by the hair-raising methods they have used on blacks and Asians in places such as Brixton. Some of these police procedures have even made the national flesh creep. For instance, Britain's white community was shocked by the 01:55 a.m. police raid on some residents living in Railton Road, Brixton, on

15 July 1981, when detectives allegedly storm-trooped homes of black people brandishing 'sledgehammers, pickaxe handles, pickaxes and crowbars' and smashed up their homes. Even the government, normally deaf to black cries of injustice, could not *afford* to ignore this blatant act of vandalism; especially after Lord 'Brixton' Scarman had visited these homes of devastation, and significantly 'commented' in the *Sunday Telegraph*, in July 1981:

... [an] inquiry [was] ordered by Mr Whitelaw, the Home Secretary, into a police raid last week in Brixton when detectives were accused of 'smashing up' houses owned by *coloured* people. [My italics. Which colour? White?]

Consequently, Brixton's all-night-soul-patrol, the recognised by all colours, lawful *peacekeeping* agents of the government, relentlessly inspecting black meat, are surprisingly stunned by the incredible results of their hit-and-run grapes of racial wrath from their permanent and persistent SWAMP squad[11].

The traditional outcome of such repeated repression, the result of which we have witnessed internationally, which 'could never happen here', *has* happened here. And the party is over. That repression has created, and is still

---

[11] Referring to immigrants before elections, Mrs Thatcher repeatedly used the word 'swamp' to panic the white voting majority. The police operation that triggered the 1981 unrest in Brixton was named 'Operation Swamp'.

creating, black and Asian rebels against a society which still smugly *presumes* their allegiance while bowling their considered 'woolly' heads against a national test-bat of racial resentment or hate.

A person who is that victimised is tutored by necessity into taking the law into his own hands. He has no problems. But this society does; by not taking crucial notice that that possibility exists. In Britain, if this individual is black or Asian, he will fall into one of two categories: either he has a 'chip on his shoulder' and stands an odds-on chance of being diagnosed a 'paranoid schizophrenic', to join the disproportionate number of blacks and Asians languishing in Britain's prisons and mental institutions, with a little help from Electro-Convulsive Therapy (ECT) and major tranquillisers; or he will (as in most societies) be labelled as a fanatic, after society considers the depth of the premeditation required to carry out what should be known as the 'victim's rebellion'. And I don't mean burglary or the like. Fanatic? That may very well be true; even though he may have arrived at his destructive way out through his consistent and persistent attempts at conversing with an Ultra ... Deaf ... Ear.

Talkers need Listeners. Conversely, Listeners need Talkers. Unless, that is, one side considers that what the other side is saying is of no interest to themselves, having already (in fact, long ago) made up their minds.

If that is the case, then some of Britain's police divisions can decisively consider who they think is most likely to be fanatical by white post-dated proxy. For example, in Brixton, where police/black/brown relationships have 'broken down' (with a little *help* from their 'friends', and through *that* political pressure), black and white residents have been pushed terrifyingly close to the point of no return. Which accentuates that these police acts have failed them conclusively and publicly by their own design. Or was it an accident? Of white purpose? So then who should be trusted to police the police? Why should the Police Complaints Board be the final arbiter of public complaints against the police? Do the police consider themselves to be a government which, through its behaviour, demands an opposition? So, what does the crisis in Brixton really signify? Will the Rule of the Cosh be the gasp in our lives?

The Police Complaints Board, a shrouded assembly, is currently surrounded by controversy. A ridiculous understatement; it is a board which has no public confidence in it. Remember Countryman?[12] What does public confidence mean, and what happens when it is lost?

Surely statutory powers investing potentially naked power on a human being demand a statutory obligation on the part of the state? That of providing a solidity of checks and balances which, in turn, checks the balance of that particular person. So that it gives more than just a 'reasonable' amount of confidence to

---

[12] Operation Countryman was an investigation into police corruption in London in the late 1970s. Eight officers were prosecuted but none were convicted. In 2018, files were unearthed that showed how senior officers thwarted Operation Countryman. They consisted of allegations of how Metropolitan and City of London police took bribes, planted evidence, conspired with bank robbers and improperly facilitated bail.

those who that naked power will possibly be used upon. Anything less than that is a mugging soul-sibling of deception. Let us mow the blue lawn of controversy. It is *not* for the public to disprove the integrity of the British police force. It is for the police to be constantly proving their own integrity to those whom they serve, the British public, regardless of sex, class or colour. In this way they could reassure them that, on the taking up of their invested succulent power, they *accept* the responsibility that goes with their *theoretically* honourable, action-man duties. That is, if they consider their moral responsibilities are in the interests of everyone, including themselves, and not just the political interest of the government. Police arrogance, implied by their instant and constant dismissals of any criticism, has served to push them farther away from those who they say they are 'protecting the rights' of. For a police force freed from public and media criticism exists only in a police state. Or is this a police state, advertising benevolence for international inspection?

It is often said that people cannot rise above the limitations of their own characters. Nations and their institutions, including their police forces, have no other choice. To some people living in Britain's community, possessing a myriad of hues and shades, the relationship between them and their police is akin to space, an unreality, and in human terms it is the hyphen between fact and fiction. Remember, this is a nation in which reality has left imagination standing. So, conversely with Britain's ethnic minorities, but always with history in mind.

When the sword of Damocles finally fell at the beginning of Britain's trade in slaves, it rooted her to the spot with myths about black people and the grandeur of herself; encapsulated today in the white fake-finger journalism about black and Asian people, making the reliability of British media reports about those peoples instantly questionable, and thus dismissible. And since a gasp is the difference between the truth and a lie, so is Britain's media.

Typical of this attitude is the regular fitting of pathetic black stereotypes inside a plethora of nascent publications with which white Britons constantly tranquillise themselves. An addiction of heroin-type proportions supports their wishful thoughts of what black people supposedly are and what they hope they are. Consider, for example, the *Daily Telegraph*, June 1981, reviewing the book *Sambo Sahib: The Story of Little Black Sambo and Helen Bannerman*. The reviewer wrote:

> It seems *extraordinary* that that harmless late-Victorian nursery favourite, 'The Story of Little Black Sambo,' should, in the last ten years have stirred up a 'racist' controversy. But so it is. It has been cast out from public libraries, *particularly in America*, removed from

children's recommended reading lists and banished from race-conscious Kindergartens.

If the author were alive today she would be both grieved and astonished, but fortunately she is not ... [My italics]

It is clear from this so-called review that this reviewer has based the critique on the wrong assumptions. What is really meant by the use of the word *extraordinary* is that white people are shell-shocked by being told, by black people, to radically change the nature of the racial chess game that they have constantly played with the black identity for centuries. Furthermore, books like the 'Sambo' series have been demolished, *particularly in American libraries*, for an obvious reason. For the price in lives of not changing the majority's racial ignorance was too high.

Contemporarily, Britain's black racial philosophy has sprung from criticism of white racial beliefs, through their seeking of logical reasons with which they then formulate logical (to themselves only) arguments to reinforce their own beliefs in the inferiority of others. A greasy attempt has been made in this review. Further still, if Helen Bannerman, the author of the 'Sambo' books, were alive today, and living in America, she would not just be 'grieved and astonished', she wouldn't *be*. *Black Slang, a Dictionary of Afro American Talk* (edited by Clarence Major), states the following: 'SAMBO any black American who accepts meekly his or her oppression; from *Little Black Sambo*, a story with stereotypes that serve the purpose of propaganda'.

Take *The Sunday Times* in April 1981, with a profile of Leslie Allen, the American tennis player:

> This black woman has a sense of humour ... The *simple truth* is that, were she not black, very few of the articles written about her in the past two months – including this one – would have appeared.

The 'simple truth' is that this reporter, with some honesty, admits that whites, including himself, have always ignored black achievement: attached is the implication that she is now successful because whites recognise her. And should he be surprised that a black woman has a sense of humour? This is yet another of the thoughtless but offensive remarks made about black people by many whites.

The *Daily Telegraph*, in an article in April 1980, highlights the negative white approach to black and Asian people which is popularly used *en masse* by the British media. The article began:

> *Immigrant* dissatisfaction with the legal system will come into acrimonious focus on Tuesday when a leading *West Indian* barrister appears before a disciplinary tribunal of the Senate of the Inns of Court and the Bar on charges

of professional misconduct and conduct unbecoming to a barrister.

Mr Rudy Narayan, a *Guyana-born* barrister, faces charges relating to a letter ... [My italics]

How about 'Black dissatisfaction' and 'leading black barrister', and do we need to know where he was born?

Notice the imaginative use of the term 'immigrant'. But when is an immigrant not an immigrant? When he is white and has it covered by being a 'settler'. Also, notice that in Britain her whites continue to insist on the term 'immigrants' for a people who came in peace by invitation.

When Britain's whites arrived to colonise Africa and Asia, with heavy immoral inspiration, on arrival, they instantly labelled themselves 'Settlers'. These houses of knowledge, hot-shots at everything and iced to other forms of humanity, created an Auschwitz-type jam-session, by proceeding to settle their score through unsettling everything else. Their militaristic jukebox played songs of massacres of hundreds of thousands of African and Asian people. They butchered their families, raped their women and squandered the lives of their children. And finally, as their Act of Settlement, through fraudulent conversion, the light-fingered white settlers robbed them of their land. That is the white man's definition of 'settler', which stands as active today as it did when they originated their kleptomania of Africans and their possessions.

This Mickey Mouse imaginative use of the word 'settler' artfully conjures up a positive image. But it stretches *my* imagination to believe that those upper-class whites possessed settling intentions. The whites converted the African and Asian victims of their immemorial deceit by creating a mugging-mystique of mythological racial absurdities into incoherent, senseless, pathetic sub-humans, entirely dependent on the white Lord of the Land, Tarzan, God's earth-bound muscle, who harnessed the raging land and its untrainable 'creatures' to lay it all at the feet of white womanhood on a pedestal.

A fanciful world of make-believe gradually became ingrained as an intrinsic component of the white mentality. With racial vanity as a yardstick, and with knowledge gleaned from Britain's history books, every white man in Africa and Asia became ten times larger than life. They were supposedly adventurous, courageous, stiff-upper-lipped, gallant, heroic, valiant, chivalrous and blue-blooded. 'Chinese' Gordon of Khartoum, Livingstone, Clapperton, Speke, Rhodes, Thomson, Burke and Wills, etc., and for evermore. The exploits of these white historical heroes gradually became intertwined and interwoven with the exploits of mythical comic-book heroes. So much so, that in the miasma of British history, the line between fact and fiction is totally indistinguishable. Notice that these white he-men died 'heroically'. Was there ever any white man in Africa or Asia who did not die, generally grossly outnumbered, 'heroically'? Interestingly, these showcase whites of Empire have a class-equivalent in British fiction of that period. Lord Peter Wimsey and Sherlock Holmes, with their razorblade upper-class cunning intellects, simultaneously exposed and undermined the so-called inferior intellects of the lower classes.

The white orchestrations performed in Africa need review. In their haven of galloping natives, negative epithets like 'darkest Africa' or 'the dark Continent' were introduced by those people who never saw light in anyone black, and relegated those ape-like, empty-headed, physical specimens into paper men and women. Those labels were used essentially to denote the helplessness of black people by conjuring up a pile of sluggish, impervious bricks in order to perpetuate the myth of non-white inferiority. When the pick-up band of contemporary white journalists arrived to make today's scene with the same patronising droppings of their forefathers, being unable to stretch their limited imaginations, the white jukebox repeated the same white negative attitude towards black people and Asians, the same hallucinations, the same labels.

In an *Evening Standard* article of March 1980, Max Hastings admitted to that biased negative approach in an article which revealed what white journalists, in general, had traditionally omitted from their reports:

... Ho ho. Those of us who have reported from Rhodesia over the years, have come to take so much for granted; the chatter about 'the munts', 'the Kaffirs', 'the indigenous' that would cause embarrassment in Enoch Powell's parlour; the weight of hatred and contempt for anyone who has voiced disagreement with 'the struggle to preserve standards'; the courage and enterprise of the farmers and industrialists; the absence of culture; the startling physical beauty...

In the past 15 years, there has been much talk in Rhodesia about the standards that Mr Smith and his army have allegedly fought to maintain. It is true that this country and its white people are marvellously clean, because there has always been an army of black workers to keep them so. The whites are reasonably law-abiding, hard-working, disciplined and hospitable ...

For ten years, there has been a growing and finally total lack of concern among most whites about the circumstances in which blacks have died in the war. Black civilians killed in crossfire were simply scribbled in the casualty lists as 'curfew breakers'. Thousands of blacks were moved from their own areas into 'protected villages' often without the slightest provision for the basic necessities of life. In some cases, their new homes were merely map references in the bush.

I discovered the tricks of Britain's white journalists in Africa, showing how these Sons of Empire became heirs to disaster. In an article entitled 'Tolerated Guests' in *New Society* November 1977, alluding to their methods of story-discovery, I wrote:

This is Zambia. Lusaka the capital. The capitals within the capital are the bars. Here at hotels like the Intercontinental on Haile Selassie Avenue, the hookers have congregated – not girls, but the journalists who, preferring the title 'foreign correspondent,' concoct the news. They are awaiting the imminent arrival of India's General Prem Chand, UN special representative. The British Commissioner-Designate for Rhodesia, Lord Carver, follows shortly.

Twelve years ago, foreign correspondents decided that the Smith regime was about to fall. According to these experts at cutting their cloth to suit the front page, it still is. 'Noise proves nothing,' said Mark Twain's Pudd'nhead Wilson, 'often a hen who has merely laid an egg cackles as if she had laid an asteroid.' The same could be said of foreign correspondents. It is, after all, due to an ingrained fanatical desire to obtain a scoop, that some blatantly exaggerate and transmit distorted facts. Not surprisingly, 'big things do have small beginnings,' especially if the small thing started off in the hands of some foreign correspondent.

This is the world of the foreign correspondent: filled with telex and alcohol. Jet lag, credit cards and craziness. Shallow, superficial and super-exciting. Super-lies, super-cliques, super flams and super ego – the Super Tramp.

Some of the most notable of these adventure story writers abide by the oldest rule of journalism: 'Never muck up a good story with facts.' The *Daily Telegraph*, considered to be the worst fantasist by many journalists out here, is nicknamed, 'the west's *Isvestia*.'

A current tale going around the bars is of the correspondent who was scouting in a light aircraft over Cabinda, Angola's oil enclave, when a MIG shot past him – at 1,200 mph. His account of this split second happening was: the steely eyes of the Cuban pilot glowered hate at *me*. His bared teeth held a Havana cigar in a vice-like grin. He flew towards me with guns spitting violence ... This earned him a week's detention in the local gaol.

Here in Lusaka, because of the fluid political situation in Rhodesia and South Africa, rumours abound and spread like wildfire. Journalists play a significant role in the spreading. Recognising this, African governments force-feed them, like Strasbourg geese, with stories they want highlighted. Smith, Kaunda and General Amin are past masters at this game. To get the correspondent, officials bait the hook with tempting stories: 'Nkomo is secretly meeting X'. The news spreads suddenly. Foreign correspondents descend like vultures from all over Africa to get a bit of the free information. For a day – or a week – they circle lazily (in ever-decreasing circles from bar to bar) and then go on to their next 'story.' Their readers may be left baffled, but the bars and the airlines go smiling all the way to the bank.

In investigative journalism there is a fine line between reporting and spying. Foreign correspondents are tolerated guests. They are entitled to comment but not encouraged to interfere with the sovereignty of a state. Hence the dearth of hard information.

By far the largest percentage of stories about the Rhodesian guerrilla war are planted from inside Rhodesia itself. Foreign correspondents are invited by the Smith regime, to show that the government has nothing to hide. A lot of native bar-bound correspondents fall for this. According to many correspondents in Lusaka, invitations to visit Rhodesia are extended to those reporters who have 'shown some sympathy' with the Smith regime. In that way, some supposedly free-thinking foreign correspondents may unwittingly become mouthpieces for the Rhodesian government. That being so, news from Rhodesia can only be one-sided and should be taken with a pinch of salt.

This is reinforced by the fact that no western correspondent has been permitted to enter any ZANU or ZAPU camps (freedom fighters opposed to Smith). Nor have they been allowed to view the fighting going on from the territories of the frontline states surrounding Rhodesia. These no-go areas are Tanzania, Mozambique and Zambia. Thus, lurid descriptions of border fighting lose their credibility.

Conversations with some correspondents yield little information of any real substance. What becomes increasingly clear is that any acquaintance with the local population is lacking. As one travel weary American journalist said, 'I would like to know where the workers live.'

At Lusaka's Intercontinental, the ambience seems to be tainted with the colonial mentality. It appears to be a bastion of a bygone era. Anyone could be forgiven for thinking that the atmosphere of Evelyn Waugh's *Scoop* was alive and thriving in Lusaka. At the sun's zenith, the swimming pool is filled with the noisy, uninfectious laughter of expatriates' wives – whiling away the length of their husbands' contracts. (There seems to be an unwritten rule that black and white must not swim at the same time.) Meanwhile, lunching correspondents huddle at the Makumbi bar and restaurant overlooking the swimming pool, gaping lecherously at the various bikinied body shapes. Waiters scurry around them, bearing exotic drinks. 'I say,' booms one correspondent, with that nasal accent that sorts out the bosses from the workers. He delivers his order with a reminiscent condescension. It is precisely this kind of attitude which has brought Rhodesia and South Africa staring full face at violent confrontation.

Meanwhile, here at the Intercontinental there may be a question of sovereignty. Outside this place, Zambia – indeed, black Africa – is independent.

So, why were the British people so shattered by the

news that Robert Mugabe was to be the Prime Minister of Zimbabwe? Were they ripped off by the twisted news of their media? They were in fact being plunged into history and not being given news. Any black man, if asked, could have told them, at the very beginning, that the information white journalists trafficked from their hotels would be white propaganda and not news.

Consequently, the white British journalistic vacuum-cleaners, so sure of a white Rhodesian victory, because it was a British-type army, weighted the news of the war in Zimbabwe against the black Zimbabweans, finally outsmarting themselves. For years the British public, with Empire mentality-infested psyches, were sucked in by the con-penmanship of their media illusionists, who impressionistically painted a daily death toll of how many black 'terrorists' had been slaughtered by Rhodesia's sanguinary white immigrants. All in all, in the entire war, if one totalled the number of freedom fighters supposed to have been killed by the white British representatives, those white butchers would have demolished the lives of at least three times the number of black freedom fighters that actually exist in the whole of Africa.

Moreover, the war was fought on two fronts, each supporting each other, each needing the other. The first front took place in Zimbabwe itself. The second front was in Britain, where the white British press constantly placed into the white public mind the 'wrongness' of the black African struggle and the 'rightness' of the white

Rhodesian immigrants by artistically and skilfully conjuring up memories of the past, highlighted by Jan Morris in *Pax Britannica*:

> The Indian Mutiny, too, had tainted British attitudes towards coloured people. It had occurred in 1857, and was one of the few imperial events which had gone into the English folk-myth, on a par with the marriages of Henry VIII, say, or the murder of the princes in the Tower. It is a favourite horror story. The British saw it in terms of cowering white ladies in fetid cellars; goggle-eyed Indians, half blood-man, half lustful, creeping unawares upon sweet English children in lace pantaloons; the massacre of innocent hostages, ambushes, orgies, treachery.

The brainwashing continued with the viciousness of the black freedom fighters, as opposed to the disciplined militarism of the whites; the glory of the Selous Scouts, as opposed to the perversion of the Patriotic Front; how the Patriotic Front had intimidated every black and brown man in Zimbabwe, while the white army of bandits spent enormous amounts of money and manpower protecting black lives. Where in history has any white power structure ever protected black lives?

The white man became the black man's burden,

when some British individuals and companies (with the British government, as usual, mouthing denials of knowledge), created a new Hollywood, with panoramic effects thrown in. The extravaganza, blockbusting motion picture in Africa was created; *The Sanction Busters*, made along the lines of *Gone With The Wind*. At black protests, the whites told black people 'Go to the wind for an answer'. And they did, in the shape of an African racial truism, which is: no white man negotiates with a black man unless he has been made to. Consequently, the white Rhodesian struggle to hold on to what did not belong to them in the first place resulted in the London Lancaster House Conference. The black Zimbabweans had brought them to their knees; and there being a very fine line between greed and defeat, the whites lost everything.

At the beginning of the black Zimbabwean War of Independence, Ian Smith's white assassins were described by Britain's journalists as the 'illegal regime' for a whole five minutes. And they quickly introduced positive and negative mind-bending images, so as to seduce Britain's white majority into siding with their homicidal cousins infesting a black man's country. A land in which the blacks had repeatedly stated that whites were more than welcome to remain, *as equals*. But the white definition of 'equality', as the world knows, is completely based on a set of immoral morals, which black people refuse to understand and can never accept. With some racially prejudiced foresight and harmony through 'the old school tie' network, overnight, the British government and Britain's media massacred the term 'illegal' and replaced it with the positive image of 'security forces'. Meanwhile, black people, who were Zimbabwe's rightful owners, instantly became 'terrorists', 'guerrillas', 'bandits', 'murderers'. All of which perpetuate an artistic negative image. But what is noteworthy is that literally none of Britain's journalists reporting from the white man's home front in white Rhodesia truthfully described Zimbabwe's black fighters the way they should have, which was 'freedom fighters', especially if that regime was as illegal as the British government claimed. Or were they 'legal in their illegality' which Africans and Asian peoples know is the white man's traditional definition of black equality with whites.

Furthermore, in their primal wish for a white victory, white Britain accidentally forgot to stop and think that the white negative reporting of the black peoples' rightful struggle for Zimbabwe was being noticed, absorbed and remembered by Britain's black and Asian peoples, who themselves were being reported by other white journalists in very much the same negative terms. The only horrendous fact for whites was that through the universality of communications systems, biased reporting against black peoples is a boomerang that will always return. For *Britain has finally colonised herself but she has yet to realise it*. The victor's toll.

Let us take a look at some of the destructive reporting on Zimbabwe that invaded the British atmosphere:

*The Sunday Times*, August 1980: 'Officials report that many tribesmen and guerrillas are unhappy to hear ministers urging *white farmers* to remain on the land.'

*The Times*, April 1980: 'There are still about 30 British soldiers in Zimbabwe helping to train former *Zanla* and *Zipra guerrillas* who are being integrated with the *Rhodesian security forces.*'

*Guardian*, February 1980: 'Five black civilians have been killed in crossfire between *security forces* and *Patriotic Front guerrillas*, a Rhodesian military spokesman said yesterday. Two *guerrillas* and one *white security force* member also were killed he said.'

*Evening Standard*, February 1980: 'As 22,000 *guerrillas* at assembly points all over Rhodesia voted today.'

*Daily Telegraph*, April 1980: 'Four men, including a *white security forces* member, held by Rhodesian police concerning a hand-grenade attack on Mr Mugabe's suburban Salisbury home, have been released.'

Michael Raeburn, author of *Black Fire! Accounts*

*of the Guerilla War in Rhodesia* published in 1978, was consciously or subconsciously image-manipulating when he wrote: 'But despite periodic bouts of fierce fighting against *Rhodesian security forces* during the latter half of the decade...'

Due to the oppressive weight of the British press image-inventing, the illegality of the white Rhodesian regime who were racing against time on a non-stop black Roman Holiday, was strategically lost sight of, by whites only. But the black question is, whose security were those white-led forces securing? 'Security', in a political sense, suggests a 'just cause' which made the misnamed 'terrorists' appear to be the impediment to the peace Britain so loudly proclaimed she wanted. So whose interests were they really 'securing'? Obviously it was the only people with any real material interests in that black country – white Rhodesian immigrants and their white British 'kith and kin'. Consider it, consider it carefully, bearing very much in mind the interminable history of Africa's black peoples at the terroristic hands of white immigrants.

The white image-manipulation of black peoples continued. 'Guerilla' as it stands, gave no political credibility to the black Zimbabwean struggle. And 'guerilla' as opposed to 'security force' implies that the black cause is not legitimate. But the 'nationalist guerilla' or 'freedom fighter' tells the world that Zimbabwe's blacks have a 'just cause' and the white immigrant opposition is the 'impediment' to their rightful rights. Especially when those white immigrants were internationally declared to be 'illegal' by Britain. In this context, the long arm of the white law suddenly became short for black people.

The white Rhodesian immigrant's struggle exploded the white mendacity of the 'protecting Zimbabwe's blacks' policy. That fabricated fantasy ultimately proved to be Africa's white parasites' jamboree, which reveals a self-evident truth in African perspectives: the more they *protect* whites from blacks, the more they are going to have to destroy blacks. So keep your peepers trained on the illegal white immigrants in South Africa, which will ultimately, universally, be known as The People's Republic of Azania.

# 6. In Cold Storage

Let me tell you something you may not know.

The upheavals that happened on the darker streets of Bristol 1980, and Brixton and Southall 1981, were the initial kick-out against a variety of second-rate white offerings by Britain's ethnic home-grown youth and their young white allies. Realistically, the relegating of Britain's ethnic community to second-class citizens also forcefully relegated their second-classness to permanency. 'Aspiration' for black and Asian adults was just a fanciful idea. It was a Promised Land ideal that gave rise to the realisation by their youth that they were just as colonised as their parents who were born in the ex-colonies.

But there exists an iron-hard streak of aggression in Britain's ethnic youth, who were, ironically, also cultured to understand the white British mentality. They were born and nurtured here, almost totally by their parents and, finally, belong here. That is why they, like much of white youth, refuse to accept blindly what many white adults consider to be their lot in life. They will rightly fight, and aggressively, for their just rights. Make no mistake: the Black Experience has taught them so.

Moreover, through the most gruelling, agonising and shameful white dismissal of young black ability, by ignoring their talent, coupled with the white discounting of the reality of their presence, the white-only body-politic was shattered to hear young blacks and browns powerfully proclaiming, 'We are black and we are British, and we have a right'. The white body slumbered on, and politics began. And they, peeking through their lace curtains of black inferiority, only saw what they had programmed themselves to see, which was 'immigrants', and 'coloureds' (which colour?) in the guise of black and brown bodies. And from the White Band of Light and Purity there arose a resounding, but resourceful, declaration: 'They have an identity crisis', as they moved in their sociological first line of attack, not yet realising that that so-called black 'identity crisis' was white.

It is you, the white Prince of Evolution, who are the crisis, through your own infinite attempts to manipulate black and brown peoples the world over; and having failed in that outlandish quest, you then tried to counterfeit the black identity by framing them into a 'coloured' facade. That failed too. For what the Superwhite all-brained-body had clean forgotten in his frantic and endless 100-metre dash to make himself rich (a euphemism for black and Asian agony), was that knowledge, in its majestic glory and purity, *has* no colour, but its users do.

Moreover, knowledge is infinite and has no owners. So why are Britain's white earthlings still utilising the identical sabotaging caricatures, created by those piratical great white fathers of Empire, on black and Asian people today? Or are Britain's whites really saying that human intellectual progress is a special preserve of whites only? But what is also self-evident to the black and Asian condition is that knowledge of the white behavioural progression *is* a special preserve to them.

Over the centuries, black and Asian peoples have taken in-depth courses on the Evolution of the White Psyche, watched the creation of white fantasies, and seen the addition of their wealth to Britain's.

They watched white men arrive, instantly claiming they had 'discovered' them, to the hinge-creaking extent that they only truly existed when propagated by whites. The holy rollers went along for the ride too, and blessed those whites as they tried to flatten African and Asian skulls into the shapes they wanted. But they never broke their spirit and never broke their wills; despite reducing the men into beasts of burden and degrading their women, by rape, into ravaged victims of white lusts. Those violent exploits became a British way of life, an attitude, an accepted behaviour requiring no more consideration. It became *the* attitude, *the* accepted behaviour.

But consider this: why have Britain's whites not yet thought themselves out of their own self-inspired present-day racial dilemma? Do they not think this is the opportune moment to begin equalising with black and Asian people, and to stop dictating to them? Or is it because the Establishment has, for so long, dictatorially dominated their own victims of lust, the white working classes, with the result that negotiation with their lowest considered forms of human life is always out of the question?

Yes, black and Asian people have watched Britain's whites inflicting injustices, with pity in their eyes; but the flame of defiance is constantly being upheld by another little item, which is, through political reality, they all possess historically transferred and exacting memories. What black and Asian people have never forgotten, with constant white British physical reminders, is the white man's alternative Darwinian conqueror's ethic, 'suppression of the considered weakest'. With this opportunistic measure, British history is laced with the black and brown human debris of their sanguinary exercises. Black and Asian people have memories.

They remember that the answer for any problems of the colonised was punitive. The answer *any* human being ever wanted to *any* problem was a solution. Those whites decided that their only solution to any problem, at home and abroad, was punishment. That is, until black and Asian peoples themselves became the problem, by merely demanding their rights. The ruling Establishment felt threatened, and white genocide of black and Asian people was repeated as their Final Solution.

In the global testing-ground of human manipulation, subjugating one's own is infinitely more manageable, more permanent and ultimately more effective than dominating another. The magnificent imperial weakness of Britain lay in her attempt to dominate other races permanently. It was made intractable by the startling fact of the universal racial victim's axiom – that they will ultimately see through all carpet-covered perjuries – because they cannot and will not accept the permanent domination of themselves by another race. All racial primal instincts, under that type of subjugation, are potently combustible and are always in opposition to it – in this instance, whites. It is also a fact that guarantees the future decimation of the Afrikaners, with the helping-hand of Her Majesty's Government, and woven into the mind-set of the black Azanian majority. And then the whites will weep.

It should therefore be of no surprise that Britain's black and Asian attitudes have been hardened by the constant rejection of their grievances. Britain is now forced to recognise that she has on her hands a resolute people who have for centuries been an essential part of the British community; who have done more than enough to justify a slice of the national cake, who have weathered degrading treatment just for being here in Britain, and just for being alive. A people who have withstood a superabundance of racialist attacks from the moment they landed, and who saw many, not all, of Britain's whites as onlookers of injustice, failing to see black and Asian ill-treatment at the hands of whites. A people who interminably walked away from confrontation, with the result that many whites proclaimed they were the cause of it, but who will not walk away again from confrontation, at the cost of losing, as they have usually lost in British hands, their human rights and their lives.

The question now is: will the rule of the cosh be the last gasp in black and Asian lives? For an answer, the history of Britain's treatment of black and Asian people from the day they landed on the shores of this 'sceptred isle' thundered NO.

Britain's black and Asian peoples and their white allies could see it; black and white America, having felt it, could see it; black Africa, still feeling it, could see it; the Afro-Caribbean peoples, who had tasted it, could see it; Asia, still paining from the effects of it, could see it; even the Soviet Union, strangely, could see it; in fact, everybody in the world could see it. Whereas, the white British psyche was shattered by it.

Having advertised continuously, internationally, her much envied social situation of 'peace and tolerance', through the 'tranquil harmony' of the most homeostatic society on earth, she bridled from the torrid weight of international derisive opinion, grating the 'pride and glory' of the Britannic trident, blasting to bits the idea that she was free from social revolution. The United Kingdom, protesting her innocence, reluctantly re-entered the mortal world.

That grand euphemism for British political opportunistic expedience, 'public confidence', suffered a setback through the uncomfortable knowledge that the governing powers had no answer for Britain's psychic pain.

In reaction, the tradition-bound white British soul buried its head back into the dust of its worshipped historical glory. Technologically, Britain is an advanced country but she is socially stagnant. Through her adulation of yesterday's glorious exploits, she momentarily re-emerged from her love of her own history books to be sustained by her imperial pride.

But the inquisitive chattering telecoms, reducing the world to seconds, prevented the sweeping of Britain's international humiliation under a carpeted facade; shattering the fantastic assumption that, universally, Britain is seen the way she sees herself. That shock in turn jolted her SAS-brain cells, which had always supported her justification for her self-image. As St Paul's, Bristol, rocked the air of stability, Britain asked why?

Why? What a late question. How could she have failed to notice the reasons for the street disturbances which lay in her doings of her own deeds? In the rhyme of her accepted reasoning, she could. Glory. Glory. Glory. She had fed her own people on it and fed other races as negative palliatives to them, thus enabling them to forget their own class-position through what they saw as positive promotion. Her people believed it through encouraged amnesia, which negated the reality of British failures, for instance, the violence of her administration of other races. Which explains another white shock on hearing blacks' and Asians' allusions to their country's colonial violence; and further explains the present-day instinctive disbelief of black and Asian cries of white injustices in Britain. Programmed excuses. What Britain had kept in cold storage suddenly sizzled spontaneously onto the delicate balance of Britain's streets.

Moreover, it was the pain of centuries which was the force behind the black and Asian reaction, equally and opposite to the very white shock. The stalking contest of the black and Asian probability, against the white-considered impossibility, now over, reinforced that the possibility of a major street disturbance is always solidly and latently potent for the future.

Britain's black community knew it, the Asian community knew it, their white friends also knew it. Even Britain's tourists commented upon it. But the sluggish white body-politic was stunned by it. *Brixton*. Ironically, just the way it was 'stunned' by the inevitable demise of white Rhodesians, it will also be 'stunned' by the guaranteed defeat of white South Africa.

Britain's black and Asian communities have always known their own minds, a fact which whites refused to believe, and which with hindsight never mattered. Black and Asian actions in Britain have severed the arteries of arrogance, steering white thought, proving that racial vanity cannot answer theirs or any racial dilemma. That is the philosophy behind the specifics.

Nevertheless, some loaded elements, with a class identity crisis and nothing to lose, colloquialised as skinheads, low-riding the streets and overwhelmed by a racial compulsion to test that slammer: 'that a nation is as strong as its considered weakest'. This physical arm of a racist reaction considered Southall to be the place to slap, to keep themselves happy. Wrong again. The slap-happy skin-beaters met a brown wall stone, which stoned them. And they were blinded by the light, that it was themselves who were always the weakest, and black and Asian peoples were always the stronger, as their identity was always concretely intact. The identity of anyone *aware* of being victimised is always clear-cut.

The message is beginning to hit home; the more the racists attack black and Asian people, the more they will have to defend whites and, in their defence, their need to exaggerate and fabricate will be greater in order to justify their dearth of solutions. A diversionary tactic. Anyone who cares enough can see that white British injustice only creates a quivering and latent potential for rebellion in black and Asian people. In another sense, life is a mixture of secure insecurities, but security must be the larger element, being the very essence for internal stability. Black and Asian stability is assured by their situation.

Media methods reflect the outmoded practices of centuries, continuing to play the bad-mouth, bad-nigger music, as is reflected in their reports of Britain's street disturbances in 1981, using positive and negative racial images. So when does a riot become a rampage? When the participants are all white.

Notice the style of the reporting and headline language on the back page of the *Guardian*, 27 July 1981:

POLICE CLASH WITH MOB IN LAKE DISTRICT

Police battled with about *1,000* motorcyclists and scooter riders armed with *axes* and *coshes*, in Keswick on Saturday.

The confrontation took place at about 10 pm at the lakeside car park, on the outskirts of the Lake District town and on the shore of Derwentwater. Police carrying riot shields moved in to prevent the youths marching on the centre of the town.

The youths, who came from many parts of the country, attacked with *bricks*, *slates* and *bottles*. The Century mobile theatre, where nightly shows are given for holidaymakers, was badly damaged, along with an ice-cream stall and parking kiosks. A parked caravan was burnt out.

Fourteen youths were arrested, mostly charged with offences under the Public Order Act, and one policeman was treated in hospital for leg injuries.

Gangs of youths had been riding around the Lake District during Saturday, but police called in reinforcements from a wide area in the evening when the riders converged on Keswick. *Some of the youths were said to be armed with petrol bombs.*

The Mayor of Keswick, Mr Claude Metcalf, described the attack as *pure vandalism* and said that everything in the car park that could be broken had been broken. There was no glass left in the theatre, and its two bars had been completely wrecked. [My italics]

Now for the *Guardian*'s front page of 11 July 1981:

BRIXTON YOUTHS GO ON RAMPAGE AS RIOTS SPREAD
Rioting erupted again in Brixton, South London, last night hours after Lord Scarman closed the first phase of his inquiry into the *riots* in April.

*Several hundred youths, predominantly*

*black, gathered in the streets and shop windows were broken, shops looted and two police cars burnt.*[My italics]

The slippery truth is out. A rampage becomes a riot when the participants are *predominantly black*. Blowing the guts off the cover-up that the racial bad-mouthing blockbusts the grey cells into seeing the accepted hypocrisy: that the artful language of headlines is a blind brother's game, being the foundations of their ground rations. Will the Rule of the Media, be the Exaggeration in all our lives? Or will they only go for Soul?

Politics is all about the art of timing. In recognition of this obvious fact, which obviously was not obvious to some who timed their politics at the wrong moment, about the wrong people and with the wrong intentions in mind, the evasion philosophy strolled in carrying a white-tonic: 'Our brainless black victims are totally incapable of standing up for themselves, it is all the doing of extremists and outside forces which have stirred them all up'. Remember the words of that 'great white disappointment', Ian Smith, and the black Zimbabwean nationalist struggle? Those whites said it was the work of communists. In any victor/victim situation, how can any 'outside influence' be responsible for the victor's racial tunnel vision, especially when the 'victim's rebellion' takes place? Based on a white belief of black incapability, 'the powers that be' could not admit that they had ignored a reality staring them in the face. Prevarication tangoes in. They preferred excuses, suggesting that if they need to rely on excuses in those situations, they had no answers; and it further means that they themselves had no understanding of the problem in the first place, which raises the question, *what is leadership?*

Leadership can only succeed if the so-called leaders themselves understand the problem. Which then gives the followers confidence that the outcome from the leaders' solution-policy is well founded.

A persecuted minority is a trembling united mass. In order to change direction, a major obstacle is the force that gives it the reason to do so. In the act of changing direction, every single component consciously or subconsciously agrees. That is why black and Asian people do not need a Moses or a white liberal or the so-called left-wing extremists or left-wing liberal friends to show them the way. Blacks and browns already know, by courtesy of the white opposition, in which direction to go. This action is called Spontaneity. The reaction that does not understand it is called Excuses, which stems from the ignorance of those whites who suggest blacks and Asians are incapable of action. Therefore, the propounded argument of why black and Asian people have reacted, through being 'stirred up by outside forces', was a lie before it left the mouths of the people who said it. But what constitutes the definition of the victim's rebellion? And when it happens, do you recognise it? Liverpool?

In an attempt to blow the guts out of Britain's 'riots' shock, the hunt for palliatives began with that infamous British word, which time had institutionalised through its constant repetition. The evasive white soul-singers struck up this greasy refrain: 'Inquiry, Inquiry', let's give them an 'Inquiry', which, it was hoped, being the natural British way of doing things, would institutionalise the problem. In any given situation, this devious mechanism usually helps the controllers not see what they don't want to see, which is the wood, the very core of society's anxieties, preferring it to the trees of pretence. Result, the drive for answers through clear alternatives is lost the moment the word 'Inquiry' is heard. In Britain, everyone is fully aware what happens to an inquiry even before the inquiry begins. Nothing. Then the grand ship Britannia recommences the same course, until the next storm.

Consequently, if the minds who set up the Scarman Inquiry don't know the reason why the disturbances happened, then they have admitted that they have psychologically, within themselves, ignored all the indicators over three decades that pointed to the explosive possibility of it. How can the black and Asian community trust the understanding of those minds they are inquiring into? Which informs us that the Inquirers themselves hold a view of Britain which is light years in distance different from the view held by those being inquired into.

Conclusively then, the Scarman Inquiry failed the

moment it was announced. Lord Scarman's statement, 'Trust me and you will not be betrayed' to the black and Asian communities would not have been said if he had understood the following, which appeared in the *International Herald Tribune* on 20 April 1981:

**Without Representation**
Now that more than 40 per cent of the country's nonwhites are born in Britain, they find it irritating to hear their troubles described as an 'immigration problem.' They have the frustrated feeling that 'no one is representing us,' as a black driver said. There are no nonwhites among the 635 members of the House of Commons, nor are there non-whites in positions of importance at Buckingham Palace or 10 Downing Street.

Offensive racial stereotypes that have long since disappeared from public view in the United States – cannibals, pickaninnies and shiftless black servants – still appear in British advertisements and cartoons, despite a government-sponsored educational campaign.

Sir David McNee, the London police commissioner, conceded that 'a multiracial society is putting the fabric of our policing philosophy under greater stress than at any time' in the past 150 years. With severe recession, national unemployment has climbed to 10 per cent; among the young and poorly educated in places such as Brixton, it may reach 20 per cent to 30 per cent.

Rejecting suggestions to increase public spending in the riot area, Prime Minister Margaret Thatcher said: 'Money cannot buy trust and racial harmony. Trust is a two-way business. No one must condone the disgraceful acts which took place. They were criminal.'

Mrs Thatcher's economic austerity policies – including rigid restraints on spending for social programs – have restricted services and facilities poor neighbourhoods had come to expect under the old Labour Party government.

'But beyond all that sort of thing, it is a question of attitudes,' said Courtney Laws, the leader of the Brixton Neighbourhood Association. 'You cannot imagine what it is like to be black in white Britain. The attitudes are going to have to change.'

Most significantly, notice the clear style of reporting. Propelling a message to our own media landscape-gardeners that their considered balance is biased against the ethnic minority. Which highlights the conclusion that they have no clear idea of the oceans of difference between balance and bias. With shears, rakes, and forks, they have dirtied a profession supposed to reflect the anxieties and true images of any society, biasing their balance with a racial edge, and tightening the noose around Britain's neck. So, if they shift their bias towards balance, it would help.

In that statement made by Lord Scarman, was he aware that he would not be believed? Most significantly, his integrity was never in question. But it was obvious he had not considered that the community he was dishing the soothing balm out to had had many headaches before. They had experience of white Britain's racially biased tonic to go with it. It never worked. It is hopeless taking a painkiller if the pain has not been correctly identified. If he knew where the pain lay, the first thing he would have done was not to make that statement. Since lawyers, like Lord Scarman, are experts on British history, presumably he is well aware of the pitiless inhumanities committed by whites against these people. Therefore, he must also have been aware of what the black and brown attitude, with well-grounded lack of confidence in Britain's system, would be to the setting-up of what they see as a Meaningless Inquiry. Black and Asian people need no Inquiries, they need the result of previous Inquiries. Hence the dishing out of palliatives is better given to the white majority, if they will accept it. What will satisfy black and Asian people are lashings of certainties. They need the certainty that their children will be given educational opportunities; they need, proportionately, a guaranteed slice of the employment market; they need the certainty that no one will burn entire black and Asian families to death in their homes; and a certainty that the fascism they also fought against, will be dealt with by the law uncompromisingly. Lord Scarman, however honourable his intentions may be, cannot *certify* any of these things. He cannot issue a certificate that *certifies* that black and Asian people walking the streets are *certain* that a cold blade of Sheffield steel will not be thrust into their bodies. That women will never again be violated. That children will stop leaving school merely semi-educated.

Another reason why the Inquiry is not needed is because the governing powers have for years now decisively shown they have no alternatives; no alternative way of talking to or an alternative way of understanding black and Asian people. The rub is that because they have used the same methods over centuries, they have no other way. The Scarman Inquiry is merely a sugar-coated pill for the white majority. Again, the Scarman Inquiry will fail because it is based on all the wrong assumptions about who black and Asian people are. As was seen in the insensitive way in which the Inquiry was formed, with its obvious balanced-bias toward white public opinion and its treatment of non-whites as naughty children. The cutting scalpel sliced the lies from a racial cover-up. If Britannia's black and brown nationals were being crudely and condescendingly treated in the full glare of her own people in Britain, what must have been perpetrated on their skulls in her out-of-sight colonies? The chicken of truth is beginning to come home to roost. The Inquiry that is desperately needed is one that will enable whites to find out who the black and brown British really are. History is wrong. Blow black, blow brown, blow understanding into white British lives.

Furthermore, in the hunt for *underlying reasons*, that Inquiry had no declared intention of consulting black and Asian women, who have held the black and Asian communities together since their arrival in Britain. In their considerations, the inquirers are well aware that colour, coupled with gender, forces them a class lower. Therefore, by attacking black and Asian women, they are attacking the roots of black and Asian communities. This is a land of fine frying slick-talk, which dismisses the savagely cultural reality; that if white Britain cuts out black and brown roots, the danger for Britain is that a great big British black oak will crash down on white skulls. You may find this ominous, but so are the white's physical and moral reactions to black and Asian people.

Finally, through historical experience right up to this very day, the black community knows it, the brown community knows it, their white friends also know it; and the entire white majority suspects it, that the Inquiry will fail to change anything. Whose interest is that in?

It is true that knowledge is power, but it is the black and Asian communities and their white allies that possess the powerful knowledge, that white palliatives are now black guarantees. It is serious to mess around with the possibility of black and Asian mass action. There has to be a massive amount of integrity in the message of the white. Anything else means the white man's mind is still stuck in the mud of historical assumptions; that black people will continue to tolerate the hot jazz of white hot air. It is time to face the music because this nation knows the score.

There are some motor-mouths in this nation who believe that political parties are there to make policy and find answers to the problems of the nation. What if the political parties themselves are the problem? What if I said that if every black and Asian voter were to join a political party, it would change nothing? Who could believe it? The answer would be dependent on their position on the ladder of class, what they have to lose, and which party they feel best represents their interests. But what if all the parties spring from the same racial foundations? And do they respect the racial interests of the other Britain?

Racial interest, which can be easily seen in the agreement they have when it comes to formulating practical, not theoretical, policy: i.e. has any party ever promoted the obvious, which is, Britain must fundamentally change the basis of her political attitude to black Africa and Asia? When it is realised that Britain has always been a one-race political party, with racial superiority attached, how could she ever hope to negotiate with those countries using *her* definition of the basis of the equality as the starting point? A state which has always represented a one-race interest cannot possibly have any of her political parties representing anything other than what she represents.

Great Britain once had an Empire, to which more than one race belonged. Outside its white members, which of the others have you heard singing hosannas of thanks, hollering the praises of Britannia and ploughing gospels of gratefulness for the golden opportunities she left embedded in their imperial memories? But there *is* agreement among them, reflected in the unwavering constancy of black and brown opinion in Britain today. Which word does that conjure up in your mind? The one in mine you know.

And the blatant truth you also know. Black and brown bodies were always used to nourish and support white interest. The old leopardess not only changed her spots, but the spotty infection increased into an ulcerated rash, resulting in a spot-less hide. Lest the spots can be identified, the cancer remains, blemishing the racial basis of each political party. Through the use of emotion as leadership, which created white Britain's racism in the first place, how do they now diffuse their emotional issue? Bertrand Russell, in his book entitled *Power*, accurately explains the build-up:

But the leader is hardly likely to be successful unless he enjoys his power over his followers. He will therefore be led to a preference for the kind of situation, and the kind of mob, that makes his success easy. The best situation is one in which there is a danger sufficiently serious to make men feel brave in combating it, but not so terrifying as to make fear predominant – such a situation, for example, as the outbreak of war against an enemy who is thought formidable but not invincible. A skilful orator, when he wishes to stimulate warlike feeling, produces in his audience two layers of belief: a superficial layer, in which the *power of the enemy* is magnified so as to make great courage seem necessary, and a deeper layer, in which there is a firm conviction of victory. Both are embodied in such a slogan as 'right will prevail over might'.

The kind of mob that the orator will desire is one more given to emotion than to reflection, one filled with fears and consequently hatreds, one impatient of slow and gradual methods, and at once exasperated and hopeful. The orator, if he is not a complete cynic, will acquire a set of beliefs that justify his activities. He will think that feeling is a better guide than reason, that our opinions should be formed with the blood rather than the brain, that the best elements in human life are collective rather than individual. If he controls education, he will make it consist of an alternative of drill and collective intoxication, while knowledge and judgement will be left to the cold devotees of inhuman science. [My italics]

The power syndrome Bertrand Russell refers to can be seen in the confidence trick the Empire builders used on their own people, by taking the weight off their minds, accidentally helping them to forget their position on the almost unclimbable vertical ladder of class. By conjuring up the power of the enemy on a religiously fearful people, the myths they created about black people took on a new status, and tales of 'Darkest Africa' with its marauding savage natives cemented it, a rich colourful legacy of negatives, which contemporarily infests white British minds. Ask any racist the basis for his beliefs. The concoction you hear will not only be baseless but based on little intelligence. Powerful is the confidence trick, if unquestioned.

Who built the misnamed British Empire? Yes, there was an Empire. White scheming provided the draughtsmen using black and brown bodies to build the draughtsmen's schemes. And true to his scheming Britishness, he had already schemed in advance to take all the credit for himself. Where have we seen that one before? Everywhere the British have schemed.

In Britain's structured class system, where the ruler's schemes divert the attentions of the majority, inhibiting their vision to notice, they have always lost out. The fact is, the empire belongs to races, who by right inhabit present-day Britain. But if they insist on still calling it 'British' then they are admitting those people were British in the past and, incidentally, the parents of the ones born here are still British. Such is the trick of thought. The British Empire was a misnomer. Black and Asian peoples built it and the ruling class minority of Britain's whites controlled it to use for their own interests. This also explains the vast differences in the division of wealth in Britain today. Why do some individuals disproportionately hold more than their needs while the vast majority hold infinitely less? Who, in real terms, reaped the rewards of other people's labours? This demonstrates that the white working classes were always as much colonised as black and Asian peoples. The unthinkable has happened. Imperialism has finally colonised itself.

Therefore, the political parties, by only representing white interests, have never represented the interests of Britain's far-flung ex-colonial constituents. They have still to 'discover' that their obvious contemporary duty is to redirect their previous racial dishonesty, with recognition of the three-dimensional race situation in Britain today.

In the liberal race against time, seeking to solve the race-condition problem overnight, some friends of non-whites have already made the classical error of asking them to join political parties. No doubt it is extremely important that that decision be left to individual choice. But remember, by retaining their foundations that reflect a one-race nation, Britain's main political parties merely use black and Asian peoples for their own interest, manoeuvring them in slightly different ways. This is known as 'Blighty's Sham' which is composed of: one party says 'Let's go back'; another says 'No, let's just avoid the minefields by looking both ways'; yet another says, 'No, let's satisfy everybody'; and the final one says, 'Don't let us say anything we believe in'. All of whom use that Great Seal, 'The British People', as their rubber stamp to attain power and develop instant amnesia.

However, the confidence in their tricks has not worked on ethnic minorities, noticeable in the activity of their absence in Britain's political life. The political skin-beating skin-users should recognise that their party constitutions in no way understand the constitution of the political party black and Asian people already belong to, created by the white racist Opposition. Also, by the outright failure of Britain's political parties to meaningfully demonstrate their opposition to that Opposition; which means they readily agree with it, through their immigrating use of it.

Contextually, that old cliché, 'actions speak louder than words', is a lie. In British politics, inaction is everything, and the actions the parties have liberated underlie the activity of their words, while continuing to consider blacks and browns as a 'soft election touch'. Additionally, the ethnic voters' natural reticence to join Britain's political parties and take their rightful place in British political life generates from their belief that they are shady set-ups, because they still do not reflect the interests of the other colour Britain. They are merely facets of elitism, proving that all oppressors shuffle in different guises, but they all look the same to the victim.

The Commission for Racial Equality is the off-shoot of a permanent tranquilliser mentality, a pre-dated programmed relief, erected in order to satisfy the programmed paranoias of the whites in their immemorial one-sided arguments. A permanent identity crisis. All nations are in a constant state of paranoia. With Britain's historical behaviour deeply rooted in your mind, is it any wonder that her paranoia has become a weapon to be used faithfully? Britannic paranoia evolves from a series of unacceptable possibilities. The unacceptabilities are, that black and Asian people are *not inferior*, that she no longer controls the universe, that she no longer possesses yesterday's political and material power, and she needs black and Asian contributions. The possibilities are that all those unacceptabilities are true. And the unacceptable becomes the paranoia, but only for the majority.

Among Britain's whites there are two views of

Britain. The view of the ruling class, who represent the past but who do not live in it, who opportunistically and politically identify a crisis, usually by 'developing' it and then feed that crisis into the identity of the nostalgia-ridden masses, thus forming the other view.

Moreover, this type of psychological trickery is used in the discussions of the white-considered racial crisis, which is supposedly due to floods of black and Asian immigrants, conjuring up the dilution of the 'quality and richness' of Britain.

The identity crisis I speak of is based on a series of unacceptable possibilities. And in this land where whites have endlessly identified themselves with superiority, the phrase *Great* Britain becomes clear and understood. The entrance of 'inferior' black and brown peoples into Britain provides us with a clear picture of the 'superior' white man's politically devised dilemma of paranoia, as he splutters '*how can I identify with that?*' The possibility that those white-considered black and brown inferiors *are* his equals is totally unacceptable. Their visible presence increases his paranoia. And because the idea is unacceptable to him, his paranoia remains. Until he understands that, the white man's identity crisis will also remain.

British governments, without remedies for potential agitation, institutionalises it with no answer at all. No answer is, 'Inquiries', Royal Commissions and Institutions like the CRE. The institution the CRE replaced is reflected in its name. The government

213

viewed two problems, with two institutions. By setting up the Race Relations Board (RRB) separately from the Community Relations Commission, (CRC) it encouraged the white majority to arrive at the view that blacks and Asians required a separate institution for a separate problem, because the crisis was only about them. The identification of the RRB as *the* institution specifically for their crisis was given more validity through isolated instances which had previously occurred, e.g. the 1958 Notting Hill Gate street disturbances.

The white majority knew it. The black and brown community knew it, and also knew what the government intended: to do nothing at all. Who has it satisfied? Those it was intended to satisfy; the institutionalised accepters followed by an institutionalised dismissal programme.

To begin with, the CRE is a platitudinal guarantee; guaranteeing that all black and Asian complaints will be cushioned by a built-in inactivity. It is carefully sculpted to sieve the heat out of black and Asian complaints, by being founded on an alien form of integrity, made certain by the exclusively white interest it represents. Being based on wrong assumptions about black and Asian people, the CRE was never in danger of losing the confidence of blacks and Asians. Because the CRE never had it. So good for the white majority.

Moreover, the relationship between black peoples and Asians on the one hand and whites on the other has always been based on aggression and condescension. This is the guts of the racial bucket in Britain today. In going high, disguised as a Commission, it went home to where it belongs. To the Great White Fathers who have timelessly infested their relationship between them and their victims with Commissions of Bad Faith. The perfidy of which is fortified by the fake-book finger artistry which required the necessity of several fangless Race Relations Acts. One should have been enough.

In relation to black and Asian people, white authority has a singular dishonesty. That is, by matching in opposition the workable against the unworkable. This tactic allows them visually to achieve the impossible: by appearing to be progressing when they are, in fact, standing still.

In cold storage is the white definition of progress; in cold relation to the black and Asian definitions of progress, which can be seen clearly in the devious intentions when forming Britain's Race Relations laws. With experience in mind, Britain's whites feel that progress has been achieved, because *they* appear to be progressing, and non-white people appear to have been conned. Whereas black people cut loose from that crumb-dropping white ideal aeons ago, and have defined progress as: *no white attempt to deceive*. The black and brown sledgehammer demand is: if a law intended to scalpel racist practices is broken, by *anyone*, that deviant must be hammered by the full force of the law, irrespective of colour or class.

Moreover, racially misconceived conceptions, if they continue unchecked and are not revamped, will always produce other conceptions which, by implication, are themselves misconceptions. The result being a contemporary inability to conceive conceptions which can murder the original misconceptions about others. Therefore, misconception becomes the order of the day, resulting in the attitude that assaulting the human rights of others will solve the original misconceived ideas about that race. So, what is the Pax Britannica? In this instance, it is the total belief in human rights. It also demands women and men with the courage, integrity and the ability required to conceive new conceptions for the actual make-up and realness of a multiracial and multicultural British body politic. Carry on misconceiving. Or use imagination to conceive optimism through the belief in, and knowledge of, *real* alternatives. Thought is food for black and white and brown grey cells, for it has no owners.

# 7. Prospects

And central to the Question of the black and Asian presence in Britain; evolving from a Message that hurricaned through the Caribbean, ran slicing into Asia, and razored the African continent, grooming the Opportunist's Ideal and thrusting impetus into the Tommy, who spoke of pastures of Britain's potent Spring, of the cowslip and the buttercup, with sparrows on the wing; and if you sail to England, where the greening meadows smile, 'neath the oak by the rivulet, where thee can rest awhile. Frantically, framing and falling apart, freezing into their brains that Britain was an inviting frolic pad, with a hustle all the same. They'll never forget red rivers wept, shrieking 'remember the centuries before'; child carried the pain loud and strong, which white chose to ignore, the enslavement of their peoples and the agony of their suppress, honing memories of devastated families, fighting Hitler for the West. 'Tis deeply etched in the Soulful, 'tis deeply etched in blood, 'twas always etched in rebelling, 'gainst further carnage of white, red and black mud. Britannia encouraged the feeling in brown people from the East, who came for hopeful prospects, to the pretence of an explosive feast; as did her other black victimised, dividing into Two, burning lashings of final midnight oils, the tropical air turned blue. But not knowing The Question would never be answered, as they climbed, clambered, chasing dreams that castles are made of, to meet the people who built those castles, with care, with motive, tended with purpose of no rights at all, cutting the expectations out of the black and brown Prospects Ball. 'I have a dream,' said one of their men, 'we also have one too, and we were also wondering if our dream will end up like you.' Their agony was stamped in a single teardrop which began what was to come, tumbling down little brown faces, those tears etched the future, represented their past, dropping the Truth into their present, and the answer came out at last...

'LET'S REPEAT THE BLACK EXPERIENCE'.

Lay down, those hearts of auspicious death knells, of final condemnations, 'rivers of blood', 'swamping' imaginations to 'backs against the wall'. Lay dead imperial product, with unreasoning for a philosophy, the sum total of centuries of absence of thought. For your answer is a rockpile of nostalgia: 'Let's repeat our history'. The Past for the Future? Run down and rocket away, for your Nothing Machine is X'ed out.

I, for one, am not a doom-merchant. Those inhabitants exist on the wrong side of the tracks of peaceful co-existence. For the distance between imagination and unimagination is the chasm in the philosophy of understanding that there *are* alternatives.

'Never in a thousand years' was the voracious and uncompromising philosophy of the dominator, of the 'white minority' illegal regime ruling a black *majority* with the rod of brutality in that black country, Zimbabwe. Curiously, those whites, holding a graveyard of bloodying projectiles to fragment and lacerate black bodies, felt threatened by Zimbabwe's unarmed black residents.

Consequently, black-majority-ruled Zimbabwe was the result of the white Rhodesian minority's bloody philosophy. Britannia's kith and kin have remained in Zimbabwe, with the ready and publicly voiced acceptance of Zimbabwe's black majority. Which announces the jackhammering irony of the racial reversal: for it is they, the blacks, who now hold the ballistics for the defence of *all* Zimbabweans. Through white Rhodesians' insatiable materialistic racist appetite, aided and abetted by inhuman British racial irresponsibility towards Zimbabwean blacks, the ultimate black victory was a phenomenally high price paid for in black and their white allies' lives. Those white Rhodesians who died killed themselves before they were dead. They did so by being extortionate parasites. Flip open your fogged blindness and focus on this: all oppressors are conclusively victims of their own beliefs, by freaking themselves into the tyrant's dogma: Me. Me. Me.

Those whites, in order to remain, have had to pledge their allegiance to the office of the black Zimbabwean Head of State. This is reflected in their visible participation in all of Zimbabwe's institutions, thus safe-guarding their racial interests by being woven into the fabric of a multicultural society. Additionally, like the black and brown British, they are also in a minority. Notice that the Zimbabwean black majority have not copped out of the racial responsibility for the human rights of white Zimbabweans.

This is a land of elitist ladders, where condescension is just a rung of 'bad taste', busting into everything, culminating in class and racial bitterness. In 1980/1, when Britain's streets were dusted by racial disturbances, we learned something; that the kinetic energy of bitterness is a powerful ladder to hate.

Nevertheless, there are racist broncos among Britain's white community who have amply demonstrated their wish to see the black and Asian experience repeated. Amazingly, *a white majority are fearful of a black and Asian minority.* Paranoia of a Christian path?

Crucially, black and brown ears have been whipped and deafened by the silence of white principle, a casually evasive guest. Or are silent principles principally silent for racial reasons? Contemporary Britain's white majority have constantly given moral justifications for any white minority dominating black and Asian peoples globally, vomiting out, 'They are not ready'. But Britain persists in conclusively excluding her black and brown community from being cemented into the fabric of her so-called multiracial society. Where is the threat? Solitarily confined in the white paranoid knowledge-box.

Britain is a land of ill-facades, where her advertised image promotes a high-powered, nut-cracking black reality. In present-day Britain, black and brown thoughts are the results of white actions constantly honing their attitudes to resoluteness. But if a chump is one who makes a quarrel out of a debate, who is quarrelling over whose interests, while encouraging the other to debate the quarrel? And what is the quarrel all about?

So, let us light the lamp in *this* Land of Darkness.

The merchants of doom merely promote ominous doom-laden theories of death and destruction. With power in the front of their political minds, and treachery in the back, they are nothing but self-centred souls, stealing away from responsibility. There are other motor-mouths, of every kind, stamping out insincerities, declaring Britain to be a 'multiracial society'. They, for whom honesty is a one-night stand, are merely dusting the air with ulterior racial motives, spiced with verbal larceny.

In a truly multiracial society, there is only one

answer that all races can live with: a collective solution. But 'Immigration', 'Repatriation' and 'Deportation' are the only answers which will satisfy those racists existing in Britain's white community, an answer which gives confidence to only one side.

And here is the blackout. With callous, but expensive, silence, calling an ill-wind and perceiving it as a soft cannonball of sane argument, the silent majority enters. Using the psychological razor blade of moral reasoning, they slashed the 'in' from 'injustice' as their belief in the rights of others took a moral holiday. Few whites seem to have seen discrimination. Blindfolded justice was the measure of the Pax Britannica, a 'peace' washed in the agonised blood of black and Asian people. And since the present morals of a country are simply a reflection of its past morality, blowing into focus the injustice that is welcomed in the present. The silence of the white majority shouts their agreement with racial intolerance, degradation and inhumanity, while they turn their deaf ear to those white, black and brown freedom believers who have the courage, the principles and the belief in the human rights of others. This silence of deafness shouts their 'belief' in humanity into silence. But the black and brown British have memories.

There's a cloud of shame hanging over this land.

Silence is what some dreams are made of. There is an anchor of pain in the heart of humanity, mugging countless minds with the memory of others' silences, boosting them on, never to forget.

Silence can also be a nightmare. In the present-day past time, the gassed-down bloodied sinews of another race forever stain the minds of Germans' wartime Silence, which also allowed the *devaluation* of the nationality of Germany's Jews. Silence seduced the fractionalisation of millions of families worldwide. In Europe, it resulted in the ever-living tragedy of broken-up, emaciated, mangled bodies; a wealth of humanity busted by the silence of the fence-sitters, culminating in the decimation of a people who just happened to be Jewish. It was called Fascism, and his bosom-pal, Silence, encouraged him. Their melted-down bodies remind the victimised and the principled with the flame of belief in human rights. Jews have memories about Germans. Such is the price of silence.

Neville Chamberlain, British pre-war Prime Minister, flew back from Munich and announced, 'Peace in *our* time'. That is Silence.

The Holocaust of the Pax Britannica broke down the bodies of countless numbers of Africa's black and Arab peoples, and Africans in the Caribbean, along with the Asian masses. Silence not only guaranteed it, but silently swallowed it into Britain's history books which, in the balance of time, were transferred into Britannic pride, strung out by story-telling.

History is what a nation wants remembered; with human expediency, it leaves out the pitiless inhumanities used on others, and sows the searing blow-torch of future conscience.

The present is the history for tomorrow, and reflection of yesterday. If it is considered that history is something to learn from and not live in, then it is sad to see how frail the human ego must be, to see people give in to their weaknesses.

Through the precedents set in history, it would seem that a nation with no obvious purpose or direction, such as Britain, passes the buck of leadership in times of recession as a diversionary tactic to those who use tactics to divert their own maladies. The Jews were the scapegoats for the Germans. Britain's black and Asian peoples are used for similar purposes. In this country, leadership is moribund due to unchanged gunboat solutions, never considering alternatives.

It cannot be in the interests of British national stability for the Hitlerite syndrome to happen in Britain. The terrible consequence of the rise of racial brutality is that, if black and brown lives are continually threatened or demolished in Britain, the defence of white lives in Asia, Africa and the Caribbean will be horrifically paramount. I, for one, do not want that and I cannot believe that any sane person does either. So blow out the afterglow.

The time will come, after the failures of Britain's whites to use principle in their stand for their famed belief in justice, that people in a thousand years will say that 'this was their finest hour of injustice'. There is a cloud of shame hanging over this land, and compassion has become a stranger. It was completely cut down yesterday. Making tracks when the merciless warriors of elitism machete in to divide and rule, thus ruling the divisions of the white majority; resulting in Britain's present-day degradation called class. Compassion is now ashamed, lingering and lurking in dark shadows of concealment. Whereas humanity, in a moral sense, was mugged by inhumanity in the out-of-sight territories of British colonies. Immorally, it returned home to the Foreign Office, with the empty corpse of humanity as a camouflage. Compassion was still in hiding in the basement of the Home Office. The two watered-down passions convened in the sweatshops of the media, instantly emerging as an aid chorus, loudly advertising Britain's veiled compassion. It is called propaganda. In the eyes of Britain's black and Asian peoples, that is the white British definition of humanity. A backdoor man.

The foundations for the loss of humanity are rooted in the beginnings of Britain's present-day advanced technology, which demanded the crushing of anything and anyone who impeded its progress, for instance, the black Zimbabwean peoples and their bulldozers, from Cecil Rhodes to Ian Smith. However, those non-white peoples of the world, without previous necessity for industrialisation, retained a large element of human compassion that still persists today. A savage culture with a psychopathic technology is the weakness crushing the strength of the strong.

Ever since the 1980/1 British street disturbances, the question which has permeated the social atmosphere is:

'What can be done to improve race relations in Britain?' The traditional British answer of creating institutions to solve a problem, in this instance, is positively negative. Because it merely dresses up pessimism to appear in the bright plumage of optimism. But first let us look at a modern-day example that continues to cement the negatives in the white race attitudes toward black and Asian people.

Decolonisation provides us with the ground rations for the continual pumping out of negative images of black and Asian peoples onto a white Britain, which never heard anything else or anything good about those people, and therefore has clearly always believed in their inferiority and gives them no reason to change those ideas. The blatancy of the racial undermining of black and brown abilities, helped by the racial vanity shown in the 'balanced' racial bias of the hack reporter, interviewing a Minister with the wishful, negative question/negative answer ingrained habit about the impending handover to a black or Asian government. It reinforces the rampant myths about black and Asian peoples, forcefully cementing them into the mindset of modern-day Britain. But this pathetic device has failed.

Traditionally, the British government's justification for retaining control of any black or Asian country and their resources was bedded in the principle of the Back-firing Caucasian Confidence Trick. Before independence, the mendacity is: 'There are not enough qualified people to run the country'. It backfires. For example, consider Her Majesty's Government, the Executive Controller of India for well over two centuries. Why were there not enough 'qualified people'? It can only point to the savage and malicious intention to create a form of government that would be perpetually dependent on Britain's white administrators. Or was it because they wanted a *permanent* white British social and political infrastructure?

Britain's definition of 'good governance' is recognised by its total similarity to Westminster, making no consideration for differences of culture and social values. All of which is based on a white crisis of identity, for they consider *identity* has value when it exists as a replica of their own.

Whites, who want a non-white government to be like their own, and non-white people to be like themselves, are implying that they want them to be simply clones. But it does not have to be like that. There are some whites who are sure of their racial identity, and wish for the identity of black and brown British to remain intact. They do not feel threatened.

This confidence trick was arrested by Britain's black and Asian peoples when Ian Smith justified his reasons for retaining power after he had declared UDI in Rhodesia. He pointed to the white 'fact' that there were not enough 'educated' black Zimbabweans. This pale deceit put a spell on Rhodesia's white immigrants, giving them a little more confidence to buy a little more time before the inevitable happened. In Asia and

Africa, have you ever noticed that that white strategy of buying 'a little more time' always results in the loss of countless black and brown lives? However, Robert Mugabe and his governing personnel, all possessed their current qualifications at the time that Ian Smith, the white farmer, spat out that boorish statement. Strangely, Her Majesty's Government and Britain's media listened to the race music of Smith, and chose to allow the British public to believe it by not significantly denying it. Furthermore, the British government could not deny the excuse she herself had used in nearly every colony, which Ian Smith thoroughly understood and used to good effect; proving that the politics guiding white actions in Asia, the West Indies and Africa is a conman's game, which always backfires. For the actions in Britain's politics had become ideas for black and brown actions, here and abroad.

Independence Day Celebrations provide another heaven-sent opportunity for more race-music of the negative kind to an ever-waiting white British public, who in turn justify their good fortune in their British nationality, stability and all that. The deed is about to be done and the British television news atmosphere is heavily laden with Sunday Righteousness. They, the Great British People, are about to *give* something away for nothing. Their pride is very British, most probably based on the 'magnificent' British gesture taking place in front of their very eyes. And the nation tunes in to a trick. The commentator begins in earnest, piling on adjectives about the 'great British presence' from the days when white men tamed that country and its peoples, giving them the benefit of British administration, education, agriculture and so on. The beat in the Independence arena is up-tempo, which also allows him the opportunity to get in 'still backward' outside the towns. The new government is in for a 'very difficult time', rumours of 'dastardly deeds' in the villages, coupled with an impending '*coup d'état*'. The rug-cutting continues with heavy emphasis on the 'fact' that the new government cannot survive 'without British aid' – carefully leaving out that that aid normally amounts to probably about ten pence per citizen. And, more importantly, the commentator totally sideslips the burning question: 'How much profit has the United Kingdom made while she was governing that colony?' The commentator now pauses, and immediately continues with something about 'the struggle' and 'not ready' and 'Britain did her best'. The waiting white millions, watching their talk-boxes, nod agreement. The 'Great' in Britain is once again justified; 'we ruled the world', as white British workers begin to get ready for their night-shift, and a take home pay-packet of £58 per week. That, I suppose, is reality. And the Independence scene they have just witnessed? 'Well, that helps take my mind off nasty realities.' An amnesia drop.

The scene is made. The Great White Giver, Her Majesty's representative, is flicked constantly on and off the screens. The mugging details about another race continue. Soon the homebound audiences are convinced that, literally, six white men ran the country, while the indolent natives were mere onlookers. But now that they are moving house, the natives are neck-breaking it to grab a piece of the action, for they only trusted the whites. But not each other.

The Giver, resplendent in his cockeyed power outfit, mounts the rostrum, all the while giving the waiting white millions his best superior smile while surrounded by those aliens, as the commentator quickly points out, 'doing their funny dances'. The Giver, with trained dignity, struts to the new Prime Minister. Meanwhile, in the foreground of the background, the commentator, with paper emotion, pans a run-down of the magnificent career of the Giver. Yes, he has had a somewhat 'rather devilish time', but he did finally bring the new leaders, who 'were practically at each other's throats', to see reason. At this point Great Britain is about to lose her newly-found friend. Sweet man sweet. The conquering Tarzans have returned to try and trust those restless natives, whose brains were always out to lunch. The White Power dance is on.

The hour draws near, then the 'fears' Britain's whites have been waiting for are pulled out of the twilight world of her dirty tricks pot. *The* statements that the white British peepers and flappers on the media beat are avidly hankering for are: 'they cannot run their country without whites', 'will the whites be safe?', 'will these peoples start killing each other?', all voiced with such professional conviction that Britain's white millions immediately believe no other human talents in that particular country exists. Only white talent and ability exist. He can play it cool, because he has an audience of willing believers. Curiously, these British television commentators never find anything positive to report about that impending ex-colony, or about its peoples, which does not explain why there was a British presence there in the first place, and for so long.

Nevertheless, all the while the white celebratory charade is happening, Britain's blacks and browns, most of whom are expert white-watchers, harden their resolve. For the celebrations, which I presume are supposed to be a momentous occasion of great joy, as per normal, merely turn into another catalogue of white British derision of black and brown peoples. Which in turn puts a little more of the non-white-inability negativity-issue into ready-to-believe white brain cells. And the show goes on.

The false moment of naked-con has risen. The Great White Giver, with insincerity, plus a delicate hint of condescension painted carefully across his face, mouths a 'moving out' speech, the Great Tenant then hands back to the Owners their 'borrowed' land and neck-breaks it out of the country. But the con almost certainly backfires. Within days, the white British residents are rudely awakened. That ex-colony may need whites; the rub is, the whites they need are not necessarily British. Great Britain has just burnt two boats. One with the newly independent country, the other with black and brown British citizens, along with a host of whites. There is no doubt that those ceremonies, or other events, must happen and be covered by the British media. But the time for thoughtless racial reporting is long over. And delivering mythical negatives, attempting to undermine another nation's integrity, is watched keenly by a determined British youth, white, black and brown, who carefully record the negatives used on another people, but which are also used on themselves. An issue has been recognised in the underhand methods that the British government and media push abroad, by way of the many negatives they peddle at Asia, the West Indies and Africa. This will always have a domino effect on British race relations. The backfire is complete.

Moreover, in nearly every British colony, true to their racial bias, Britain's whites erected a set of race laws (written and unwritten) which practically deprives that colony's black and brown citizens of their land rights, education and equal opportunity. Where have we heard that before? And, as usual, those race laws were always biased towards whites.

The smart stuff is repeated. Back home in Britain, where 'fair play' is the name of the game, the Race Relations laws, with colonial experience of skin-beating and separate development, are biased towards whites by carefully omitting the naked power of the law (which in the colonies was carefully woven in), even when a racist white deed is clearly blatant and legally proven. The offender, if white, is given a gentle slap on his wrist. Outside, in the white, white world, his conviction in some cases is merely 'battle honours'. But this legal racial bias towards white pigmentation explains the vindictive powerlessness of any British Race Relations law where blacks and Asians are concerned. Consequently, what we see happening in Britain today reinforces the aggression emitting from Asian, West Indian and African peoples, about the vindictiveness, through material greed, of Britain's violent and racist methods in the legal administration of those nations. The white British Stormtrooper action towards Britain's non-white nationals comes sizzling hot from her memory. For it is merely a reflection of Britannia's negative attitudes which she used to keep her colonial non-whites independence struggles within British perspectives. At that time, she was doing what is known as 'taking care of business'. She was only treading water in the balance of time. On the streets of present-day Britain, in the hearts of black and Asian peoples, there are devastating moods; a community crawling with clues for quality time. It tastes like this in the tearful world of 'capital competition', where 'winning and losing' is the name of the game. If you prefer to think that being an Imperial Coloniser means you have 'won', then the blatant truth is, since decolonisation, Great Britain has been heavily engrossed in losing all the 'winnings'. She is now in a reactive rapid transfer stage, when governments with few answers usually end up saying: 'Let them eat cake'. Let them know this in Liverpool, Southall, Brixton, Bristol and anywhere else riots and tragedy takes place.

I broke into numerous visions when I noticed, through the railings of a kindergarten, a multiracial class of kids playing with life, never minding luck. They were gardening, sitting around discovering each other. In one corner of the garden, I perceived a group of three or four free souls, all holding Union flags with Prince Charles and Lady Diana stamped in the centre. For me, children are half a stretch away from imagination. In a way, it is promise-food for my dream-box. It was a brightening scene and I felt good.

The importance of that scenario only hit home when a white kid, with resolve as per his size, grabbed the Union flag out of the hand of his black friend. Watched by two others, a brown and a white, the black, all of four or five, put a spell on his ideas and snatched his property back. Encouraged by his success, he began to run the changes, proudly waving his flag as his sign of victory. Gradually, with a little support from their teacher, peace returned to the play space.

Awareness flooded my imagination. From that simple scene, I focused on Tomorrow. Transferring that child through the hustle of time, I placed him a few years hence. I pondered a moment to get to the effect. I bounced a little with my thoughts. 'What,' I asked myself, 'if that child grows up to discover the Union flag he was holding would one day stone him in the guts?' Or maybe, wouldn't even let him get up off the ground floor?

Feeling I was onto something, it wasn't time to mess around. I headed for some conniggeration, for other opinions. Later on that day, I breezed back home and began to think, constitutionally. If that child, in that not far-off time, has only heard the insecurities of whites, with their personal aces constantly grinding in on his head, through the labels 'immigrants', 'repatriation' and 'deportation', while still calling him the derogatory term, 'coloured', he will in less than half the time it takes to form a thought, become *another* rebel.

The reality is that in any of Britain's ex-colonies, white racial and material interests have always been safeguarded by virtue of being an inherent part of the fabric of that society. Let us also remember that whites, in setting up the infrastructure of government, land ownership and commerce in those then colonies, cunningly weaved themselves in, to become *the* structure itself. A white sit-in. They belonged to everything, and every club there was, to keep an eye on things. They were *the* government, and owed allegiance to the British monarch. So did all the black and Asian peoples. Her Majesty's 'subjects' they most certainly were, but 'British' in name only. Notice that for Britain's black and Asian peoples, being a 'British subject' was pure theory, while the practice of citizenship, when applied to colonised peoples, always came first. Thus, *subject to Britain* was the order of the day. Consequently, when Britannia needed compulsory volunteers to fight for 'King and Country', the use of her 'subjects' was a foregone conclusion. But in white Britain, after *her* danger was over, racial 'accidental amnesia' suddenly occurred. The only wartime contribution she 'suddenly' remembered reared up with a vengeance when Ian Smith announced a Unilateral Declaration of Independence. A national white British Spasm Band, sensing the spark of international cries for British military action, especially from African and Asian countries, streaked into action and pumped into a black hide-beating refrain: 'kith and kin, kith and kin, they fought beside us during World War Two'. The heat was too much for a British government, who never had any intention of sending British troops to quell the white rebellion. Incidentally, the government did offer the Aldershot Regiment to Nigeria's Prime Minister, Sir Abubakar Tafawa Balewa, who was at almost the same moment undergoing a successful *coup d'état*. The Aldershot Regiment was placed on seventy-hour alert, but was never used, not having been requested by the Nigerians.

When Ian Smith and the white Rhodesian immigrants became white Zimbabweans, the British government was most insistent on the protection of white lives and the racial interests of Zimbabwe's whites. And in order to give more foundation to white Zimbabwean interests, the Great White Father trumpeted in unison with those whites: how they had built the country, as usual with their bare hands, from nothing, forgetting that the black Zimbabweans performed *all* physical tasks. They now delivered what all of Africa's whites consider *their* killer-punch: 'the country will fall into rack and ruin without whites'. Why those particular whites? There are others, who most probably possess far more integrity. The black peoples of Zimbabwe and Azania (South Africa) know very well that there is a fine line between black necessity for those particular whites and the destruction of blacks by those same whites.

Today, Zimbabwe, with the help of Britain's government, essentially protects the racial interests of Zimbabwe's white minority — who are also very much part of the fabric of the State.

Black and Asian peoples have, for several centuries, contributed to the British economy, even more so than Zimbabwe's whites have done for Zimbabwe. Significantly, countless black and Asian lives have either been butchered at the hands of Britain's whites, or lost in numerous wars fighting for Britain, especially World Wars One and Two. Why then, are their racial interests not being reflected in the social and political life of Britain? Is it because they cannot totally look like, speak like, or eat the same foods as the whites; in fact, murder their own identity? The truth is, when Britain's whites arrive in *any* colony, they practised the same white-superior-implacable attitudes in others' territory. They kept themselves strictly apart, while making the local inhabitants house-serfs. And those 'Gods on Earth' required an army of pathetically-paid interpreters to make themselves understood, not being able to speak any of the languages. Most of those whites, strutting in boots of arrogance, even after twenty years' residence could still not speak the local language. Local citizens were made to learn English. Yet, in Britain, cries of 'we can't understand what they are saying' highlights a major hypocrisy. For those colonial whites kept the truth of their attitudes and their brutalities from those whites at home. However, black and Asian people, having suffered the self-same treatment from whites who have never even ventured out of this sceptred isle, can, with some justification, believe that racial injustice to be part of the white British body politic.

In previous times of crisis, Her Majesty's Government announced 'we want you to fight in the coming war, because the life of the Empire is threatened'. What the Great White Father meant was that white lives were threatened; so black lives must defend them and be sacrificed, if need be, in their defence. That Walt Disney-type idea of 'answering the call' will not work again until the black and brown British community can visibly see what interest they have in the state of Great Britain. If they are part of the fabric of the State, through its institutions, then they will possess a reason for allegiance. At this point in time, holding a racially-devaluing British passport means absolutely nothing. I would have thought it makes sense. Surely Britain's internal stability is paramount?

Consider this idea. What does the British government intend to do, in the event of a military crisis, with an element in its population whose loyalty it is not sure of? Internment? Almost two million people? Or is there some ambitious scientific programme planned in order to subdue a large section of that population?

If the allegiance of Britain's ethnic minorities has already been decided, then keeping their parents out of the fabric of Britain's multi-racial(?) society defeats the object. This is confession time, and the period for performing conjuring tricks is over. And so are cut-rate citizenships.

Imagination is useful, for those who have a use for it. There are some cut-rate word artists for whom imagination is a tedious stumbling block and reality a misconception. Therefore, their conception of reality stretches my imagination. Clean out of sight.

Will the rule of the newspapers be the lie in our lives? Who will believe it? Why? Editor of *Race Today*, Darcus Howe, has for years been speaking out about the reality of life in Brixton for black and Asian people. This has earned him the static label 'Race Leader' from the artistic race word-weavers of the balanced-bias-towards-white press. The abundance of this style of reporting suggests that these thinkers have the same thoughts, which again suggests sheep who also move in the same direction when the thoughts of their identity are in racial crisis. But we need the press to be significantly free in order to guarantee *all* of our freedoms, liberty, and freedom of speech. The ethnic community is also an integral part of the British community, and requires those journalists to use equality for ink in their nibs. Therefore, why have those race reporters failed to put the boot into the race leaders of the House of Commons, who *are* race leaders in the strictest sense? They represent the interest of only one race, thus cutting another large chunk out of the quality time of those other British people, who happen to have a different colour of skin. So what happens to the 'special relationship' with the white, brown and black British people?

That 'special relationship' is a bring-down. For a moment, just for a moment, six years ago, the black community thought that it had a positive commitment from a British institution. The British Broadcasting Corporation. It lasted a moment. Paranoia, in the form of a series of unacceptable possibilities, came heavily into play. There was the possibility that 'Black Londoners', presented by Alex Pascal, might be a success. The programme, to be heard five days a week with a captive audience of Londoners reflecting a black British view, quickly became unacceptable –

that is, financially. Surely, a programme which reflects the views of the other Britain should be considered a priority for real financial backing? Or are there so many programmes reflecting black views all over Britain that 'Black Londoners' is not considered a paramount social investment? And the possibility of the black community having a stake in state institutions fades away into star-dust. Is 'Black Londoners' a SOG? Save Our Guilt.

They're building rainbows in the white-house tonight. At the Commission for Racial Equality, the corridors are full of hunters helping the hunted. To give answers to questions, through no understanding, desks full of assumptions, the community asks: 'What do we do now? You are our racial Valium.' They tread water in vain, without thinking why they are no nearer the hues and shades that brought them to fruition, for they know that the future of the other Britain is also the decider of social stability. Have you ever tried walking a tightrope a million miles in the air knowing whatever happens, you must only come down on one side?

The attitude of Britain's ethnic community to the CRE is conclusively reflected in an article in the *Caribbean Times* in July 1981:

**Equal Opportunities**
The single biggest disaster area of the CRE's activities has been the failure of its white

dominated Equal Opportunities Division (EOD) headed by Ex-Colonial Peter Sanders, to make headway in their formal investigations in eliminating racial discrimination, despite the massive powers given to it by Parliament and the generous resources allocated to it in terms of staff and access to outside lawyers.

After four years, only ten puny investigations have been completed.

## Employment

In *Employment*, the most important area affecting blacks, not a single major investigation has been completed nor is likely to be completed in the foreseeable future. The E.O.D. is reluctant to take on the Civil Service or the powerful professions.

## E.S.N.

NOT a single education investigation has been completed! Nothing has been done about the disadvantage suffered by black kids as a result of racial stereotyping on the part of education authorities and teachers, which so seriously undermines the future of whole generations of blacks. Not a single investigation has been completed into the educational policies and teacher attitudes which condemn black kids to the school dustbins of remedial classes and their categorisation as educationally sub normal.

**Advertisements**

THE reluctance of Sanders and his investigators to act decisively and effectively in using the law to confront discriminators is best illustrated by the manner in which they take great pains to avoid taking out legal proceedings against those who place racially discriminatory advertisements.

In 1980, the CRE 'disposed of' 32 advertisement complaints. 18 were found to be unlawful, but they were all settled *informally*!

When fear knocks on the door, a stranger on the other side is not necessarily a saviour. Until now the CRE has had few saving graces. It has failed to become an organisation that all communities have confidence in. If the nation needs agents of balm, so be it. But it is clearly obvious that the black and brown communities have no confidence in the personnel of the CRE.

The directed task for the CRE of creating racial stability based on the white race assumptions of non-whites is impossible. The possibility of confidence in the CRE, coupled with equal representation of all communities, has been made impossible because the race conflict within it gives even less confidence to the black and brown communities. The possibility that the CRE began with an assumed misconception of Britain's black and Asian people dismisses it.

If this fangless institution is to gather any heavy momentum, then why has it not begun hide-beating all authorities who possess every single historical document on African and Asian history to be housed in its own archives, e.g. records of the slave trade, colonial history, and all contributions of black and Asian people in all wars fought for Britain, in order that all British people are given the benefit of such vital historical research.

So, what is ladled into the skulls of school pupils is highly questionable. Voltaire clarifies what can be considered to be *the* African and Asian dilemma about British history. He wrote:

### The Certainty of History

Any certainty which is not a mathematical demonstration is only extreme probability: this is all that historical certainty can ever be.

Marco Polo was the first and at that time the only person to speak of the greatness and of the population of China; he was not believed and he could not expect to be believed. The Portuguese, who entered this vast empire several centuries later, made its existence probable. It is now certain, with that certainty which arises from the unanimous testimony of a thousand eyewitnesses of different nations, when this testimony is challenged by no one.

Using Voltaire's thoughts, therefore, to Britain's whites, Britain's history is a certainty. To European countries in the family affair of white oppression of the world's non-white peoples, it is almost a certainty. To those whites who have no other source, it is only possibly true. For the thoughtless, it is extreme probability. But to those non-white peoples of the world, it is extremely probable that British history is a cover-up, based on an extreme certainty, that *any* cover-up of *any* oppression is a camouflage for falsehoods. So what is the truth of British history?

Moreover, the CRE sets the scene by what it has not done. The pathetic myths still perpetuated about non-white peoples are damaging to the social and intellectual structure of Britain, and this does not seem to be too high on its list of conference-going activities.

It's on the beam. Without a doubt the great British youth shall inherit the mistakes of the (mis)leaders, who load up and make tracks for better horizons when the going gets tough. They leave behind them the same magical statements to give courage and optimism to British youth: 'greater productivity', 'fewer strikes', and 'more efficiency'; meaningless phrases conjured up, out of sight, back in historical time. They have listened to the droppings of the paper party men and women. How can Britain's youth relate to leaders who are an experience and two classes removed? They have every reason to rebel, with no jobs, no prospects but a guaranteed place in the great British dole queue. Today, they have witnessed defiance in black and brown youth and they are allies. The ethic of white superiority means nothing. They see action, they see refusal, and a future for refusal. A unification of the victimised is twice as bad in retaliation.

I have a ten-year-old white friend. Recently, his homework studies required him to write a project on 'Stanley finds Livingstone' from *The True Book of Great Adventures*, published in 1978. He wrote:

As I have been writing about David Livingstone for my school project I would like to criticise a few things about the book I was working from. For my first criticism I shall quote from the book. All words and sentences underlined show that they are either ridicule and impossible or that they are trying to make out that whites are superior to blacks.

'In 1844 a group of *frightened* natives implored Livingstone to drive off a savage lion that was attacking their sheep. Livingstone wounded the lion with his first shot, but before he could fire the second barrel, the enraged animal pounced on him and shook him like a terrier shakes a rat. Lying helpless on the ground, Livingstone was mauled by the lion *for several minutes*. His life was saved by an elderly African named Mebalwe, who reloaded the gun and fired. He missed the animal which promptly savaged both him and a native, before finally dropping dead as a result of the first shot.'

The first underlined word is 'Frightened', the reason for this is that I myself do not think a tribe of natives, whose fathers had been living in the jungle for thousands and thousands of years, would be frightened by a lion and would ask a European who knows nothing about lions to kill one. The second underlining is also unlikely. I wonder if there really was a lion.

This young opinion shows the changing face of Britain. It also shows that each generation is one more moment removed from the traditions that can hold a nation back.

The past is a dead living entity to be perceived with totally honest objectivity. Youth is better placed to do just that.

The answer was stamped on black and brown faces, who weathered storm deaths as their Time stood the test. Remember New Cross and Southall's burning surprises, and white history still remained covered, yet wet. There's a time for reflection and a time for regret. A time when race violence may not be over just yet. But the answers will stand firm; their future is cast. The Great British People, viewed their Question again, looked into their colonial past, stared twice at the future, as *their* answer came out at last — the permanent presence of the black and brown people is the answer.

Otherwise, if the small black community in the UK has been allowed in on a provisional basis, then a shocking outcome awaits us all. Will African and British governments begin taking tit for tat actions over immigration? And that cannot be blamed on Britain's masses. Like so much else in British history, it will only be due to the blunders of a public-school ruling minority.